"This book is a powerful diagnosis of the church's illness and sound antidote to the virus found in our body and institution. May God 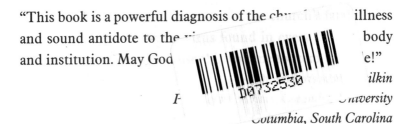 e!"

—ilkin

F   University
Columbia, South Carolina

"Evangelical Protestant leaders throughout North America will be well served by reading this timely volume."

—*Dr. George Bullard*
Executive Director, New Reformation Solutions
Columbia, South Carolina

"I had a hard time putting this book down. It is a journey through ecclesiastical reality."

—*Dr. John Hull*
Senior Pastor, Peoples Church
Toronto, Canada

"Dr. Cook has done us a favor. . . . Let's heed his warning and reverse the moral and spiritual decay of our times."

—*Dr. Erwin W. Lutzer*
Senior Pastor, The Moody Church
Chicago, Illinois

"This book is a clarion call for a needed change in direction that will bring spiritual renewal to Christ's Church and glory to our Heavenly Father."

—*Dr. Peter Nanfelt, President*
The Christian and Missionary Alliance

HISTORICAL DRIFT

Must My Church Die?

How to Detect, Diagnose and Reverse the Trends

Arnold L. Cook

CHRISTIAN PUBLICATIONS
CAMP HILL, PENNSYLVANIA

Christian Publications, Inc.
3825 Hartzdale Drive, Camp Hill, PA 17011
www.cpi-horizon.com
www.christianpublications.com

Faithful, biblical publishing since 1883

Historical Drift
paperback edition
ISBN: 0-87509-901-7

LOC Catalog Card Number: 00-090167

© 2000 by Christian Publications, Inc.

All rights reserved
Printed in the United States of America

01 02 03 04 05   6 5 4 3 2

Unless otherwise indicated, Scripture taken from the HOLY BIBLE:
NEW INTERNATIONAL VERSION ® .
© 1973, 1978, 1984 by the International Bible Society.
Used by permission of Zondervan Publishing House. All rights reserved.

Scripture labeled "KJV" is taken from the Holy Bible: King James Version.

Scripture labeled "The Message" is taken from *The Message: The New Testament in
Contemporary English*, Eugene H. Peterson, Navpress Publishing Group, P.O. Box 35001,
Colorado Springs, CO 80935.

Scripture labeled "Amplified" is taken from The Amplified Bible.
© 1965, 1964, 1962 by Zondervan Publishing House,
© 1958, 1954 by The Lockman Foundation. All rights reserved.

Scripture labeled "NKJV" is taken from the New King James Version of the Bible.
© 1994, 1982, 1980, 1979 by Thomas Nelson, Inc. All rights reserved.

Figures #5 and 6 ("Stages of Church Life" and "Types of People"): Permission granted
by author, Dr. Robert D. Dale, of *To Dream Again*, Broadman Press, Nashville, TN. (Out
of print, copyright returned to author. Permission granted by telephone, March 23, 2000.)
Figure #7 ("Life Cycle and Stages of Congregational Development"): Permission granted
by author, Dr. George Windrow Bullard, of *New Reformation Solutions*. (Permission
granted March 6, 2000 when we received the illustration on disk.)

Dedicated to my all-star team—

Mary-Lou, my godly, loving, consistent and encouraging wife
of forty-six years and twenty-seven moves
and mother of five
Our children—my mentors
Charles—teacher, missions, organizer, innovator
Darla—counselor, helper, joy in trials
Timothy—pastor, family, people, servant to all
Sandy—mother, athletic, gift of helps
Michael—teacher, family, coach, athletics
Sandy—mother, teacher, enthusiasm
John—missions, quiet leader, humor, creativity
Beth—nurse, missions, sensitivity
Beth-Ann—spirited, artistic, refresher of people

Bench Strength
(The five greatest grandchildren)

Jeremy, Jessica, Katelynd, Cody, Taylor

Contents

Part I: Historical Drift Defined

Part II: Historical Drift Diagnosed

Part V: Historical Drift Reversed

Part VI: Historical Drift Reviewed

List of Illustrations

Foreword

Arnold Cook and I have been lifelong friends. He stood up with me when my wife and I were married in 1959. In fact, I have known him for forty-six years. We graduated from Canadian Bible College together, and later in life, when I went back to school, he was my professor at the Canadian Theological Seminary. Now, I am his publisher.

The term "historical drift" has been part of our mutual vocabulary and thinking for so long and has become so intertwined in our lives that I cannot remember when I first heard it.

Briefly stated, historical drift is "the inherent tendency of human organizations to depart over time from their original beliefs, purposes and practices, which in the Christian context results in the loss of spiritual vitality" (page 10).

The book concept has been at least ten years in the process. It now comes to us as a carefully considered and mature word to local church leaders and to the Church at large—the passionate heart-message of a missionary/churchman who deeply cares about Christ's kingdom.

As president of one of Canada's fastest growing mid- to large-size denominations, Cook is writing about an immense idea—certainly the equal of Church Growth or Renewal as concepts in the evangelical mind. I have privately wondered, *What would happen if impedances to historical drift were applied as enthusiastically as reorganizational or Church Growth methods are?* Or again, *What if our passion to see authentic revival in our day were equaled by a like passion to impede historical drift until revival comes? Would not the Church be much different?*

As I write, I am into the twelfth year of my tenure as Publisher here at Christian Publications, founded in 1883. Since we first published

Tozer's *The Pursuit of God* in 1948, *Historical Drift* is, in my opinion, the most significant book to be issued in the intervening years.

The prophet Daniel talks about the "lengthening of [our] tranquility" (4:27, KJV). *Historical Drift* unfolds an opportunity to do just that by extending godly and aggressive ministries of churches and denominations well past the common point of drift, decline and departure from truth.

Applying these words has the potential for extending the power and influence of churches and their attendant organizations. It also offers a lifeline for rescuing the Church from its seemingly incessant infatuation with the world, and for alerting leadership which finds itself on the slippery slope to the precipice ahead. And it presents the prayer rationale for restoring Christ's Body to vibrant spiritual life and for claiming authentic revival in our day.

K. Neill Foster, Ph.D.
Camp Hill, Pennsylvania
April 28, 2000

Preface

There are a host of people, beyond these special "hands-on" helpers, whom I want to acknowledge and thank. But first and foremost, in the words of the Apostle Paul, "I thank Christ Jesus our Lord who has enabled me, because He counted me faithful, putting me into the ministry" (1 Timothy 1:12, NKJV).

I thank The Christian and Missionary Alliance (C&MA) in Canada and the C&MA U.S. prior to Canadian autonomy in1980. They gave me an incredible platform for forty years of ministry during the most significant period of missionary expansion in the 20th century, 1960-2000. This book has emerged slowly but surely over those years as this denomination provided me with worldwide exposure to the fascinating cultural mosaic of the Christian Church.

I thank the Boards of Directors who have encouraged me in my research and writing. Through my reports, many aspects of *historical drift* have been tested on these boards over a twenty-year period.

I thank the National Leadership team who have been my colleagues and who grapple with the challenges of church life at even a closer level than I do. Without these gifted overseers, my job would have been impossible. And to the vast host of godly lay people, without whom nothing in Christian ministry would happen.

I thank all the pastors, the practitioners, who are privileged to have both the most difficult and the most rewarding role in Christian ministry. May this book help them in the building of the only institution that Jesus guaranteed would succeed—the Church.

I thank the National Office Staffs with whom I have worked shoulder to shoulder over a twenty-year period. They have been our extended family. Mary-Lou and I have been enriched spiritually as together we have shared our trials and our triumphs, our dreams and our disappointments.

Last, but not least, I want to recognize a great friend of forty-six years, Neill Foster. He is the man who caught the vision of this book many years ago. His encouragement and incessant feeding of materials to me carried me through three manuscripts over a ten-year period. Marilynne, his wife, also encouraged me with the reminder that a book must be written at least three times. She graciously pushed me through the minutiae of revisions, holding me to deadlines which made the final product a reality. *Muchisimas gracias, amigos.*

Acknowledgments

- Research Assistance: Menno Fieguth, Roy Hall, Arnold Reimer, Sandy Ayer, Ralph Willison, Bert McBride, K. Neill Foster
- Editing and Proofing: Marilynne Foster, Judy Harris, Esther Goodwin, Mary-Lou Cook, John Hull
- Secretarial Assistance: Juliet Allman

"Is there no way to prevent this—this continued decay of pure religion?"

— John Wesley

Introduction

A Tale of Two Churches

THE LEADER WAS AN ENTHUSIASTIC young businessman, the worship service upbeat. I couldn't believe that church could be so exciting! Perhaps most importantly, the song leader also taught my class of senior teen boys. My stalled Christian life quickly began to move forward. This dynamic Sunday school teacher became my first mentor, and I took the step of baptism.

So what made this church so special to a lanky sixteen-year-old? Here's the context.

Our family had been attending a small rural church that was in the throes of a slow and painful death. Despite its condition, however, God gave me two good experiences there. The first came through special children's meetings where I, at age eleven, became a Christian.

Then there was Mrs. Fleming, a godly woman, who taught Sunday school in the back pews of the one-room church. I always managed to maneuver my way next to the window so I could scrape the frost off the pane while Mrs. Fleming did her best to capture and hold my attention.

But here's the bad news. It seems like it happened every Sunday. I was always anxious for church to end so my playtime could begin. Church at best was boring. But those long after-service members-only meetings were killers. I can still see the old deacon standing by the window so he could see to read in the dim light. In a halting voice, he would read letters from the denomination to this tiny dying country church. Today a small plaque marks the site.

Why this tale of two churches to introduce a book for Christian leaders? Here's the story behind the story, the contrasting contexts of these two churches.

The country church that died was part of a denomination which was fast becoming liberal in its theology and was in the midst of a messy split over critical doctrinal questions. The eye of the storm centered on their seminary.

In contrast, the lively church to which my parents moved us was part of a new association of churches. They had broken away from the old dying denomination that was becoming liberal. This was my first encounter with a church that drifted from truth.

Why the Fascination with Drift?

As a young pastor in my first churches, I observed that growth came primarily through people moving from mainline churches. These transfers were usually unable to articulate what went wrong, but they were certain of one thing: that their churches had drifted into operating like secular institutions which just happened to bear a Christian name.

A Christian leader in a Lebanese church once commented on this trend. "Arnold, we don't use the term 'Christian' anymore. We prefer to call our people 'believers.' " The tendency to drift seems endemic in all social structures.

Robert H. Bork, in his volume titled, *Slouching Towards Gomorrah*, addresses drift in the context of the American culture:

> With each new evidence of deterioration, we lament for a moment, and then become accustomed to it. . . . So unrelenting is the assault on our sensibilities that many of us grow numb, finding resignation to be the rational, adaptive response to an environment that is increasingly polluted and apparently beyond our control. . . . As behavior worsens, the community adjusts its standards to that conduct once thought reprehensible but is no longer deemed so.[1]

Bork echoes the concern which everyone who works with social structures echoes. The tendency is for the fire of passion, commitment and excellence to go out. This is the common experience of corporations, academic institutions, governments, social agencies and religious movements. Over time, vision dims, core values shift and passion fades.

Yes, time is the chief culprit in the drift process. The following historical anecdotes demonstrate how the passage of time changes vision, values and passion.

Lifesaving stations were simply organized along the Atlantic seaboard. Selfless volunteers, committed to rescuing victims of shipwrecks, staffed them. But over time they improved their facilities. Introduced some games. Upgraded their boats. And finally they became plush yacht clubs pandering to the penchants and pleasures of their affluent membership.[2]

A mission was opened in a storefront near a steel mill. It was strategically located between two taverns. Many mill workers were converted. Then a notorious gambler was saved, and overnight the little mission was famous. The volunteers became distracted. Soon they lost interest in evangelism. So they hired some preachers to win the souls. They raised the questions whether "winning souls" was really their purpose. The majority concluded it was not. The minority left and rented a storefront across the street and began services with only crude chairs and a small pulpit. [3]

He was pastoring in the inner city of Chicago. He had a passion to reach the needy people around his church. After some years he lamented: "Fifteen years ago our church had a fisherman's club. Ten men regularly went out to preach on street corners and win souls. We were concerned about men going to hell. Now our flaming witnesses are gone. These same men are now respectable property owners."[4]

It was John Wesley who decried "this continual decay of pure religion":

> Wherever riches have increased, the essence of religion has decreased in the same proportion. I do not see how it is possible, in the nature of things, for any revival of religion to continue long. For religion must necessarily produce both industry and frugality, and these cannot but produce riches. But as riches increase, so will pride, anger, and love of the world in all its branches. [5]

Throughout history, vision dims, core values shift and passion fades in organizations. To describe this common pattern I have coined the term *historical drift*.

Based on my observations over forty years of ministry, I resonate with the blunt *ad hoc* suggestion of an elderly and unidentified bishop: "All Christian organizations should be scrapped every 100 years and started over, except for the women's missionary prayer circle." I wonder what accumulation of experiences and observations would have triggered such a radical and irreverent proposal from a venerable churchman?

Although it is only conjecture, I suspect that in his journey to the bishopric he had pastored several geriatric churches—in denominational jargon often referred to as the "Old First Churches," e.g., The First Baptist Church of Dallas, The First Nazarene of Toronto, etc. Or perhaps he's recalling those late-night church board battles with leaders suffering from the "hardening of the categories." As a bishop he had wrestled often with elders who had been "in the way" for a long time, the kind who not only love visiting the "hall of fame" but actually preferred to live there!

Why Not Celebrate Drift?

Some younger leaders will zero in on the second part of the old bishop's idea, i.e., start over with new movements. Let drift do its work, they say, as a benevolent form of euthanasia to remove worn-out wineskins which have lost their elasticity. Bring on the new wineskins! History is replete with case studies where this has occurred, sometimes effectively, sometimes with great loss. So why not celebrate drift, new leaders ask, and always move forward with new structures?

I believe there are two short answers. First, if this became our first response to drift, we would be doing an end run around the Holy Spirit's commitment to renewal. Unlike secular structures, the Church is first an organism and secondly an organization. God designs organisms for renewal. Organizations can only be restructured.

Second, much of drift is intertwined with generational issues. God is committed to working through generations, not around them. The art of Christian leadership is the challenge of blending generations into dynamic synergism as a witness to a watching and fragmented world.

Why Focus on the Darker Side of the Church?

I have full confidence in the triumphant future of Christ's Church—capital C.[6] He will present to Himself a "radiant [C]hurch, without stain or wrinkle or any other blemish, . . . holy and blameless" (Ephesians 5:27). My concern is for the earthly reflection—churches, small c. For this reason, I am addressing the drift issue.

The major focus of this book is on evangelical churches, their related agencies and their leaders. I will grapple with what I call *historical drift*—the tendency of churches to move away from their original moorings over time. In this context, I am addressing leaders, primarily clergy, but also key laity.

My thesis regarding leadership is this: "Organizations don't drift, only their leaders." Whether a Christian organization thrives or dies depends on the caliber of its leaders. I will describe how courageous godly leaders can take a firm stand on the slippery slope of culture and move Christ's Church through this millennium with renewed strength and spiritual integrity.

This book is a twenty-first-century call for a contemporary army of Christian leaders who, like the sons of Issachar (1 Chronicles 12:32), understand their times and know what God's people should do.

~

Discussion Questions

1. Take a few minutes to review your personal church journey. Can you identify with any of the experiences of the author in dying churches?
2. He speaks of organizations, which have drifted over time and changed their purposes. Do you know of any?
3. John Wesley laments the "continual decay of pure religion." If this is true, what do you think God's answer is?

4. The author states, "Organizations don't drift, only their leaders."
   What does he mean?

". . . I will build my church, and the gates of Hades will not over-come it." (Matthew 16:18)

Part I

HISTORICAL DRIFT DEFINED

We have looked at some brief anecdotal evidence of historical drift in the introduction. In this part, I want to define the term. First, we will look at some of the many biblical references which illustrate this troublesome phenomenon. Then, in the second chapter, we will consider theories which both secular and Christian researchers have developed to analyze the problem and propose solutions.

"Every generation must stand on the shoulders of the previous generation and reach higher." This insightful statement is attributed to St. Augustine. Certainly the role of successive generations is a major player in historical drift. The Bible provides a rich source for the study of generations with its numerous listings of genealogies.

Early in the Old Testament, God introduced Himself as the God of Abraham, Isaac and Jacob (Genesis 50:24). He made it abundantly clear that generations would be His vehicle for the propagation of faith throughout the history of His people. In His "book of remembrance,"

He reminds parents to teach their children all the miraculous works He has performed to bring them into the land (Deuteronomy 11:1-21).

The failure of one generation to communicate effectively its faith to its children results in loss of personal experience with the living God. Out of this generational slippage comes my basic definition: *Historical drift is the inherent tendency of human organizations to depart over time from their original beliefs, purposes and practices, which in the Christian context results in the loss of spiritual vitality.*

"Organizations tend to lose vitality rather than gain it as time passes. They also tend to give greater attention to what they 'were' rather than what they are 'becoming.' "

—Charles Swindoll

1

Joshua, Jesus, Peter and Paul Did It

God's People Have Lamented Historical Drift

SUCCINCTLY STATED, HISTORICAL DRIFT IS the inherent tendency of human organizations to depart over time from their original purposes. In the Christian context, worst case scenario, it looks like this: The vision of the founders has faded, yet the organizational machinery grinds on. With corporate management by objectives in place, enhanced by the latest gimmicks of marketing and with a suave touch of public relations, many of these churches not only survive but also grow and prosper economically.

What has been the reaction of God's people to historical drift over the centuries? The following figure, which I have adapted, helps me to visualize drift. The top half of this clock face reveals the progressive steps of historical drift.

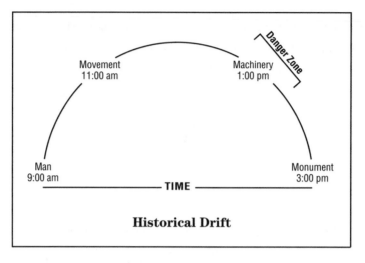

Figure 1: Historical Drift

A Predictable Cycle

"The second generation holds its convictions less fervently than pioneers of the sects. . . . With each succeeding generation, isolation from the world becomes more difficult."[1] We may adversely react to such cold and calculating analysis as this from secular social scientists like Richard Niebuhr. We protest: "But Christian organizations are different. This predictable curve of man/movement/machinery/monument doesn't apply to true Christianity!" Agreed. It should not, but in reality it does. God speaks very openly in His Word concerning this tragic reality.

In the Old Testament books of Joshua and Judges this propensity of God's people to comply with the predictability of the sociological pattern is clearly documented. Judges picks up the history of the children of Israel just after the death of Joshua. He had led the people into Canaan. As a wise leader, he understood God's strong commitment to transmitting faith through successive generations. Early in their settlement of the land, he took deliberate action to insure that every future generation would know what God had done in his day.

> And Joshua set up at Gilgal the twelve stones they had taken out of the Jordan. He said to the Israelites, "In the future when your descendants ask their fathers, 'What do these stones mean?' tell them, 'Israel crossed the Jordan on dry ground.' . . . He did this so that all the peoples of the earth might know that the hand of the LORD is powerful and so that you might always fear the LORD your God." (Joshua 4:20-22, 24)

Despite Joshua's careful visionary action, Judges records this tragic sequel:

> The people served the LORD throughout the lifetime of Joshua and of the elders who outlived him and who had seen all the great things the LORD had done for Israel.
>
> Joshua son of Nun, the servant of the LORD, died at the age of a hundred and ten. . . .
>
> After that whole generation had been gathered to their fathers, another generation grew up, who knew neither the LORD nor what he had done for Israel. (Judges 2:7-10)

Judges narrates the next 300 years of the nation's history, characterized by the refrain, "Every man did that which was right in his own eyes" (17:6, NKJV). This gave rise to a tragic cycle:

- "The Israelites did evil in the eyes of the LORD." (3:7)
- "The anger of the LORD burned against Israel." (3:8)
- "[Israel] cried out to the LORD." (3:9)
- "[God] raised up for them a deliverer" [a judge]. (3:9)
- "[God gave them] peace [until the judge died]." (3:11)

This cyclical response of Israel became the pattern for centuries. Although their grumbling for forty years in the wilderness manifested drift, now in Canaan it became a pattern. The spiritual level reached a new low under Eli the priest and his godless sons. Then, with the miraculous birth of Samuel, new hope came to Israel. But Samuel's sons became corrupt. This fed the growing demand among the people to have a king like the pagan nations did. This is historical drift, defined and demonstrated by the children of Israel living under theocracy.

Under the monarchy, little changed. Kings replaced judges, but the cycle became endemic. The godly leadership of one king frequently was followed by the less-than-godly leadership of another who led the people back into idolatry. This drift became the lament of the prophets. Despite their warnings, fewer kings led their people in repentance. Judgment through captivity proved inevitable and finally, in captivity, was eradicated in the remnant.

Spiritual Pharisees

How does spiritual pharisaism connect with historical drift? Jesus reserved His most caustic condemnation for the Pharisees of His day. Consider His outburst in Matthew 23, shortly before the cross: He labeled them "hypocrites" six times, "blind" on five occasions, "whitewashed tombs" and "snakes." We are left with the distinct impression that He considered them less than spiritual!

His target for these searing rebukes was an old religious movement established 200 years earlier. Hit rewind and visit the Pharisees during their early history. What a sweet/bitter discovery! Here's a glimpse of their glory days.

The sect of Pharisees is thought to have originated in the 3rd century B.C., in days preceding the Maccabean wars, when under Greek domination and the Greek effort to Hellenize the Jews, there was a strong tendency among the Jews to accept Greek culture with its pagan religious customs. The rise of the Pharisees was a reaction and protest against this tendency among their fellow-countrymen. Their aim was to preserve their national integrity and strict conformity to Mosaic law.[2]

In their early history, the Pharisees were likened to the Puritans of the 17th century who became the nonconformists of the 19th century in England.[3] As pacifists, some became martyrs during the Maccabean wars. Initially, the Pharisees jealously protected the uniqueness of Judaism from Hellenistic influences and established themselves as zealous students and teachers of the Scriptures. Their early history reflects a strong Messianic focus.

How, then, could such a zealous orthodox Jewish group with such a commendable history become the object of Jesus' verbal wrath? Short answer: It was one more victim of historical drift. Few organizations survive 100 years with religious integrity. As third-century geriatrics, they had been parked at the monument stage for at least 100 years. Jesus chose well the descriptive term "whitewashed tombs" for a movement which had long ago outlived its original purpose.

Yes, we can understand how drift takes its toll over three centuries. Now, let's look at what can happen in just over a decade.

The Foolish Galatians

What evidence, if any, do we find of historical drift in the New Testament Church? The Galatians are but one of many case studies.

Acts, which spans a period of thirty-three years, describes small, struggling yet vibrant churches—no doubt including the Galatian churches—enjoying their "first love." However, the Pauline letters, addressed to these same young churches, reflect evidence of significant problems among them.

During his first missionary journey (A.D. 45-48), Paul established several churches in the region known as Galatia in Central Asia Minor. Acts 13 and 14 identify them as Iconium, Lystra, Derbe, perhaps Pisidia and Antioch. Paul's letter, written about A.D. 57, expresses his grave concern for their spiritual condition.

> I am astonished that you are so quickly deserting the one who called you by the grace of Christ and are turning to a different gospel. (Galatians 1:6)

> You foolish Galatians! Who has bewitched you? Before your very eyes Jesus Christ was clearly portrayed as crucified. I would like to learn just one thing from you: Did you receive the Spirit by observing the law, or by believing what you heard? Are you so foolish? After beginning with the Spirit, are you now trying to attain your goal by human effort? (3:1-3)

> My dear children, for whom I am again in the pains of child-birth until Christ is formed in you, how I wish I could be with you now and change my tone, because I am perplexed about you! (4:19-20)

New Testament Church history promptly reminds us that Christians can rapidly drift from truth. External factors play key roles in the rate of historical drift. These churches had barely reached their tenth anniversary! In Galatia, the major drift contributor was a sect of Jewish Christians known as Judaizers. Their perversion of the gospel consisted of teaching Gentiles that they had to comply with the ceremonial laws of Judaism to be truly Christian. Persecution of Christians by Jews was another contributing factor in the Galatians' fall back into legalism.

Those Elusive Hebrews

We turn now to Jewish believers who were drifting from their new-found faith. The epistle to the Hebrews "is in many respects the riddle of the New Testament."[4] "Who wrote the *Letter to the Hebrews* only God knows for certain."[5] I will defer to God regarding the authorship. However, questions of to whom and when are germane to this study.

Barclay develops the following rationale for identifying the original readers as:

- a long established church: "In fact, though by this time you ought to be teachers, you need someone to teach you the elementary truths of God's word all over again" (Hebrews 5:12).

- a church which had some time in the past suffered persecution: "Remember those earlier days after you had received the light, when you stood your ground in a great contest in the face of suffering" (10:32).

- a church which had had great days and great teachers and leaders: "Remember your leaders, who spoke the word of God to you. Consider the outcome of their way of life and imitate their faith" (13:7).

- a church which the apostles had directly founded: "This salvation, which was first announced by the Lord, was confirmed to us by those who heard him" (2:3).

In summary, Barclay concludes:

Hebrews is a letter written by a great teacher to a little group or college of Christians in Rome. He was their teacher; at the moment he was separated from them and was afraid that they were drifting away from the faith; and so he wrote this letter to them.[6]

When was it written? The most helpful clue is found in the references to persecution. It appears that some of their leaders had died for their faith (Hebrews 13:7). But they themselves had not: "In your struggle against sin, you have not yet resisted to the point of shedding your blood" (12:4). A.D. 64 marked the first persecution. The next was in the time of Domitian about A.D. 85. Lacking a strong consensus on most aspects of this book, A.D. 80 is a reasonable date. But one of the few areas of considerable consensus relates to the first of five major warnings.[7] Note the following renderings:

> We must pay more careful attention, therefore, to what we have heard, so that we do not drift away. (2:1, NIV)

> Therefore we ought to give the more earnest heed to the things which we have heard, lest at any time we should let them slip. (2:1, KJV)

> Since all this is true, we ought to pay much closer attention than ever to the truths that we have heard, lest in any way we drift past [them] and slip away. (2:1, Amplified)

> It's crucial that we keep a firm grip on what we've heard so that we don't drift off. (2:1, The Message)

The warning centers around two key Greek words: *prosechein* and *pararrein*. Note the intent of *prosechein* in three other uses in the New Testament: 1) Acts 5:35, Gamaliel's warning to the Sanhedrin regarding the apostles: "Men of Israel, *consider carefully* what you intend to do to these men." 2) Acts 20:28, Paul's charge to the Ephesian elders: "*Guard yourselves* and all the flock of which the Holy Spirit has made you overseers." 3) Second Peter 1:19, Peter's strong admonition to believers: "And we have the word of the prophets made more certain, and *you will do well to pay attention to it*, as to a light shining in a dark place (emphasis added)."

The word *pararrein* is used only once in the New Testament, and is translated *drift*. It has several meanings in classical Greek, i.e., to flow beside, to glide aside from, to fall off, decline and to make forfeit of faith.

> It is used of something flowing or slipping past; it can be used of a ring that has slipped off the finger; of a particle of food that has slipped down the wrong way; of a topic that has slipped into the conversation; of a point which has escaped someone in the course of an argument; of some fact that has slipped out of the mind; of something that has ebbed or leaked away. It is regularly used of something which has carelessly or thoughtlessly been allowed to become lost.[8]

Both of these words are linked to the nautical world. *Prosechein*—paying careful attention—can apply to the docking of a ship. *Pararrein*—to let something slip away—can describe a ship which drifts by the dock due to the carelessness of the mariner who failed to calculate carefully the wind or tide.

Barclay offers this translation of Hebrews 2:1: "Therefore, we must the more eagerly anchor our lives [*prosechein*] to the things that we have been taught lest the ship of life drift past the harbour [*pararrein*] and be wrecked."[9] The elusive Hebrews, we must agree, represent generational drift over thirty to forty years.

Christ Comes to Church

We come now to the Head of the Church. How does He understand historical drift?

The book of Revelation promises a specific blessing to all who read it, "hear it and take to heart what is written in it" (Revelation 1:3). In contrast to the book of Hebrews, the authorship and audience of the

Revelation are clearly identified. But the seven churches raise a couple of questions: Who are these churches? Are they simply a literary device, i.e., one message to the church at large broken arbitrarily into seven parts? Do they represent seven periods in church history, i.e., Ephesus being the first century; Laodicea, representing the apostasy of the last days. Or are they real churches?

The observation that each message has relevance for the specific conditions in the cities named supports the interpretation of real churches. Leon Morris amplifies this position:

> This does not mean that the letters originally circulated as individual units. They were probably in this from the first form, and intended to be read by others than members of the churches named. John has addressed himself to the needs of the little churches but has dealt with topics which have relevance to God's people at all times and in all places. He is writing to the churches, but he is also addressing the church as a whole.[10]

Who is the angel addressed in each church? Are they guardian angels of the churches? Are they earthly representatives of the churches, e.g., bishops, pastors, etc.? Are they representative of the essential spirit of the church?

Matthew 18:10 speaks of children having "their angels in heaven," but there are no suggestions that churches have such angelic representatives. Addressing the bishop or head pastor rings logically to our 20th-century thinking, but it is highly doubtful that these early churches had developed such roles. The third interpretation—representation of the essential spirit of the church—has the least problems.

The Revelation has traditionally been considered the last to be written. John's statement in Revelation 1:9 indicates he was writing from the Isle of Patmos. Apostolic tradition linked his banishment to the persecution of Domitian around A.D. 95. John was released in A.D. 96.

Two of the churches, Ephesus and Laodicea, were founded during Paul's third journey, A.D. 54-57. We assume that Pergamum, Sardis and Thyatira were similar in age. Christ detected sufficient evidence of drift to command five of the seven churches to repent after only forty years of ministry.

Summary

The not-so-good news from this survey is that historical drift is biblical! It moves in cycles. The length of this cycle from man through monument can be a decade or a century or more. The result, however, is essentially the same—a departure from original beliefs, purposes and practices resulting in a loss of spiritual vitality.

~

Discussion Questions

1. Turn to Judges 2:7-10. Identify the three generations. What were the characteristics of each?
2. Read Revelation 2:1-7. About how old was this church? What is meant by "first love"? How do you suppose they lost it?
3. Check Hebrew 2:1-4. From what were they drifting?
4. What is the good news (see pages 22-23) in the story of the Brooklyn Tabernacle about drift?

Good News

"You will never have a building large enough. . . ."

Jim Cymbala has been the pastor of the Brooklyn Tabernacle in New York City for twenty-seven years. He describes the church in its early days as a "woeful church that my father-in-law had coaxed me into pastoring."[11] It was a shabby two-story building in the middle of a downtown block on Atlantic Avenue.

He recalls that the first Sunday morning offering amounted to $85. But the church's monthly mortgage payment was $232. Then there were the utility and other bills. Whatever might be left became the pastor's salary. Jim felt inadequate. He did not know what he was doing. He had never attended Bible college or seminary. As he grew up in Brooklyn in a Ukrainian-Polish family, going to church on Sundays with his parents, he never dreamed of becoming a minister.

During the early days of discouragement, God met Jim at a retreat. Venting his frustrations, he prayed: "Lord, I have no idea how to be a successful pastor. . . . I haven't been trained. All I know is that Carol and I are working in the middle of New York City, with people dying on every side, overdosing from heroin, consumed by materialism, and all the rest. If the gospel is so powerful. . . ."[12]

He could not finish. God broke in. Then, in words not heard by ears but deep within one's spirit, he sensed God speaking: "If you and your wife will lead My people to pray and call upon My name, you will never lack for something fresh to preach. I will supply all the money that's needed, both for the church and for your family, and you will never have a building large enough to contain the crowds I will send in response."[13]

Jim Cymbala returned to his people restored in body but more importantly with direction from God for the Brooklyn Tabernacle. Then he shared God's response to his searching heart: "From this day on, the prayer meeting will be the barometer of our church. What happens on Tuesday night will be the gauge by which we will judge success or failure because that will be the measure by which God blesses us."[14]

Today, more than 6,000 attend the Brooklyn Tabernacle each Sunday in multiple services. Perhaps, more importantly, between 1,000 and 1,500 meet for corporate prayer Tuesday evenings. Their 240-voice Brooklyn Tabernacle Choir continues to fill auditoriums such as Madison Square Gardens for concerts. The church has also given birth to several daughter churches.

"The institutional church will either choose to die, or it will choose to die in order to live."

—Mike Regele, *Death of the Church*, Grand Rapids, Eerdmans, 1970, p. 20.

2

Bad News from Barna and Company

The Social Sciences Have Lamented Historical Drift

W E HAVE VISUALIZED THE TRAGIC demise of Christians with a passion for evangelism as they sell out to conflicting cultural values. Laments from New Testament leaders remind us how quickly God's people can drift from truth and slip into dead traditions. Now let's consider some analyses of this phenomenon of historical drift by social scientists.

On the broader scale of religion, Karl Marx dismissed all religions as "the opium of the people." The religious experiences of leaders and the rise and demise of the movements they founded have intrigued sociologists for centuries. Max Weber has written extensively in this field. His particular interest was the Protestant Reformation in the 16th century. In his books *Sociology of Religion* and *The Protestant Ethic and the*

Spirit of Capitalism, he develops theories for the emergence of Baptist sects and the rapid growth of the Protestant Reformation.

How should the Christian church evaluate the research and theories of sociologists, psychologists and cultural anthropologists? Are they friends or foes? Historically, the church has been critical, and rightly so, of Freudian psychology and atheistic Marxism. In the field of cultural anthropology, Margaret Mead has been a long-term critic of missionary work as an intrusion into indigenous cultures.

However, I would argue that many Christians, trained in the humanities and committed to the absolute authority of the Scriptures, do bring helpful understandings to the Church and are particularly insightful in the discussion of historical drift. Although we rightfully attribute it to spiritual causes, the process is inseparably intertwined with a shifting culture. Let me illustrate this by looking at the works of a few writers whom I have found particularly significant.

George W. Barna

George Barna, in his extensive marketing research, analyzes culture and its incessant impact on churches. He suggests that the only constant in society is "the slow drip of constant change."[1] In his book, *The Frog in the Kettle*, he draws on the most-used analogy of historical drift from the high school biology lab—the frog. We can all remember those naïve frogs we dissected. But I can't recall doing this experiment which Barna describes:

> Place a frog in boiling water and it will jump out immediately because it can tell that it's in a hostile environment. But place a frog in a kettle of room temperature water and it will stay there, content with those surroundings. Slowly, very slowly, increase the temperature of the water. This time, the frog doesn't leap out, but just stays there, unaware that the environment is

changing. Continue to turn up the burner until the water is boiling. Our poor frog will be boiled, quite content, perhaps, but nevertheless dead.[2]

What is the lesson here for the Christian Church? Answer: Change is a slow and incremental process. The dripping of water over time can alter even the contour of a granite rock. The Church, although by definition a called-out body of Christians, lives in a shifting culture. How does a church whose spiritual foundation must never move resist the societal pressure to accommodate to the surrounding culture? This challenge has never been more difficult.

In earlier periods, governments in the Western world supported Christian values. This is no longer true. Now, aberrant and sinful practices such as abortion and homosexuality evolve as tiny subcultures, grow and are embraced by the main culture with government recognition and funding. How can a church be relevant to non-Christians yet remain faithful to God's revelation, the Bible? These are the tough questions Barna addresses in his books.

Barna, however, has his critics. He has been labeled the "guru of evangelicalism." In his book, *Marketing the Church*, some see him as promoting corporate Wall Street principles in the management of churches. In fact, the truth is that this growing mentality among evangelical leaders, as I will later demonstrate, is a significant factor that feeds historical drift.

These critiques may be valid, especially if based upon certain parts of Barna's prolific writings. But I would argue that his more recent works are sounding a prophetic voice of warning to the evangelical church. David Bryant, international leader of the Prayer Movement, quotes Barna: "If revival does not come to America by the year 2003 we will have anarchy." And Henry Blackaby, coauthor of a best-selling Bible study, *Experiencing God*, cites Barna's survey indicating that in each of 150 lifestyle areas, including divorce and abortion, "the church is no different than the society around them [sic]." Barna adds, "Survey data shows that most Americans believe that you cannot tell a born-again Christian from nonbelievers because there is no difference in the way they live."[3]

In developing the analogy of the frog in the kettle of water, he warns Christian leaders of the greatly accelerated cultural changes. But his concern is always for the effective future of the Church. This is the thesis of *The Frog in the Kettle*:

> The objective of this book is to help you to perceive the condition of the world, and the outcomes toward which we are careening. Unless we acknowledge where we are headed and develop insightful strategies for redirecting the nation's path, we will find the church to be just another ineffective if well-intentioned institution.[4]

Despite the constant reminders by social scientists that we live in the vortex of the fastest pace of change known to humanity, our most vigorous reaction is benign neglect. In the pivotal hinge decade of the 1990s, Barna suggested that change was doing a number on us in at least six areas:

- Values. We will become more self-centered, more materialistic, more driven to play.
- Currency. Time will replace money as tomorrow's currency of choice.
- Beliefs. Religion will be viewed as less of a corporate experience and more of a self-fulfilling process.
- Background. [North] Americans will be darker, more wrinkled and from more widely divergent economic backgrounds. (Toronto, where I live, is home to people from 169 different countries, with over 100 languages spoken. American cities such as New York and Los Angeles would be even more diverse.)

- Tools. The result (of shift from an emphasis on innovation to application) will be increasing acceptance of technology as a means to an end, bringing new attitudes and lifestyles into being.
- Institutions. The local church will have to earn its place in people's hearts. Institutional loyalty, the presumption of their credibility and altruistic support of them, will largely disappear. Only if the institution provides high quality benefits to the individual will it stand a chance of gaining attention and support.

How do we as leaders balance understanding our culture and understanding God's commands? Jack Hayford, pastor of The Church on the Way, suggests the following:

> To target today's "lost soul," we'd better tune in to both the Holy Spirit and the realities of our culture. Focusing on one to the exclusion of the other will fail to penetrate the present with eternity's power, values and blessings. Barna is helping church leaders keep in touch with both.[5]

I am well aware of the danger. It seems easier to read a Barna book or take one more seminar on "How to Reach the Postmodern Society" than to fast and pray for a week to discern God's answers. But one of the fruits of the Spirit is self-control—biblical balance. Barna is one of the prophetic voices of our day. Here is another voice from the social sciences which has impacted my leadership. Meet Dean Kelley.

Dean M. Kelley

"Of the reading of many books there is no end." Some I start and fail to finish. Some are hard to set down once you start them. Dean Kelley's book, *Why Conservative Churches Are Growing*, was one of the latter. I read it during my graduate studies at Fuller Seminary twenty-five years ago. His powerful thesis returns every time I assume the leadership of any organization from a Sunday school class to a denomination.

Who is Dean Kelley? He is a sociologist and a member of what we call an ecumenical church. As part of an older historical denomination in decline, he, a social scientist, was intrigued by the growth of conservative movements. His interest grew out of an observation of contrasts. His ecumenical church sought to be "all things to all people," but they were dying. In contrast, he observed narrow, sectarian groups extending beyond evangelicals—including the Jehovah Witnesses and the Black Panthers—waving politically incorrect flags. They required their followers to live counterculture lives, and yet they were growing rapidly. (Obviously, Kelley uses "conservative" in the sociological sense of "adhering to very strict regulations and requiring high commitment from their members.")

So what are his theses? He begins by listing some unfulfilled expectations:

> 1. It is generally assumed that religious enterprises, if they want to succeed, will be reasonable, rational, courteous, responsible, restrained and receptive to outside criticism; that is, they will want to preserve a good image in the world (as the world defines all these terms).
>
> 2. It is expected, moreover, that they will be democratic and gentle in their internal affairs (and will want to work cooperatively with other groups to meet those needs).
>
> 3. They will also be responsive to the needs of men (as currently conceived), and will want to work cooperatively with other groups to meet those needs.
>
> 4. They will not let dogmatism, judgmental moralism or obsessions with cultic purity stand in the way of such cooperation and service.[6]

Based on Kelley's research, the above four expectations "are a receipt for the failure of the religious enterprise."[7]

Out of this conclusion emerged his basic thesis: "We may suppose that the higher the demand a movement makes on its followers, the fewer there will be who respond to it, but the greater the individual and aggregate impact of those who do respond." (We witness this principle in the book of Acts. Luke records that some minority of believers empowered by the Holy Spirit were perceived as having "turned the world upside down" [Acts 17:6, KJV].)

Kelley's thesis has been challenged by many since the book was published in 1972. Much of the critique focuses on the question: "Why does high demand attract some and repel others?" Max Weber responds briefly in *Sociology of Religion* by suggesting that those who are willing to give religious concerns such significant proportions of their energies as "virtuosi of religion."[8] For Christians, the statement of Jesus comes to mind: "Many are called, but few are chosen" (Matthew 20:16; 22:14, KJV).

In summary, Weber identifies the characteristics of a strong religious movement:

> The strong religious organization makes very high demands upon its members. They must give it absolute and unswerving allegiance; be willing to work, suffer, and die for it; abandon all competing activities, allegiances, and responsibilities in its favor; tell its Good News tirelessly and unselfconsciously to strangers; wear its stigmata of humiliation on their bodies; submit to its strictures, conformities, and disciplines; go where they are sent and do what they are told.[9]

Of the many religious groups Kelley studied, the Anabaptists and Wesleyans especially impressed him. He felt that they excelled in giving guidance in shaping and preserving the integrity of the religious organization without violating the dignity or integrity of persons.

Up to this point, we have considered Dean Kelley's hypotheses for what constitutes strong social structures. But much of his study focuses on the causes of decline in social structures. What I call historical drift, Kelley refers to as "slippage" or "decline." His theory is essentially the reverse of what constitutes strong structures, i.e., that subtle diminishing of demands contribute to slippage and decline.

He notes, too, that the uniqueness of a movement *and* the stronger the commitments of the adherents are both secrets of their strength and their Achilles' heel for compromise.

Another illustration of slippage would be the Congregational churches in New England which made concessions called the "halfway covenant." This made provision for partial membership, an effort to accommodate the lukewarmness in children and grandchildren of believers who could not meet the demands of conversion. Commenting on the impact of this compromise, Frankland H. Littell, an authority on the origins of Protestantism, noted that they not only "halved the covenant" for their children again and again until there was scarcely a sliver left, but also progressively relaxed the standards of membership for those coming in from outside who could make no filial claim.[10]

Compromising on expectations contributes to slippage.

Ironically, success is another factor. With success comes the pressure of upward social mobility. John Wesley called it "the pride of life." By this he meant a danger which overtakes even the most zealous movement: success. Kelley explains:

> The same broadening of interests and concerns is apparent in churches as well as in their members. Some churchmen have, for the most commendable of motives, concluded that God desires His servants to seek justice, freedom, and truth as well as obedient faith. In fact, they may have reached the heretical conclusion that there are obediences more important to God

than maintaining the social strength of a particular institution—even His Church![11]

The subtle shift from stringency to stricture indicates loss to slippage. Early in strong movements, members admonish and encourage other members to adhere to the core values. All members feel they have a personal responsibility to preserve the discipline and purity of the organization. This is healthy stringency. However, later in the movement's history, these actions lose their spontaneity. Members tend not to monitor one another. It now becomes the responsibility of the leaders. This is stricture which is imposed. "The Old Order Amish would be a strictured survival of Anabaptist stringency."[12]

In conclusion, Kelley states that "entropy is the simplest explanation"[13] sociologically for slippage in a movement. Organizations do run down and social strength does ebb away.

What value for today's church leaders can be derived from Kelley? I suggest two concepts, neither of which Dean Kelley mentions but which his writings trigger.

When he speaks of strong commitment and high level of demands, my mind immediately gravitates to Christ's call to His prospective disciples: "If anyone comes to me and does not hate his father and mother, his wife and children, his brothers and sisters—yes, even his own life—he cannot be my disciple. And anyone who does not carry his cross and follow me cannot be my disciple" (Luke 14:26-27). This has been the basic secret to the survival of the church over a 2,000-year period.

Although Kelley is helpful as he addresses the human factor in forming strong social structures, the power of God in the lives of believers must be added. This helps to explain the role of persecution: "The blood of the martyrs is the seed of the church." One communistic government finally learned this principle. Their counsel to similar regimes was: "Whatever you do with Christians, don't persecute them.

They only grow stronger." More on this when we examine how to impede historical drift.

The second key principle which Kelley fails to factor into his thesis is the innate ability of the Church to be renewed spiritually. A major aspect of impeding historical drift is frequent times of revival. This is an important theme which will be considered in Part V.

The most helpful aspect from Kelley's work is, in my opinion, that of asking and expecting high commitment. If Kelley is right, the current strategy which seeks to attract nonbelievers through making the church user-friendly appears flawed. Certainly unnecessary barriers must be removed, but no matter how we rework the core message of Christianity, there's a cross. In God's economy the high cost of Christianity becomes a powerful attraction when the Holy Spirit is at work in our lives.

I have seen Kelley's commitment theory work with highly successful Bible studies. They require homework—done before you arrive. If not, you do it while the rest are in their discussion hour. And, if you miss three times during a twelve-week period, you are dropped from the group. What's the impact of such demands? A waiting list for those who want to join!

I have too often seen his theory proven true in groups that fail. They were based on the popular but erroneous principle, "Don't scare people off with high demands; homework is optional; come when you can."

Donald A. McGavran

I have introduced you to two people from the social sciences: George Barna, who is a current voice, and Dean Kelley, who is an ongoing mentor from an earlier period. Now, I want to introduce one more—a man who would be in my version of "Who's Who in the 20th Century," Donald A. McGavran. His message to the Church may be summed up in the following quote: "Men like to become Christians without crossing racial, linguistic, or class barriers."

As my professor, his teaching on the mission of the Church gave me a blueprint for the rest of my ministry. As a scholar of cultural anthropology, he skillfully harnessed the social sciences for the propagation of the gospel, all the while carefully subjecting them to the queen of the sciences, theology. In this, he has modeled a critical balance I endeavor to emulate. As a Christian gentleman, his gracious public critique of those who disagreed with him was an example I never want to forget. He held tenaciously to biblical truth, but did it with grace.

So what's so special about his thesis—"Men like to become Christians without crossing racial, linguistic, or class barriers"? Don't all churches and missionaries believe that? To McGavran's credit, many more today do, but in mid-20th-century India, where McGavran worked, many didn't. Many believed faithfulness to God was adequate. Missions were just emerging from the colonial era in 1955 when McGavran compiled a little book entitled *The Bridges of God*. Some missionaries still believed that natives needed to learn English or German (depending on the missionary's mother tongue) in order to become Christians.

In it, he began to probe various mission operations to discover why evangelism was ineffective and churches were not developing. Many were involved with schools, but few were effective in evangelism. Confusion reigned as to what was the task of the church. McGavran declared as fact "that eighty per cent and more of the activities of missions (in 1970) are organized good deeds and social action that take the attention of many younger churches off the propagation of the Gospel."[14]

As he researched mission fields, utilizing the tools of anthropology, sociology and theology, he developed what he later called "church growth eyes." His initial conclusion? Receptivity of the gospel had never been greater, and that most people aren't resistant but neglected due to the missionaries' inability to understand cultures and to strategize for results.

McGavran returned to North America and established an Institute for Church Growth in Eugene, Oregon. In 1965, he accepted the invitation to move it to Fuller Seminary. This gave him a worldwide platform as leaders of younger churches came to study at The School of World Mission, a division of Fuller Theological Seminary. In his basic text, *Understanding Church Growth*, McGavran explains his understanding of the need:

> What priorities are correct? Among many good enterprises, which has preeminence? Which should come first and which—if any have to be—should be omitted? How is carrying out the will of God to be measured? What has really been accomplished as the Church has spread on new ground? Considerations of anthropology, sociology, theology, and organizational complexity pile up one on the other. Never was a clear mission theory more needed than today—a theory firmly rooted in biblical truth.[15]

McGavran insisted on a solid theological basis. He believed that the planting of churches (assemblies of baptized believers) was pleasing to God. He also was convinced of the anthropological dimension of this task. The size, number, ethnic and cultural composition of the undiscipled people must be known and can be measured. Undefined faithfulness was unacceptable.

He became the architect for the new discipline of the 1970s called "missiology." It has been correctly defined as "the harnessing of the social sciences," i.e., sociology, anthropology, education and psychology, but always rendering them subservient to the queen of the sciences, theology.

When Peter Wagner introduced Church Growth to the North American churches in the mid '70s, evangelical interest in the social sciences exploded. What had been a helpful tool in assisting the missionary to understand his target culture now became the bottom line for "doing church" in the North American context. This resulted in burnout for two decades of pastors, caught up in the numbers game. (The penchant of North Americans to discover a good idea and then market it into a heresy is well documented. This explains the backlash to the Church Growth Movement now common among evangelicals. Donald McGavran, from the beginning, warned against this. He insisted that theology must always be preeminent over the behavioral sciences.)

Mike Regele

This title, *Death of the Church*, caught my attention. Mike Regele, the author, writes with his theological degree from Fuller in one hand and a sheaf of demographic surveys in the other. His thesis is blunt and clear: "The institutional church will either choose to die or it will choose to die in order to live."[16]

Because of change, he believes the Church is moving rapidly to a "defining moment." Stating his thesis even more pointedly, here are the options: "Simply, we can die because of our hidebound resistance to change, or we can die in order to live."[17] He suggests the first is easier, since the church left to its propensity to drift is on an express route to death. The second option is difficult: "We will experience many forms of fear and discomfort. Anger and frustration will plague our efforts. Recalcitrance will thwart plans. Uncertainty will be a constant companion."[18]

Regele uniquely approaches the issue of historical drift. He agrees that exponential change and the church's inability to cope effectively has led to the irrelevance of most churches. He leans heavily on generational theory as developed by Strauss and Howe in *Generations: The History of America's Future, 1584 to 2069*. Their research of a four-century period indicates a generational cycle of eighty years. Quoting

Strauss and Howe, Regele states: "When we look at a broad sweep of history, it appears that there is a regular and repeated cycle that is roughly eighty to ninety years in length. This cycle, in turn, can be divided into four periods of approximately equal length, hence four generations of twenty to twenty-two years each."[19]

By identifying six spiritual awakenings and five secular crises over the last four centuries, they believe we can predict the ebb and flow of the Church and its effectiveness. They cautiously predict an impending crisis around 2003 which will produce a growing sense of insecurity. This, in turn, will move our culture away from its inner directed values of self-indulgence and back to a renewed communitarian spirit. Based on this theory, we may expect the seventh spiritual awakening around the year 2035-2045.[20]

Summary

In summary, these three proponents of harnessing the social sciences to increase the harvest—Barna, Kelley and McGavran—have been helpful in my ministry both as a missionary and a churchman in North America. Mike Regele is new to me. I am attracted to his perspective on generational theory which links secular crisis and spiritual awakening.

Later, as I diagnose historical drift, I will lay considerable responsibility on evangelical leaders for buying too deeply into the social sciences. Earlier in this chapter, I raised the question: "Social sciences—friend or foe of the Church?" Many Christians, especially in the field of cultural anthropology, have been openly hostile to the missionary enterprise. Much of psychology has been negative for the Church. But the authors I have profiled in this chapter are definitely friends.

~

Discussion Questions

1. George Barna uses the analogy of the "frog in the kettle." What is the application for the Christian church?
2. Dean Kelley suggests four commonly accepted guidelines for Christian organizations which he believes lead to *historical drift*. How does your church relate to these? Do you tend to endorse or reject these?
3. What does Mike Regele mean when he says, "The institutional church will either choose to die or it will choose to die in order to live?"
4. What's the good news (see pages 40-41) from the 18th-century church in England? Are there parallels to the conditions in North American society today?

Good News

In the Darkest Hour,
God Does His Greatest Work

In 1750, Francis Asbury, colleague of John and Charles Wesley, described the spiritual condition of both the English Church and nation as "a very dark, dark, dark day and place."[21]

> Many English ministers were tinged with deism but would not go so far as to reject the orthodox creeds. The clergy became coldly intellectual, unconcerned with the low morals of the majority of Englishmen. In the clergy's books the learning was vast, but in the pulpit it was deadly. "Dull, duller, and dullest" was an estimation of their appeal. Rationalism made the ministers afraid to utter anything that might be construed as an emotional statement or appeal. Deistic tendencies, rationalism, abject worldliness within the churches, indolence, infidelity—all of these characteristics and more described the eighteenth-century English church scene.[22]

This dismal scenario of the Church of England plunges the tragic impact of historical drift to a new low.

But "English society was even worse, and one may wonder if the church's weaknesses contributed to the grossness and immorality, or if it simply reflected it. England from the Restoration to the Colonial War was course, lawless, ignorant, and vain."[23]

Into this dark hour came three men. John and Charles Wesley and George Whitefield had studied together at Oxford. They joined a deeply religious group which fasted twice a week, had frequent communion and helped prisoners in a local jail.

God was about to impact two continents by these men.

Wesley developed the society as a way for encouraging converts. By means of prayer and Bible study among a small group, the society leader could discern if each member was growing in grace. Smaller "bands" of five to ten persons were formed for those who wanted even closer fellowship. . . . The Methodist movement grew with great rapidity as a revival movement within the Church of England. . . . John was assisted by his brother Charles in several aspects, particularly in the composing of hymns that sang their way into the hearts of the English-speaking world.

In North America,

Francis Asbury . . . had taken John Wesley as his model, for he duplicated in his own wilderness diocese of America what Wesley had accomplished in England. . . . In 1780, there were 42 preachers and 8,504 members. In 1820, by which time Asbury had passed on, there were 904 preachers and 256,881 members.[24]

"Rarely does a second-generation hold the convictions it has inherited with the fervor equal to its fathers."

—Richard Niebuhr, sociologist and author of
The Social Sources of Denominations, p. 20.

Part II

HISTORICAL DRIFT DIAGNOSED

During my teaching ministry in Latin America, this theme of historical drift surfaced periodically. In my attempt to emphasize the inevitability and consequences of the drift pattern in organizations, I referred to it as "la curva maldita." ("The cursed curve" would be an acceptable English translation.) Fifteen years later, this rendering came back to haunt me.

One of my students, now a leading pastor in Latin America, came to Canada in 1992 as our guest at a biennial church conference. While interviewing him at a men's luncheon, I asked him to comment on the unusual ability of his national church to sustain a strong passion for evangelism. Although he spoke good English, he had not been to North America for many years. He began to respond to my question, then paused.

"Yes," he finally continued, "I remember that you spoke about this tendency of organizations to lose vitality over time. I recall you referred to it as a curve. I think you called it the 'damn curve'!"

I lost the interview right there! Some of the conferees were almost literally rolling off their chairs with laughter. In an attempt to recover, I scrambled to explain to my friend that his translation was "a little strong," that the literal translation would be "the cursed curve," to which he responded by again calling it "the damn curve!" Indeed, it is a bad curve!

One of my theses pertaining to this curve is that, in social structures, it is inevitable. This includes secular corporations, Sunday school classes, denominations, local churches, parachurches (now better known as "enabling agencies"), secular universities, seminaries, etc. My second thesis is, "With good leadership, historical drift can be curbed, and the curve can be extended."

In this section, as I diagnose the curve of historical drift, I will address my first thesis—its inevitability. We will view this in three venues: first, in the context of similar curves; second, in the marketplace of the corporate world, and third, in Church history.

"For religion must necessarily produce both industry and frugality, and these cannot but produce riches."

—John Wesley, as quoted in Dean M. Kelley, p. 55

3

The Cursed Curve

Why Historical Drift Is Inevitable

S INCE DEVELOPING MY OWN CURVE some years ago, I have since discovered several other versions. Some describe the process as a

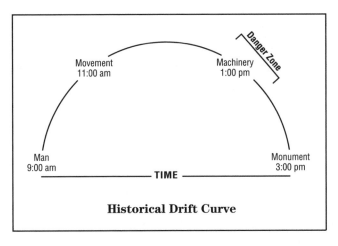

Figure 2: Historical Drift Curve

cycle instead of a curve. But the basic concept remains constant—the loss of vitality over time.

Rags-to-Riches-to-Rags

Richard Niebuhr, a sociologist, develops this cycle in his book, *The Social Sources of Denominationalism*:

> The children born to the voluntary members of the first generation begin to make the sect a church long before they have arrived at the years of discretion. For with their coming the sect must take on the character of an educational and disciplinary institution, with the purpose of bringing the new generation into conformity with ideals and customs which have become traditional. Rarely does a second generation hold the convictions it has inherited with a fervor equal to that of its fathers, who fashioned these convictions in the heat of conflict and at the rush of martyrdom. As generation succeeds generation, the isolation of the community from the world becomes more difficult.[1]

Niebuhr's use of the term "sect" reflects Ernst Troeltsch's terminology where he sees churches beginning as a sect, then evolving into an institution and finally into a denomination.

The Sociological Cycle of Church Growth

Elmer L. Towns, researcher of rapidly growing American churches, has developed a sociological cycle. By his own confession, he expanded the basic cycle employed by Ernst Troeltsch, David Moberg and other secular sociologists.[2]

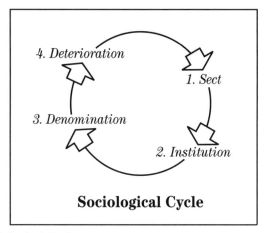

Figure 3: Sociological Cycle

Moberg describes the cycle as "a process by which cults originate, develop into sects, and then change into denominations, perhaps to finally emerge from the process as churches." Towns has simply added a fourth phase to the cycle, i.e., deterioration. His adaptation is designed to serve as a grid to study the dynamics of fundamentalism (the sect), evangelicalism (institution) and denominationalism (mainline denominations or the position of theological liberalism). The last phase he identifies with "deterioration."

At the time of his study of the ten fastest growing churches in America (1972), all were in the category of "sect" or "fundamentalism" based on Town's categories.[3] The dictionary defines "sect" as "a dissenting or schismatic religious body."[4] This cycle, although helpful thirty years ago, is of limited value today.

Evangelicalism now dominates the conservative landscape in the Western world, and denominationalism needs to be subdivided between the evangelical and non-evangelical groups. However, what it does is display the constant shifting from one structure to another.

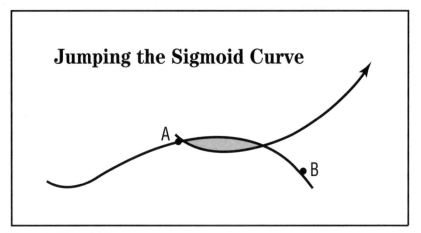

Figure 4: Sigmoid Curve

Charles Handy, an English structural theorist, developed what he called the "sigmoid curve." This curve derives its name from the 18th letter of the Greek alphabet, *sigma*. Its uniqueness lies in the dual curves moving in opposite directions. Bob Buford of Leadership Network comments: "One of the most useful tools in understanding the natural life cycle of a product, an organization, a church or even a relationship is the sigmoid or S curve."[5]

Most versions of the basic bell curve focus on taking strategic action just after high noon prior to the slippery slope territory. Handy's theory argues that such action is too late. Change must be initiated before the peak point. Take the initiative while there is still energy, time and resources. Do not wait for the inevitable dip toward point B. Take action at point A, prime time—and develop a new upward curve.

I like this concept, although the following implications present a formidable challenge:

- Implication 1: It requires different thinking because it challenges the conservative adages, "Don't fix it if it ain't broke," "Don't tinker with success," "Don't believe insiders who assure us that everything is fine, no need to change anything."

- Implication 2: The second curve, whether it is a new product, a new strategy or a new program, will be different from the first curve "and so will most of the people who lead the new curve!"
- Implication 3: For a time, new ideas and new people will need to work together. Note the shaded area between A and B. There will be necessary overlap until the second curve is established and the first one begins to wane and ultimately vanish.
- Implication 4: This shaded period has great potential for tension. Imagine new innovative personnel working with long-term employees—new ideas competing with old ideas for the future of the organization.

This sigmoid curve challenges institutions not only to identify their location but also every leader within the organization to ask the tough personal career questions.[6] Only avant-garde companies who consistently work with consultants to keep current can execute this curve successfully. Most organizations are well on their way to the danger zone of the slippery slope before reaching out for help.

To Dream Again: The Organizational Life Cycle

The organizational life cycle bell curve was developed by Robert D. Dale, Professor of Pastoral Leadership and Church Ministries at Southeastern Baptist Theological Seminary.

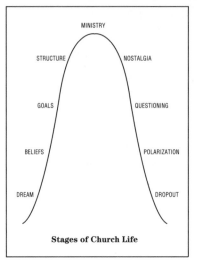

Figure 5: Stages of Church Life

Every bell curve tells the same tale: vitality is lost over time. Dale's last category on the downward side of the curve is "dropout." Professor Dale submits that there are four ways to revitalize a church organizationally:

- The easiest area is policy change. You simply adjust the way you do things.
- A second strategy is to change personnel, firing the minister or electing new lay leaders.
- Another change tactic is to create new program structures. Reorganizational plans are familiar in institutions of all kinds.
- The fourth way to revitalize a church is to define and act on its fundamental purpose. A new dream awakens a congregation.[7]

In the last chapter entitled *Planning for Vitality*, Dale recommends a psychohistory profile of the congregation. Everyone, according to age, is categorized under four areas of need—religious, developmental, family and vocational: "Strong ministry to strategic needs helps a con-

gregation minister effectively and appropriately. A psychohistory profile of your church may help you focus on key ministry issues with
more awareness and confidence. Healthy ministry is the product of
planning to meet real needs."[8] The Dale curve becomes a helpful device in assessing the human resources needed to revitalize a church.

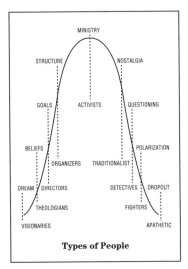

Figure 6: Types of People

Note the nine distinct types of people on the inside of the curve.
How many of each are in the congregation? Which are the largest
groups? How many people are in the smallest groups? He suggests that
the answers to these questions become the indicator to the next step toward restoring vitality—dreaming again.

In describing the tensions of a church in decline, Dale zeroes in on
organization, the typical scapegoat. He refers to it as a "descent into organizational hell." Victims of historical drift gravitate toward various
forms of conflict. This corresponds to the downward side of the
curve—handling the conflict of nostalgic members. Organizational
conflict follows three predictable stages:

- Questioning: The goals of the organization come under fire.

- Polarization: Conflict is now open, escalating and messy.
- Dropout: Some members give up and drop out.[9]

Two of the most helpful aspects of Dale's work are these: 1) the developing of a psychohistory profile of the congregation. This identifies the breakdown of needs based upon categories of age (p. 141); and 2) the critical matter of choosing the key issue and the most strategic group which represents it in the congregation.

He begins with nostalgia, which he defines as "organizational homesickness." The nostalgia issue is critical in three areas: diagnosis, cure and prevention (p. 26, 107). He sees a congregation "dream again."

Congregational Passages

George Bullard, consultant and head coach of New Reformation Solutions, brings to the challenge of church renewal a long and effective track record of ministry in the Southern Baptist Convention. In recent years, he served as the architect for a very successful strategy developed by the South Carolina State Convention. He has identified ten stages of congregational development as seen in Figure 7:

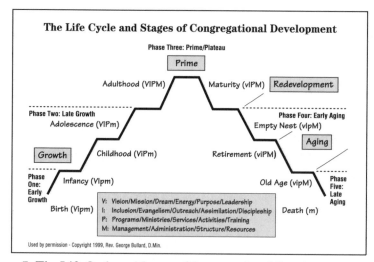

Figure 7: The Life Cycle and Stages of Congregational Development

These stages correspond to five phases of the life cycle:

Phase One: Early Growth
Phase Two: Late Growth
Phase Three: Prime/Plateau
Phase Four: Early Aging
Phase Five: Late Aging

Bullard's basic thesis is as follows: To understand the life cycle of a congregation "is to understand the pattern of the organizing principles that make up the various stages of congregational life. This life cycle is principle driven."[10]

The four organizational principles are:

- Vision: "The current understanding of God's strategic spiritual direction for the local congregation that is cast by the leadership and owned by the membership."
- Inclusion: "The relational processes by which persons are brought to faith in God through Jesus Christ, become involved in a local New Testament church, are assimilated into the fellowship life and care ministry of the church, have opportunities for spiritual growth and leadership development, and utilize their gifts and skills through kingdom involvement.
- Programs: "The functional attempts to provide ministries, services, activities, and training for people related to the congregation by membership, attendance, fellowship, or through inclusion processes."
- Management: "The administration of the resources of the congregation, the decision-making structure of the congregation, the formal and informal culture of the congregation, and the openness of the congregation to change and grow."[11]

He goes on to provide seven observations on the growth side of the life cycle and seven on the aging side. The following are slightly abbreviated versions of his fourteen observations:

Growth Side of the Life Cycle

- In order for a congregation to keep developing it needs to focus on the organizing principle formula of the next stage of development.
- Congregations can become dysfunctional and stop developing.
- Vision and inclusion fuel congregations on the growth side.
- No more than twenty-five to thirty-five percent of congregations are on the growth side of the life cycle.
- The change and growth style utilized is different for different stages of the life cycle.
- The leadership style of congregational leaders is different for different stages of the life cycle.
- The issues to be addressed are different for different stages of the life cycle.

Aging Side of the Life Cycle

- The vast majority of congregations who do strategic planning or attempt some journey of change and growth are on the aging side of the life cycle.
- As a result of their position on the aging side of the life cycle, congregations are being sustained by their management rather than fueled by their vision.
- The change and redevelopment strategy is different for different aging stages.

- The length of time it takes to produce lasting change is different for different stages of the life cycle. Generally, the more aged the congregation, the longer it takes to produce lasting change.
- Some people feel there should be no aging side to the life cycle because congregations should redevelop with a new vision, a new life cycle or an explosive curve of new, positive change and growth. This is ideal. The ideal may happen less than twenty percent of the time.
- Death is not inevitable. The life cycle and stages of development are not deterministic. Having said that death is not inevitable, congregations who are aging are dysfunctional, and those who will wait until Phase Five: Late Aging to seek a turnaround are unlikely to experience a positive, successful future.[12]

I have found Bullard's Life Cycle and Stages of Congregational Development the most helpful grid for analyzing the current status of an organization. Although this diagram is designed for congregations, I have seen it used effectively in the evaluation of a denomination. A common malady of denominations is their propensity to become self-serving. Congregations quickly sense that "they exist for the denomination." For denominations to have a future, that perception in the churches must be changed. This simply means denominations must change.

One example of positive change is exemplified in the South Carolina Southern Baptist State Convention to which we previously referred. The denomination began to listen to the congregations. They stopped cranking out programs for the churches and started discovering what would help them. They developed what is known as EKG: "Empowering churches to fulfill their vision for Kingdom Growth." Over a six-year period, they saw a thirty-eight percent increase in the number of growing churches.

Why Is Historical Drift Inevitable?

To concede that historical drift is inevitable sounds negative. In all other aspects of life we expect and pay professionals to tell us the truth even if it's terminal. Only in the church do people want just good news. Current popular evangelical leaders skillfully downplay anything potentially negative. To affirm the inevitability of the loss of spiritual vitality falls into that unsavory category. To simply ignore the possibility of drift is to reject major sections of the New Testament: e.g., the ministry of Jesus, the admonitions of Paul, the warnings of Hebrews and the final exhortations of Jesus to the seven Asian churches, to name a few.

Biblical Causes of Historical Drift

Congenital Defect

Mankind is born flawed. Original sin is both a theological and experiential fact. "Therefore, just as sin entered the world through one man, and death through sin, and in this way death came to all men, because all sinned—for before the law was given, sin was in the world" (Romans 5:12-13). And Psalm 51:5: "Surely I was sinful at birth, sinful from the time my mother conceived me."

Evidence of original sin in society abounds—from the most heinous crime committed by culturally refined persons to the lament of small merchants who cannot find honest employees with commitment and integrity. The corruption in governments and business attests to the total depravity of mankind. But in the church we work with redeemed humanity. The question is: Does that make an obvious difference in matters where the rubber meets the road?

Theologians continue to debate the degree to which Christians can live beyond the pull of original sin. Pastor-turned-professor, Eugene Peterson, reminds us that pastoral ministry must start with this premise:

An understanding of people as sinners enables a pastoral ministry to function without anger. . . . If people are sinners then pastors can concentrate on talking about God's action in Jesus Christ instead of sitting around lamenting how bad the people are. We already know they can't make it. We already have accepted their depravity.[13]

He had lived to be 104. During his life, he sat under fourteen pastors. He served as church treasurer for thirty-seven years and had participated in church ministries for fifty-one consecutive years. He admitted to disagreeing with his pastors at times and recognized that they too were fallen creatures. But he chose to handle such occasions in two ways: first, he prayed for them and, secondly, he never put them on a pedestal.

A sophomore Bible college student, cutting his teeth in campus leadership, lamented to me: "I delegate responsibility, but they don't carry through." My response, "Welcome to leadership!" Many leaders quickly buy into the old adage: "People don't do what is expected but what is inspected."

Yes, mankind is born flawed.

The Toll of Time

Time is a great healer *and* a greater eroder. It dilutes commitment, blurs vision, undermines values and destroys virtues. The darker side of generation theory would remind us that in questionable ethical issues what one generation rejects the second one tolerates and the third one embraces.

At every level of Christian living and ministry, time takes its toll. Complacency gradually replaces commitment. The desire to be served subtly displaces the desire to serve. Monetary motivation slowly takes priority over ministry. Wants evolve into needs. And, through it all, historical drift becomes the winner.

Passing the Baton

Transition in leadership has been a common contributor to drift. With few exceptions, this was the pattern of the Old Testament kings. Discerning leaders and boards believe that the loss of spiritual vitality can be curbed and even reversed in the process of choosing a new leader. A few astute boards of directors, aware of the tendency for institutions to drift, deliberately choose a new leader "just a little to the right" of the incumbent.

Both secular history and church history frequently remind us of the evils of nepotism, but a case could be built for some exceptions. Recent evangelical church history demonstrates several very positive transitions from fathers to sons, extending the curve of the ministry's effectiveness for several more decades. Later, we will look at several examples of this.

On the other hand, contemporary theology in this century, especially coming out of Europe, reminds us how truth is lost in the passing of the torch. A number of contemporary theologians are products of evangelical parsonages who took their graduate studies in Europe. Upon their return, they chose to follow their fathers' calling, but not their theology.

Incompetence Syndrome

Peter Laurence's humorous yet serious book, *The Peter Principle*, grows out of his study of the hierarchy of organizations. He fingers the system of promotions as the major contributor to obsolescence—historical drift. He observed that in an organizational hierarchy, people tend to be promoted to the level of their incompetence. Apart from the pressure to promote is the matter of false assumptions, i.e., good sales personnel make good sales managers; quality teachers make excellent principals; effective pastors make outstanding bishops. The victims of this flawed system often find themselves both ineffective and trapped. Unfortunately, the corporate system provides no dignified way to back down the ladder. One company created twenty-one vice presidents, thus providing a lateral move to resolve their corporate blunder! In more recent times, companies create attractive early retirement incentives to move out the incompetents with dignity.[14]

The Myth of Redemptive Lift

"Doesn't the gospel lift people socially?" one may ask. Although lift is not the initial intent, it is reality. In the class-conscious society of Latin America, the early missionaries reached only the lower classes. The upper classes were resistant and seemingly inaccessible. The middle class did not exist. Within a generation, however, evangelical churches were full of middle-class people, a testimony to the fact of redemptive lift.

How does it happen?

Meet my friend José. He's the father of eight children. He regularly left half of his paycheck at the bar. He also supported a mistress on the side. He couldn't afford shoes for his children. This meant that they couldn't go to school. Then José met Christ. His life was radically changed. He no longer drinks. He brings home the paycheck. He dropped the mistress on the side. He now has money for shoes. The children are in school. This family unit has been lifted socially. But there's even more good news. Since the gospel spreads best through family webs, soon his extended family experienced redemptive lift. This is the quiet social revolution of the gospel.

Why then did John Wesley lament redemptive lift? True, he rejoiced that the scum of English society had been transformed by the gospel, but as they became productive, frugal, industrious citizens, they became affluent. Then, with riches came pride, covetousness and selfishness. The very gospel that lifted first-generation believers socially now appeared to be destroying second and third generations by the resulting affluence.

Organizations Don't Drift—Only Their Leaders

Organizations, although managed by living beings, are inanimate structures. As such, they are impervious to culture, change and climate. We speak of organizations having a life of their own apart from people. One mutual fund does twenty-two percent. Chrysler has their worst quarter ever. A local church is dying. A denomination is plateaued. These are all helpful euphemisms employed by CEOs, bishops, pastors, presidents, elders, etc., to deflect personal responsibility for the drifting of their organizations.

Weakened Commitment to Scripture

The Christian's commitment to Scripture, historically, is rooted in Christ's endorsement of the Old Testament passages. We identify with His exclusive commitment when He declares to Satan: "Man does not live on bread alone, but on every word that comes from the mouth of God" (Matthew 4:4).

We agree with Paul's understanding: "All Scripture is God-breathed and is useful for teaching, rebuking, correcting and training in righteousness, so that the man of God may be thoroughly equipped for every good work" (2 Timothy 3:16-17). And we endorse Peter's teaching that the New Testament is on par with the Old Testament Scriptures, when he states:

> Bear in mind that our Lord's patience means salvation, just as our dear brother Paul also wrote you with the wisdom that God gave him. He writes the same way in all his letters, speaking in them of these matters. His letters contain some things that are hard to understand, which ignorant and unstable people distort, as they do the other Scriptures, to their own destruction. (2 Peter 3:15-16)

We accept the decisions of the Patristic Fathers of the 4th century who acted with divine wisdom in the closing of the canon of Scripture, including sixty-six books. We rejoice in the restoring of Scripture as the only rule for faith and life by the Protestant Reformation of the 16th century, and returning the Bible to the common man.

We heartily agree with the summary statement of the Chicago Commission on the Inerrancy of Scripture as being adequate, clear and understandable for the laity: "The Bible says what God says, through human writers without error." I heartily agree with the following statement: "Scripture, plainly read by plain people, should be plainly understood.... Yielding to the temptation to explain [away certain texts] is being done on all sides. We indulge it at immense peril."[15]

Although all evangelicals profess to hold to a high view of Scripture, their approach to interpreting it betrays their profession. The Spanish adage from the days of the chalkboard applies here: "What they write with their hand they erase with their elbow."

This weakened commitment to the authority of Scripture, whether conscious or unconscious, fails the following simple five-point test of a high-view hermeneutic:

- Go with the clarity of Scripture, not with the obscure passages.
- Listen for the Spirit of Scripture on any given issue.
- Let Scripture interpret Scripture to find consensus and harmony.
- Follow Christ's handling of Scripture, e.g., referencing issues back to the Old Testament, especially Genesis.
- Hold tenaciously to a literal interpretation of Scripture wherever possible.

A weakened commitment to Scripture, more than any other factor, has facilitated historical drift. It renders us vulnerable to the subtle accommodation to culture. Currently in evangelicalism there are three battle-for-the-Bible fronts: the ordination of women, divorce and remarriage for pastors and the ordination of homosexuals. On all three fronts, the first and most basic hermeneutical principle is being ignored: i.e., the clear passages of Scripture must be used to interpret the obscure—not vice versa.

~

Discussion Questions

1. Why does the author call this the "cursed curve"?
2. He considers this curve to be inevitable. Why? Do you agree with him?
3. Do some of the other curves give hope for reversing it? Which ones?
4. Where would you pinpoint your church on the "Life Cycle and Stages of Congregational Development?"

Good News

The Miracle of EKG

The South Carolina Baptist Convention is 175 years old. It predates the Southern Baptist Convention by twenty-four years. In 1996, they had 1,884 churches in South Carolina. In 1990, they discovered that seventy-five percent of their churches had plateaued or were declining and dying.

A staff, committed to change, began to pray and plan. With unanimous support of the State Convention, a ten-year emphasis (1992-2002) was launched. They named it "Empowering Kingdom Growth (EKG)." "Empowering churches to fulfill their vision for Kingdom Growth" became the mission statement. George Bullard, quoted earlier, served as the architect, while Carlisle Driggers executed the plan.

So what has God done since 1990?

Since we first began back in 1990 to talk seriously about a new direction for our work, we have seen an increase in average Sunday school attendance; a 38% increase in the number of growing churches; no plus or minus percentage change in plateauing churches, and a 13% decrease in declining and dying churches. At the same time, we have witnessed the starting of 110 new church-type missions with a net increase of 60 new churches.[16]

The budget was surpassed. "We have also seen monies from the churches steadily increasing to the point where we surpassed our budget requirements in 1995 for the first time since 1990. This past year, we received the largest total receipts in our history."

Tensions have been reduced: "In addition, we have watched with gratitude and some degree of amazement as tensions among our Baptist people across the state have reduced."[17]

Four words summarize these positive results:

- Image: Changed from churches serving the denomination to the denomination serving the churches.
- Simplicity: Keeping a singular focus: Empowering Kingdom Growth (EKG) one church at a time.
- Networking: Commitment to team ministry, drawing on the resources of other churches.
- Service: "Our staff does not exist for the churches to serve the convention, but the convention exists to serve the churches. That is our business, and we are hard at it."[18]

"A charismatic leader is not an asset but a problem to recover from."

—Jim Collins, Built to Last Organizations

4

Clock Building, Not Time Telling

Learning from the Corporate World

I HAVE LAUDED THE CONTRIBUTIONS of several Christian social scientists. We now turn to a related but different question. What, if anything, should we learn from the secular corporate world? The cyberspace-oriented church world has greatly expanded the reason for this old question. The Internet has reduced the universe of information to a global village mentality, and the advent of church growth theory in the '60s has catapulted many churches and their leaders into the pursuit of sociology, anthropology, psychology, etc. In some cases, it has thrown church leaders into a bungee binge. We jump to the latest high-tech church seminar skillfully marketing thinly veiled principles from the corporate world, then rebound to the occasional seminar on prayer and renewal.

So, what does Jesus say about worldly wisdom?

Plenty. He sees the world—cosmos—opposing His purposes. "My kingdom is not of this world" (John 18:36). Instead, He directs the majority of His remarks to remind His disciples that this world is their mission: "You are the light of the world" (Matthew 5:14).

There were, however, two occasions when Jesus seems to encourage His people to learn from the world. One is in the context of commissioning the twelve: "I am sending you out like sheep among wolves. Therefore be as shrewd as snakes and as innocent as doves" (10:16). Another is found in the parable of the astute manager. It has to be the most difficult of all parables to understand.

The boss fires an irresponsible manager who, in the process of leaving, pulls off a creative plan to recover a part of three bad debts. Listen to a boss change his mind: "The master commended the dishonest manager because he had acted shrewdly" (Luke 16:8). But more amazing is Jesus' comment: "For the people of this world [age] are more shrewd in dealing with their own kind than are the people of the light. I tell you, use worldly wealth to gain friends for yourselves, so that when it is gone, you will be welcomed into eternal dwellings" (16:8-9).

I certainly don't believe we have to encourage Christian leaders to learn from the world. The world's values are already seeping into our churches, and our leaders all too often embrace them unconsciously. But it is true that "all truth is God's truth." Occasionally, in His sovereignty, He affirms His truth even in a secular context. Jim Collins, a secular author in the corporate world, is an illustration of this exception.

The Successful Habits of Visionary Companies

Published in 1994, the book *Built to Last: The Successful Habits of Visionary Companies* was for several years a best-seller in the corporate world. James C. Collins and Jerry I. Porras, the authors, are professors from

Stanford Graduate School of Business. For more than six years, they re-searched eighteen successful and enduring companies. These companies had an average age of almost 100 years. The authors also studied the pri-mary competitor of each company to determine why those companies had not attained the same level of success. Their bottom-line question was, "What makes the truly exceptional companies different from other companies?"

Bill Hybels, senior pastor of the Willow Creek Community Church, interviewed James Collins at the 1997 Willow Creek Association lead-ership conference. Collins, a self-confessed "seeker" versus "believer," responded with some success principles which might apply to the Christian church.

Clock Building, Not Time Telling

> Imagine you met a remarkable person who could look at the sun or stars at any time of day or night and state the exact time and date. . . . This person would be an amazing time teller and we'd probably revere that person for the ability to tell time. But wouldn't that person be even more amazing if, instead of tell-ing the time, he or she built a clock that could tell the time for-ever, even after he or she was dead and gone?[1]

Is there any application here for the Church? We see many success-ful megachurches with charismatic leaders. Collins shocked the lead-ership conference, stating: "A charismatic leader is not an asset but a problem to recover from."[2]

The Tyranny of the "Or" and the Genius of the "And"

The tyranny of the *or* pushes people to choose one or the other:

- You can have change *or* stability.
- You can be conservative *or* bold.
- You can have low cost *or* high quality.
- You can have creative autonomy *or* consistency and control.

- You can invest for the future *or* do well in the short term.
- You can progress by methodical planning *or* by opportunistic groping.

"Balance" implies going to the midpoint, fifty-fifty, half and half. A visionary company doesn't seek balance between short-term *and* long-term, for example. It seeks to do very well in the short-term *and* very well in the long-term. A visionary company doesn't simply balance between idealism and profitability; it seeks to be highly idealistic *and* highly profitable. A visionary company doesn't simply balance preserving a tightly held core ideology and stimulating vigorous change and movement; it does *both* to an extreme.[3]

Evangelical pastors, struggling with tension between change and tradition quickly identify with the last illustration. Missionary movements, wrestling with short-term missions versus career missions discover an option in this principle: The tyranny of the *or* and the genius of the *and*.

Preserve the Core and Stimulate Progress in All Areas

One of the surprises in the Collins/Porras research was that all successful companies did not share the same core values. But whatever they were, they held tenaciously to them and in all other areas were aggressively progressive.

We've found that companies get into trouble by confusing core ideology with specific, non-core practices. By confusing core ideology with non-core practices, companies can cling too long to non-core items—things that should be changed in order for the company to adapt and move forward.[4]

The application that immediately emerges is the challenge to separate core values from cultural issues.

Seek Consistent Alignment

It's become fashionable in recent decades for companies to spend countless hours and sums of money drafting elegant vision statements, value statements, mission statements, purpose statements, aspiration statements, objectives statements, and so on. Such pronouncements are all fine and good—indeed, they can be quite useful, but they're not the essence of a visionary company.[5]

Corporate Life Cycles

I have demonstrated the inevitability of historical drift in the realms of ecclesiology, sociology and cultural anthropology. Now, let's meet Ichak Adizes, the director of the Adizes Institute in Santa Barbara, California, who focuses primarily on the phenomenon of drift in the corporate world. The subtitle of his book, *Corporate Lifecycles*, reads: "How and Why Corporations Grow and Die and What to Do about It."

His interest in the subject grows out of more than thirty years of consulting with several hundred companies including some non-profit organizations such as churches and denominations. Out of his observation of living subject-to-life cycles organisms, he has developed his thesis: "Organizations have lifecycles just as living organisms do; they go through the normal struggles and difficulties accompanying each stage of the Organizational Lifecycle and are faced with the transitional problems of moving to the next phase of development."[6]

Although his theory initially appears complex, it is helpful to remember that he is constantly focusing on two main factors—flexibility and self-control. When organizations are young, they tend to be very flexible, but difficult to control. As they age, controllability increases but flexibility decreases, e.g., the contrast between babyhood and adulthood. However, as people and organizations age, they eventually lose both flexibility and controllability.

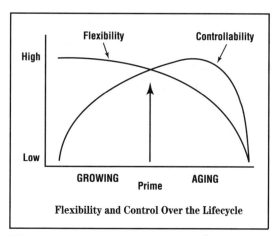

Figure 8: Flexibility and Control Over the Lifecycle[7]

For example: Young organizations are very flexible.

> "We used to commit 80 percent of our resources during break-
> fast, sitting on the stairs of the shop," one of the founders of
> Logicon, a large high-tech company in Southern California,
> told me. "Now that we have grown, even a small investment
> takes months and reams of paper to approve."[8]

The following rather complex bell curve further explains the life cy-cles and roles of growing and aging. In my curve of historical drift, I begin with vision and finish with monument. Adizes initiates the curve with courtship and concludes with death.

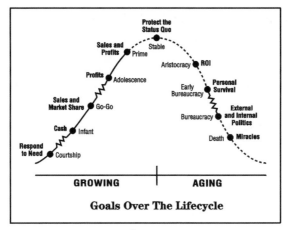

Figure 9: Goals Over The Lifecycle[9]

The ideal stage on the above curve is "Prime." Adizes describes it this way:

> In Prime, the organization knows what to do and what not to do. They know when to pass up an opportunity and why to pass on it. The organization has both talent and discipline. It has vision and self-control. It is oriented toward quantity and quality. Both the form and the function are balanced, and they are functional. The organization can grow profitably.[10]

This is the good news. But there are two challenges: The first, of course, is to get into Prime, and the second is even more difficult—staying in Prime. Let's look further at the characteristics of Prime.

Characteristics of Prime

- functional systems and organizational structure
- institutionalized vision and creativity
- results orientation; the organization satisfies customer needs
- the organization makes plans and then follows up on those plans

- the organization predictably excels in performance
- the organization spins off infant organizations.

Prime organizations know what they're doing, where they're going and how to get there. In Prime, a company has an aggressive
budget and the variance of actual over budget is tolerable. . . .
Usually, a company in Prime does not complain about being
short on cash. That does not mean that they have plenty of it.
Cash shortage for Prime is an expected and controlled event. It is
a sensation, not a problem.[11]

The normal complaint of companies in Prime is that there are not
enough well-trained people. Their abnormal complaint? Complacency.

Challenges of Prime

Before speaking to the challenges of companies in Prime, I have a
question: Why in Figure 9 is Prime before the zenith? His answer: "If
it's green, it's growing; if it's ripe, it's rotting."[12] If Prime were at the
top of the mountain, the only option is down. Then why does the curve
continue up? The short answer: momentum. This increase in viability
comes from the organizational momentum that was generated in
Courtship, tested in Infancy, refueled in Go-Go, institutionalized and
channeled in Adolescence and is being fully capitalized on in Prime.

Here is the challenge of Prime: Complacency must be treated as abnormal. If the Prime organization does not refuel its momentum, if
they lose entrepreneurship, if they keep capitalizing on the momentum rather than nourishing it, they will lose the rate of growth and
eventually the organizational vitality will level off. The organization
will proceed to the phase called Stable, which is the end of growth and
the beginning of decline. The challenge of Prime is to stay in prime.

When Stable Is Unstable

Stable becomes the first of the aging stages in the Lifecycle. "The company is still strong, but it is starting to lose its flexibility. It is at the end of growth and at the beginning of decline. Organizationally, it suffers from an attitude that says, 'If it ain't broke, don't fix it.' The company is beginning to lose the spirit of creativity, innovation and encouragement of change that made it into a Prime organization."

Subtle shifts

> creep in on cat's paws like London fog: >flexibility declines >organization mellows >less to fight about >reliance on the past >stable niche in the market >creativity rare >occasional urgency >orderliness prevails >conservative approaches protect past achievements >more time in office—less with customers >meetings prolonged >formal climate >finance people overshadow marketing, research and development people >return on investment becomes dominant >entrepreneurial spirit dwindles.

Adizes summarizes the characteristics of Stable on the Lifecyle as follows:

- has lower expectations for growth
- has fewer expectations to conquer new markets, technologies and frontiers
- starts to focus on past achievements instead of future visions
- suspicious of change
- rewards those who do what they are told to do
- more interested in interpersonal relationships than taking risks.[13]

These descriptions of Prime and Stable resonate with anyone leading a Christian church or organization. Many will no doubt confess that they have slipped from Prime to Stable. Perhaps even now you are looking for Adizes' book or hitting his website (www.Adizes.com *or* www.AdizesUSA.com) to discover how to avoid falling down the curve to Aristocracy.

We have taken a brief but enlightening dip into the secular corporate world to see what, if anything, we should learn about coping with historical drift. In the theories proposed by both Collins and Adizes, I sense we are grappling with very similar issues in our nonprofit organizations—loss of vitality. But there's one major difference: They have only human might and power, while we have the power of the Holy Spirit. Before probing this distinction further, let's look at some common questions which emerge from both worlds.

What Is Vision?

Porras and Collins identified four successful habits of visionary companies. Is vision different from a mission statement? Some would define "mission" as who we are (our core values) and "vision" as where we are going. However, these authors combine both concepts into vision. They state: "We see vision as simply a combination of an enduring core ideology plus envisioned progress for the future."[14]

George Bullard, a church consultant, gives a different but refreshing spin on vision: "Vision is not a statement which is memorized, but an experience which is memorable." This connects vision to the vitality of current personal experience versus the memory of a supernatural past.[15]

How does one consistently align? Consistent alignment only becomes possible when core values have been clearly enunciated. Christianity's major struggle continues to be keeping the main thing the main thing. Our apparent uncertainty in understanding the nonnegotiable core values as clearly taught in Scripture makes alignment impossible. Alignment to what? Wherever core values are not identified and tenaciously embraced, historical drift moves Christian organizations unchallenged toward dead Christendom.

Will present findings and structural theories become obsolete in the third millennium? When asked this question, Porras and Collins replied with confidence:

> No. If anything, we believe our findings will apply *more* in the twenty-first century than in the twentieth. In particular, the essential ideas to come from our work—clock building, the Genius of the AND, preserving the core/stimulating progress, and alignment—will continue to be key concepts long into the future.[16]

My response is similar but from a vastly different perspective. Christian leaders believe in an immutable God. Christ, the head of His Church, "is the same yesterday and today and forever" (Hebrews 13:8). He resolutely declared: "I will build my church, and the gates of Hades will not overcome it" (Matthew 16:18). This has been happening over two millennia despite every conceivable tactic of Satan. I heartily agree with Ralph Winter, one of the great missiologists of the 20th century, when he states concerning the Church: "Is there any other trend lasting 2,000 years of documented history which is as unshakeably true and unquestionably significant?"

Wise leaders will look back and study Church history to discover the core ideology that under God has served as a rudder to keep the Church on course through the storms of history.

The Bottom Line

What is the bottom line? Can we learn from the corporate world? In sampling just two of the many consulting agencies, I have learned that their diagnostic tools are insightful and relevant. The parallels between the Church and the corporate world are many.

In an interesting and somewhat current historical coincidence, the spheres of the church and the corporate world have intersected. Timothy Eaton, founder of one of Canada's foremost leading department store chains, was a man of Christian principles. For instance, he insisted that drapes be drawn on all display windows in his stores on Sunday. In 1999, Eaton's filed for bankruptcy. None of Timothy's four sons profess a living faith in Christianity. Ironically, the coming of Wal-Mart, founded by Sam Walton, a Christian, had at least some part in the demise of Eaton's.

Christian principles are effective in both worlds. But given today's proliferation of secular resource options, we must identify up front those aspects of these resources which set Christian organizations apart from the secular world. The two most obvious factors are faith and prayer. This leads to some very basic questions.

Are Our "Customers" the Same?

"Our customers are our people in our churches." I constantly hear this statement at church seminars focused on success. It is quickly expanded beyond our people to the community we want to attract. This inevitably leads into a discussion on relevance.

David Wells, a professor at Gordon-Conwell Theological Seminary, responds by contrasting the potential church constituency with the marketplace clientele.

The assumptions are that

- both must expand in the marketplace
- both must meet needs
- both must have customers.

The similarities are that

- growth is good
- we need to understand culture
- we should be hospitable to outsiders.

There are, however, differences between the marketplace and the church:

- The consumer defines his own needs—God defines our needs.
- The consumer has many hidden motives—with God, all motives must be open.
- In the marketplace, the customer is sovereign—we must come on God's terms.
- The market defines the product—only bad churches do that.[17]

What's the Focus?

Business must first find its niche in the market. The church, however, is unique in its inclusivity and breadth. Everyone from the cradle to the coffin forms the potential market of the church. It ministers to the entire family. This creates a distinct ambivalence and requires professional leaders with a special gift-mix.

Is Our Philosophy of Economics the Same?

What drives corporations? Answer: the marketplace. They live by the bottom line of profitability. This stands in stark contrast to Christ's philosophy. He owned nothing. He specifically sent out His followers wholly dependent on God's provision for them through strangers (Luke 10:1-17). Paul, the first missionary, had limited financial support. When that failed, he took up his trade of making tents and continued to minister. Many faith missions born in the last century followed a radical principle. Their commitment was to only share their financial need when asked. Certainly, in this century, the role of church finances has been revolutionized by the corporate world. Today's Christian organizations have bought into direct mail and the most recent fund-raising techniques.

In closing this section, let me quote the leading theologian of the 20th century. Carl F.H. Henry, in *Fund-Raising Management* magazine, comments:

> As budgets spiral ever upward, ministries often look for leadership skilled in public relations and in raising funds from large foundations. Sophistication is required in preparing grant proposals, and personal contacts in the financial world are important. All of this tends to treat God as a peeping Tom in economic affairs, except when deficits so threaten survival that no earthly hope remains but to return to the prayer meeting.[18]

Are the Bottom Lines the Same?

Companies with success surpassing a century continue to impress the corporate gurus. However, with the acceleration of change powering the communication explosion, long-term planning has been reduced from decades and years to months and weeks.

Historically, the bottom line of financial profit set church and state apart. Terms for "profit" and "nonprofit" were coined. Today, this distinction at best is blurred. The issue greatly exceeds money. Christianity's uniqueness rests forever in its focus on another world. It is a two-world religion: This world determines everyone's destiny for the next world. This is what sets true Christianity a world apart from visionary companies built to last. Herein lies the bottom bottom-line difference.

Yes, we can learn from the secular world. All truth is God's truth. Modern-day Jethros continue to pass by with helpful input from the world of common grace. The words of Jesus are too often embarrassingly true: "The people of this world are more shrewd in dealing with their own kind than are the people of the light" (Luke 16:8). But there is "wisdom that comes from heaven" that must be distinguished from that which is "earthly, unspiritual, of the devil" (James 3:13-17).

Discussion Questions

1. How do you feel about borrowing principles from the corporate world? How do we differ from the corporate world? Are there areas of similarities? (Note David Wells' comments.)
2. Which of the four success principles from *Built to Last* most readily apply to the church?
3. Historical drift is all about growing and aging. According to Ichak Adizes how do you keep an organization in "prime" versus "slipping into stable"?
4. Where do you see your church on his "growing and aging" curve?

Good News

Back to the Essentials

The Church of England, referred to as Anglicans in Canada and Episcopalians in the United States, predates all other extant Protestant churches by several centuries. They trace their roots to the 4th century. (Three British bishops attended the Council of Arles in A.D. 314, and St. Augustine [not the Bishop of Hippo] came as a missionary to the English in 597.) Formally, its origin dates back to the 16th century under the reign of Henry VIII. In 1534, the Act of Supremacy made the king head of the national church.

The Church of England is home to a vast variety of people around the world. The Lambeth Conference (August 1998) in England drew over 700 bishops. Theologically, the church is equally diverse. Ten years ago, they debated vigorously the issue of the ordination of women. Currently, about half of the national churches within Anglicanism ordain women as priests, and three, including Canada, have consecrated female bishops.

The leadership of the Anglican Church of Canada has been moving with the liberal wing within the Church of England. Canadians have been actively promoting a gender-inclusive hymnal. One conference focused on the ordination of homosexuals, and several Canadian bishops supported it. The motion was ultimately defeated.

Meanwhile, the Anglican Church has been declining rapidly in Canada. In 1991, 61,000 attended Anglican Sunday schools in the province of British Columbia alone. By 1993, there were only 67,000 in Anglican Sunday schools all across Canada. There was also a growing sense among many parishioners that their national church was not championing key tenets of the faith with vigor or conviction. In addition to dwindling membership rolls, they faced severe financial difficulties.

But in 1994, unexpectedly and from the grass roots, God showed up at a small conference in Montreal. Members of three organizations, the Anglican Renewal Fellowship, Barnabas Ministries and the Prayer Book Society of Canada, teamed up to sponsor this historic conference. Essentials '94, as it was called, optimistically anticipated 375 delegates. Over 700 registered. Their agenda was to promote and preserve biblical, orthodox teaching within the Anglican Church of Canada. The Archbishop of Canterbury, George Carey, known as an evangelical, addressed the conference. He was applauded in his affirmation of the uniqueness of Jesus Christ and the primacy of Scripture.

The renewed delegates approved a four-page, fifteen-point Declaration. It included the following doctrinal articles:

- authority of the Bible: "living and powerful as God's guidance for belief and behaviour"
- Jesus is the only Savior
- priority of evangelism
- challenge of global mission
- challenge of social action
- standards for sexual conduct: the only sexual relations that biblical theology deems good and holy are between wife and husband.

"The Montreal Declaration of Anglican Essentials," edited by University of Toronto historian, George Egerton, has been printed by the denominational publisher, Church House.

Since 1994, a series of regional Essentials Conferences have spread across the country. In May of 1997, a meeting at the University of Ottawa attracted 130 theologically conservative Anglicans committed to developing young leaders. Even a decade ago, half of the new clergy in the Church of England were coming from the evangelical wing.

Renewal is alive and growing in one of the world's oldest denominations.

"Leaders see what others don't see, see before others see and see farther than others see."

—John R. Mott, prominent leader of
the Student Volunteer Movement in the 1890s

5

Memory Is a "God Thing"

Learning from Church History

ON THEIR FORTIETH ANNIVERSARY IN 1996, *Christianity Today* published the following quotes from first-year articles of the magazine (October 5, 1956—September 30, 1957).

- Billy Graham: "I think it was Goethe who said, after hearing a young minister, 'When I go to hear a preacher preach, I may not agree with what he says, but I want him to believe it.' Even a vacillating unbeliever has no respect for the man who lacks the courage to preach what he believes."[1]
- Elisabeth Elliot, speaking on behalf of the five widows of slain missionaries to Ecuador one year after their deaths: "We have proved beyond any doubt that He means what He says—His grace is sufficient, nothing can separate us from the love of Christ. We pray that if any, anywhere, are fearing that the cost of discipleship is too great, that they may be

given a glimpse of that treasure in heaven promised to all
who forsake."[2]

- Frank E. Gaebelein: "The supplanting of sound values by
  the world's methods of popularity and success may be cloud-
  ing the influence of the Bible upon our writing. This is a difficult problem. Christian writing needs the note of
  contemporeity, but never at the expense of truth."[3]

- L. Nelson Bell: "We live in a time of unprecedented discov-
  eries, many of which tend to make life longer and living
  more comfortable and enjoyable. But with change and progress the inexorable law of change and decay also operates.
  Strange that so few in this world prepare for the inevitable."[4]

The question may be asked, "So, what's new?" These four reminders
touch four critical issues still facing us today: 1) preaching with conviction; 2) embracing the high cost of discipleship; 3) balancing relevance and truth and 4) coping with progress and drift. Will we as
evangelicals listen and learn? Mankind is notorious for its refusal to
learn from the past. But if we would, here are some things we could
learn.

God Remembers—Man Forgets

- God is into memory. He remembered Joseph in prison
  (Genesis 39:21). Man is into forgetting. "The chief cup-
  bearer, however, did not remember Joseph; he forgot him"
  (40:23).

- God works through covenants. "[He keeps] his covenant of
  love to a thousand generations" (Deuteronomy 7:9). He
  made His first with Noah. And He continually reminds all
  peoples on earth of that first one. Every time we behold a
  rainbow, He reminds us of His covenant never again to
  judge the earth by a flood.

- God reminds us through nonverbals. Festivals are big with God. Of the many, the Passover was central—a powerful reminder of God's delivering Israel from bondage. For the Church, the Lord's Supper reminds us of the New Covenant.

Memory Is Powerful

Although the Jewish people experienced memory lapses in the wilderness, memory played a major role in their enviable record of cohesiveness. Having experienced the diaspora as few other nations, they have exhibited remarkable resistance to acculturation. L.L. King comments:

> Moses in his final charge to the Israelites said, "Remember all the way which the LORD thy God led thee these forty years" (Deuteronomy 8:2, KJV). . . . He recognized the influence of memory. He well knew that properly used, it best serves as (1) a perpetual warning, as well as (2) a perpetual inspiration for present endeavors, and as (3) one of the great forces that makes for the future.[5]

The word "deuteronomy" means "repetition of the law." The key phrase in the fifth book of the Pentateuch is "remember." God included this book to focus on the power of memory as final preparation for Canaan. The book of Joshua follows Deuteronomy. It records that God fought the battles of the children of Israel and gave them victories. The stones of memorial reminded every generation to come of Israel's miraculous entry into the land.

Then comes Judges. Joshua had died. The elders who followed him were gone. A new generation "grew up, who knew neither the LORD nor what he had done for Israel" (Judges 2:10). "[They] did not re-member the LORD their God" (8:34).

Historical Drift Thrives
When Memory Dies

The Church desperately needs to rediscover the Holy Spirit. One of His key ministries is to remind and prompt the believer. He gives us the word to speak in a crisis moment. "But the Counselor, the Holy Spirit, whom the Father will send in My name, will teach you all things and will remind you of everything I have said to you. . . . He will not speak on his own; he will speak only what he hears, and he will tell you what is yet to come" (John 14:26; 16:13). Because of this reminding role, lying against the Holy Spirit becomes a special category of sin (Matthew 12:31-32; Acts 5:3-11).

God Is into Generations

God describes Himself as "[the God of] Abraham, Isaac and Israel [Jacob] (Exodus 32:13). God has but one plan: to work through succes-sive generations to "fill the earth with His knowledge." Man thinks in days, weeks, months, years and occasionally in decades. God thinks in generations.

The English term "generation" translates into six distinct concepts:

- Circle. Depicts the cycle of generations (Deuteronomy 32:7), a people of a particular period (Genesis 7:1) or people of a particular sort (Deuteronomy 32:5).
- Births. Refers to the procreation account of man and his de-scendants (Genesis 5:1); a successive number of families in a lineage (Genesis 10:32) or genealogical divisions (Numbers 1:20).

- Begetting. Describes successive members of a genealogy (Matthew 1:17); a race or class (Matthew 17:17); the people of a period (Luke 21:32); and an age period (Colossians 1:26).
- Source/Origin. Alludes to the generation of Jesus Christ (Matthew 1:1).
- Offspring/Progeny. A figurative use, e.g., "O generation of vipers" (Luke 3:7, KJV).
- Stock/Race. Refers to a spiritual concept, e.g., a "chosen generation" (1 Peter 2:9, KJV).[6]

Moses, in his book on remembering, specifically reminds parents of their responsibility with the next generation: "And the words which I command you today shall be in your heart. You shall teach them diligently to your children" (Deuteronomy 6:6-7, NKJV).

Joshua too was diligent in establishing the memorial of stones from the middle of the Jordan. This was for the purpose of communicating God's truth of their supernatural history to their children (Joshua 4:6-7).

The history of Israel showcases the power of godly generations and the tragedy of ungodly generations. When the fathers obeyed, the manifestation of God's power and might was manifested and transmitted. When they failed, the next generation was placed in jeopardy. This prayer of an aging psalmist puts God's strategy of generations in perspective: "Since my youth, O God, you have taught me, and to this day I declare your marvelous deeds. Even when I am old and gray, do not forsake me, O God, till I declare your power to the next generation, your might to all who are to come" (Psalm 71:17-18).

Organizations Don't Drift!

"What do you mean? I thought that is the issue of this book!" you may be saying. Practically speaking, organizations are inseparable from their leaders. It is well said: "Organizations are only as good as their leaders." But to get to the nub of the issue of historical drift, leaders must be addressed apart from their organizations.

Alert organizations recognize the distinction. Solid seminaries annually interview each professor prior to a new contract in order to detect and correct any unconscious or conscious theological drift. CEOs do it with their VPs, VPs with managers, governing boards with CEOs and presidents—*if* they accept the thesis that only leaders drift, not organizations.

Drift Is *Poco a Poco*

"Beginning today I am adopting a weaker commitment to biblical authority."

"This company, beginning today, will no longer hold to our historic core values."

"From today forward, I am going to adopt more contemporary moral standards."

"As a government we will, as of today, grant full rights to same-sex marriage partners."

No such changes occur overnight. The process of historical drift is insidious and deceptive because it happens *poco a poco* (Spanish for "little by little"). It moves slowly over an extended period of time, incrementally breaking down the barriers by softening the opposition. It happens unconsciously like the proverbial frog in the kettle.

Governments understand well this *poco a poco* process and employ it skillfully. To locate a land fill site (euphemism for "garbage dump") in a community, they publish twenty possible locations. Twenty communities react. Over several months, the number is reduced to two or three. Opposition has been reduced. Morale breaks down through weariness over time. Pessimism sets in. A site is identified and approved with only a whimper of protest from a few persistent opponents.

Robert Bork, in his book, *Slouching Towards Gomorrah*, comments on the power of culture to unrelentingly squeeze us into its mold:

> With each new evidence of deterioration, we lament for a moment, and then become accustomed to it. We hear one day of the latest rap song calling for killing policemen or the sexual mutilation of women; the next, of coercive left-wing political indoctrination at a prestigious university; then the latest homicide figures for New York City, Los Angeles, or the District of Columbia; or the collapse of the criminal justice system. . . . So unrelenting is the assault on our sensibilities that many of us grow numb, finding resignation to be the rational, adaptive response to an environment that is increasingly polluted and apparently beyond our control.[7]

The Gay Movement worked the system effectively in 1998. In February, city council extended same-sex health benefits to all City of Toronto employees. In May, the federal government provided funding for the first national survey of the gay and lesbian communities. Eleven smaller victories led to the following decision, beginning with this social event in 1965: The Melody Room opens on Church St. and same-sex dancing is encouraged with the help of a front-door security system that alerts patrons to the arrival of police (see Appendix II: "Lonely Path Leads to Gay Rights").[8]

The media plays a key role in such devious plots. X-rated movies are euphemistically called "adult entertainment," but appear earlier and earlier in the evening schedule. Profanity is incrementally increased and gains acceptability. Television captures our children with humorous cartoons which become increasingly violent, thus insidiously conditioning them to accept violence in the real-world movies.

No Exemptions for Churches

This *poco a poco* approach to change works equally well in the church. The fact that most evangelical denominations become liberal well before their centennial attests to the effectiveness of incremental change. The largest denomination in Canada is a tragic case study of this process. Within less than seventy-five years, that denomination, founded on twenty solid theological truths, has moved to the ordination of homosexuals. Officially they have never altered their solidly conservative doctrinal foundation, but they have chosen to simply ignore it for the greater cause of being a "truly uniting church" for all (see Appendix I: The United Church of Canada).

Denominations such as the Presbyterian Church U.S.A., the United Methodist Church and the Episcopalian Church, to name some of the larger ones, are experiencing conference by conference the unrelenting pressure of growing vocal minorities. Typically it begins with the pro-choice movement on abortion. Over time it evolves into debating euthanasia. Then the question of women in ministry is raised. This quickly shifts to women in leadership and naturally into the ordination issue. Most denominations, as illustrated by the Episcopal Church, gradually move from women's issues to homosexual issues.

Pastors are astute change agents and sometimes employ this system of incremental change rather skillfully. For example, church leadership committed to moving toward the inclusion of women as elders will soften the opposition through a subtle conditioning of the congregation for such change. One method may be the including of elders' wives in serving the Lord's Supper.

A church's position on the controversial question of divorce and remarriage becomes a frequent agenda item at a denomination's annual meeting. I traced the discussions of one denomination on this subject back to 1921. Each of the three times they reopened the topic, the net result was a weakened position from the clear biblical teaching of Scripture.

Curves Can Be Extended

History tells those who will listen that the man/movement/machinery/ monument trajectory will be their predictable future. But two caveats must be appended to that statement.

First, the length of the curve can be extended. A cursory glance reveals a wide margin of time variance. Jesus pinned the extension at thirty-five to forty years when He audited the seven churches of Asia Minor (Revelation 2-3). One old Moravian bishop eyeballed this cycle at around a century. Result? The Moravian church has held to their core value of missions for several centuries, slipping only in the latter half of the 20th century. The fact is that few movements enjoy effective ministries into a second century.

Second, the down side of the curve can be reversed. History would caution us that reversals rarely occur, but are possible. Radical revivals have restored spiritual vitality to denominations, reversing drift for a time. The Great Awakenings impacted society beyond the Church. The influx of new believers renewed those churches which were able to accommodate them.

In the 1990s, new leadership in the Worldwide Church of God, after almost half a century, dramatically reversed their direction. They have literally restored what was a cultist movement to the orthodox Quaker/Baptist roots of their founder. Other organizations in North America have become two. In Canada, churches have gained autonomy from United States entities, a *kairos* moment for structural change and spiritual renewal.

Although these churches have inherited long traditions, they seize the opportunity to write their own history. The process also offers the opportunity to reverse drift and extend their curve of effectiveness into the future. For instance, The Christian and Missionary Alliance in Canada, which became autonomous in 1980, can say that they have 103 years of tradition, but only twenty years of history.

History would tell us one more thing about historical drift: Withdrawal from a movement is more common than reversal of drift within it. At some point on the downward side, God seems to birth a new organization from the old. This happens frequently. Methodism emerged out of the Church of England as the revived John and Charles Wesley, along with George Whitefield, developed new methods of proclamation. These were unacceptable to the Mother Church. Over the two centuries of Methodism, the withdrawal phenomenon continues. Historians speak of the "200 sons of John Wesley," a reference to denominational spin-offs from the original movement.

C. Peter Wagner implies in his book, *The New Apostolic Churches*, that revivals are effective only if they find their expression in new wineskins.[9] Historically, it could be argued that the existence of a credible evangelical church today is primarily due to groups seeking renewal spinning off from aging denominations which were approaching the monument stage.

Church history, ancient and modern, brims with lessons. Certainly one of God's purposes in giving us a written record of His workings in the Old Testament was to warn us of pitfalls. He tells us that "the way of the transgressor is hard." Nevertheless, teenagers from evangelical homes protest: "But I want to discover it for myself." To the credit of the mother of Moses, she taught him well—and he listened. Moses "chose to be mistreated along with the people of God rather than to enjoy the pleasures of sin for a short time" (Hebrews 11:25).

We as adult Christian leaders too often adopt the attitude of our teenagers. New mission organizations enter new fields and repeat the mistakes initially made by existing groups which they never bothered to consult. Committed to change, new denominations emerge, but within a decade have fallen into the same self-serving mentalities of their previous traditions.

Summary

What can we learn from history if we would only listen? It is trite but true: "We would learn that we don't learn from history." Those who live in the past are blind in one eye. Those who never consult the past are blind in both eyes.

~

Discussion Questions

1. Read Joshua 4:20-24. What other events were the Israelites to remember?
2. What does the word "Deuteronomy"mean?
3. The author states "*historical drift* thrives when memory dies." What lessons from history does today's church tend to forget?
4. God is committed to working through generations. Does your church integrate generations or segregate them? Why?

Good News

We've Been Wrong!

Ruth Tucker documents the cultist nature of the Worldwide Church of God:

> For most of a half-century, no book on cults was complete without a chapter on the Worldwide Church of God (WCG) and its founder, Herbert W. Armstrong. The late Walter Martin, in his classic, *The Kingdom of the Cults*, devoted 34 pages to the group, documenting how Armstrong borrowed freely from Seventh-Day Adventists, Jehovah Witnesses, and Mormon doctrine.[10]

Following the founder's death, Joseph Tkach, Sr. became the leader in 1986. He led a process of evaluating their doctrines based upon Scripture. In 1995, a new covenant was issued which enunciated clearly that the church had departed from Armstrong's teachings. The Bible would be allowed to speak plain truth for itself. Half of their membership left, many joining splinter movements. But the core of the Worldwide Church of God has returned to orthodoxy. They are now members of the Evangelical Associations in both the United States and Canada.

Joseph Tkach, Jr., current Pastor General of the Worldwide Church of God, summarizes:

> We've been wrong. There was never an intent to mislead anyone. We were so focused on what we believed we were doing for God that we didn't recognize the spiritual path we were on. Intended or not, that path was not the biblical one. . . . So we stand today at the foot of the cross—the ultimate symbol of all

reconciliation. It is the common ground on which estranged and alienated parties can meet. As Christians, we all identify with the suffering that took place there, and we hope that identification will bring us together.[11]

I was part of a small group session at a Meta Church Cluster Conference. Each of us shared one recent significant spiritual crisis. A pastor of the Worldwide Church of God, ironically named Armstrong, riveted us to our chairs as he related the details of his crisis:

My wife and I were reared in the Worldwide Church of God. It was all we knew. When the new leadership asked every pastor to do a biblical evaluation of our doctrinal system, I struggled greatly. Finally, I went to an older pastor for counsel. He told me, "Buy a new Bible without notes. Get alone with God and the Scriptures and deal with each issue." I did that, and God brought me through.

"Remember that the greatest strides in Christianity's history—the first century—were taken when the church had no money or property."

—Joseph Bayly, contributing editor
to *Eternity* (October 1985, p. 79)

Part III

HISTORICAL DRIFT DETECTED

We have been examining the loss of vitality which I am calling historical drift. All agree that it's an incremental, *poco a poco* organizational malady. Observe the downside of any of the curves. The loss of vigor and vitality increases as people and organizations drift with the passage of time.

The consultants all accede on this point: If historical drift is addressed early, recovery is easier and faster. In this aspect, it is analogous to cancer in the human body. Take, for instance, the following not-so-good news item: "A slow and silent killer, prostate cancer strikes four out of ten men over age fifty. But it progresses slowly, and panic-driven surgery may be a mistake."

Then comes the good news: "Male-specific cancers can be caught early and treated."[1]

This information also applies to breast cancer in women and all other types of the dreaded "C" word. Early detection is critical.

How, then, can Christian leaders become skilled in early detection of historical drift? This is the key question to which we now turn.

"Every generation must stand on the shoulders of the previous generation and reach higher."

—Augustine

6

The First, Second and Third Chairs

Tracking the Trail to Nominality

ORGANIZATIONS DON'T DRIFT—ONLY THE people who lead them. Historical drift is all about people—people who live and relate intergenerationally, people who function in the context of changing environments called cultures, people who organize themselves into societal subsets for a wide range of purposes ranging from work to worship, from recreation to revolutions.

This fascinating mosaic of people intermingling cross-culturally and cross-generationally is grist for sociologists and anthropologists. I specifically want to address the generational aspect, but in the context of the church.

God Has No Grandchildren

Grandchildren are wonderful. A provocative plaque suggests: "Grandchildren are God's reward to parents for not killing their children!" Contrary to current churchianity, God has no grandchildren. Consider this early statement by John in his Gospel regarding Jesus: "He came to that which was his own, but his own did not receive him. Yet to all who received him, to those who believed in his name, he gave the right to become children of God—children born not of natural descent, nor of human decision or a husband's will, but born of God" (John 1:11-13).

"He came to that which was his own." The Jewish people believed they were descendants of Jehovah. Later, they protested to Jesus: "We are not illegitimate children. . . . The only Father we have is God himself." Christ's answer shocked them and provoked even greater anger: "You belong to your father, the devil, and you want to carry out your father's desire" (8:33-44). Still, later, Jesus explained how everyone, including the most devout Jews, could become true children of God. Responding to Nicodemus, He described the new birth as being accomplished through the work of the Holy Spirit (3:1-8).

Three Chairs

Bruce H. Wilkinson, founder and president of Walk Through the Bible Ministries, graphically illustrates intergenerational drift with three chairs, each representing a generation. In his book, *First Hand Faith*, he realistically explains how a vibrant faith in Christ held by one generation can be lost in the next.

Joshua and his life and times provide an instructive period for understanding the roles of generations. The man comes to the end of his leadership. The people are assembled to hear their leader's final challenge. He speaks as God's voice. "This is what the LORD, the God of Israel, says" (Joshua 24:2). He rehearses God's mighty deeds in the lives of their forefathers, and they are reminded that God gave them this land for which they did not toil (24:13). Then Joshua closes with this powerful challenge to the next generation: "As for me and my household, we will serve the LORD" (24:15). He was clearly representing the strong commitment of the First Generation Chair. He had experienced God firsthand.

The response of the next generation was enthusiastic, "Far be it from us to forsake the LORD to serve other gods" (24:16). But Joshua, the veteran leader, was unimpressed. He urged the crowd to repent: "Throw away the foreign gods that are among you and yield your hearts to the LORD, the God of Israel" (24:23).

There are two additional references to this second generation, following Joshua's death. "Israel served the LORD throughout the lifetime of . . . the elders who outlived [Joshua] and who had experienced everything the LORD had done for Israel" (24:31). The other is found in Judges 2:7. It too affirms that the elders who outlived Joshua served the Lord. These are Second Chair children raised by First Chair parents. How do these children differ? For most, their experience was not firsthand. They had heard and even seen what happened in the parents' lives. But it tended to be a secondhand faith.

Once these second-generation parents had children, they found themselves sitting in The Third Chair. Note their characteristics: "After that whole generation had been gathered to their fathers, another generation grew up, who knew neither the LORD nor what he had done for Israel" (Judges 2:10). Result? "Then the Israelites did evil in the eyes of the LORD, and served the Baals. They forsook the LORD, the God of their fathers . . ." (2:11-12).[2]

How can a people move from godliness to godlessness in just three generations? The answer to this question lies in early detection of the symptoms. We are dealing with the tragic process—historical drift—that moves successive generations into nominality, i.e., Christian in name only.

In Name Only

Webster's Dictionary defines "nominal" as "existing or being something in name or form only." Eddie Gibbs, in his study on nominality,
In Name Only, traces the typical trajectory.

> In Christian denominations, nominality begins to emerge in
> the second generation and becomes endemic by the fourth gen-
> eration. By this time, the nominal person will either have re-
> jected all claims to membership or will have been reactivated.
> The lifespan of an organization is between sixty and eighty
> years, by which time it will have reached the point of no return
> unless intervention strategies are in place.[3]

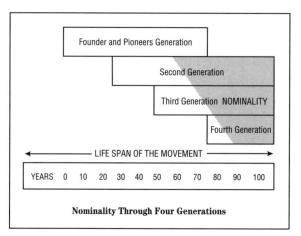

Figure 10: Nominality Through Four Generations

Gibbs believes that this explains, in part, the crumbling of Marxist
societies in Eastern Europe, seventy years after the Russian revolution.
Their nominality eventually turned to disillusionment and cynicism.

Surface Evidence: Loss of Commitment

A Lausanne Committee studied the problem of nominality in the context of evangelical Christianity and focused on commitment. They sought to define authentic commitment to Christ for those who had experienced a transforming encounter with Him. The criteria for evaluating their level of commitment was based upon the following expressions: "Love, joy, peace, a desire to study the Bible, prayer, fellowship with other Christians, a determination to witness faithfully, a deep concern for God's will to be done on earth, and a living hope of heaven to come."[4]

Based upon this definition, they identified five types of nominal Christians who behaved as follows:

- Attend church regularly and worship devoutly, but who have no personal relationship with Jesus Christ.
- Attend church regularly but for cultural reasons only.
- Attend church only for major church festivals (Christmas, Easter, etc.) and ceremonies (weddings, baptisms, funerals).
- Hardly ever attend church but maintain a church relationship for reasons of security, emotional or family ties or tradition.
- Have no relationship to any specific church and never attend but yet consider themselves believers in God (in a traditional Christian sense).[5]

Although helpful, this approach has limitations. It ascribes motivations to individuals based upon church-related activities. It also limits authentic faith to the standards of classic evangelicalism. Nevertheless, it serves to remind us that the loss of commitment is symptomatic of deeper root causes as historical drift leads to nominality.

Given the emerging division in evangelicalism, we need to revisit the Gospels and review Christ's nonnegotiables for discipleship. Consider these issues He identified:

- Singular allegiance: "If anyone comes to me and does not hate his father and mother, his wife and children, his brothers and sisters—yes, even his own life—he *cannot be my disciple*" (Luke 14:26, emphasis mine).
- Identity with the cross: "Anyone who does not carry his cross and follow me *cannot be my disciple*" (14:27, emphasis mine).
- Exclusive commitment: "Any of you who does not give up everything he has *cannot be my disciple*" (14:33, emphasis mine). Compare also His response to the rich young man (Matthew 19:16-24).

Christ's conditions for a true disciple clash with various evangelistic approaches of our day. Jesus required lordship up front. Some movements, with a strong focus on the deeper life (a post-conversion encounter with the Holy Spirit), have been legitimately criticized for their failure to present lordship in their gospel presentation; i.e., Christ is presented as Savior, and lordship is relegated to a post-conversion experience. Based on Christ's example in the Gospels, these truths are inseparable.

This matter of lordship becomes particularly critical for Christian movements without a theology of deeper life/higher life teaching. It is often completely bypassed. The slide toward nominality is virtually unchallenged in such a flawed theology.

Below-the-Surface Causes

How did the Ephesian Christians lose their first love? Their conversions from a demonized society had been radical (Acts 19). Paul described them as being "dead in . . . transgressions and sins" and dominated by the "ruler of the kingdom of the air" (Ephesians 2:1-2), but ones who had been "made . . . alive with Christ" (2:5).

Then, just thirty years later, Jesus revisited their church. His response? A mixed review. He commends them for hard work and perseverance, but asks them to repent for having forsaken their "first love." Somehow that exclusive commitment to love Christ supremely had been seriously compromised. He called them back to "the things [they] did at first"—responding to Him as Lord (Revelation 2:1-7).

Loss of commitment is analogous to an iceberg. The public lack of lifestyle commitment to the church becomes what is seen—the public tip of the iceberg. But the contributing causes of an eroded belief system are buried below the surface. The following is another version of the typical evidence of loss of commitment:

- inconsistent Sunday morning attendance
- token giving but not tithing
- no apparent desire for serious Bible study
- no interest in corporate prayer
- no public verbalization of faith
- no involvement in outreach or missions
- no apparent interest in becoming godly
- considered as a respectable adherent
- appreciative of family services provided by the church

Assuming a true spiritual conversion has occurred, what has happened below the surface? Upstreaming the steps, beginning with the tangible loss of commitment and working back to the core causes, let's consider the following.

The Greatest Commandment

"Love the Lord your God with all your heart and with all your soul and with all your mind" (Matthew 22:37). The Pharisees were seeking to trap Jesus with their question, "Which is the greatest commandment in the Law?" (22:36). He disarmed them by quoting from the law: "Love the LORD your God with all your heart and with all your soul and with all your strength" (Deuteronomy 6:5).

At the very core of our Christian faith is a supreme and uncontested love for God. God underlines this truth by referring to our heart, our soul and our mind. Theologians, seeking to define the essence of our spiritual being, have vigorously debated these terms. Despite the studies, they remain imprecise, overlapping at times or representing all three concepts in other Scriptures.

Paul employs the term "mind" (*dianoia*) in his appeal to the Romans for full commitment:

> Therefore, I urge you, brothers, in view of God's mercy, to offer your bodies as living sacrifices, holy and pleasing to God—this is your spiritual act of worship. Do not conform any longer to the pattern of this world, but be transformed by the renewing of your mind [*dianoia*]. Then you will be able to test and approve what God's will is—his good, pleasing and perfect will." (Romans 12:1-2)

The Battle for the Mind

In the early detection of historical drift we must focus on the Christian mind. I would argue that this battle began with our first parents in the Garden of Eden where Satan's strategy was quarterbacked by deception. (Deception and historical drift work hand in glove.) Satan addressed his crafty question to the mind of Eve: "Did God really say?" (Genesis 3:1) The question is subtle because it affirms that indeed God has spoken, but questions what He really meant, thus inviting multiple interpretations. Here are but a few of the modern versions of this ancient, demonic device:

- Did God really say He created the world in six days out of nothing? (1:2)

- Did God really say, "Let us make man in our image"? (1:26)
- Did God really say, "I hate divorce"? (Malachi 2:16)
- Did God really say, "You shall not murder"? (Exodus 20:13)
- Did God really say, "Man does not live on bread alone"? (Matthew 4:4)
- Did God really say, "Friendship with the world is hatred toward God"? (James 4:4)
- Did God really say that He does not want anyone to perish? (2 Peter 3:9)
- Did God really say that hell is eternal? (Matthew 25:46)
- Did God really say, "Be holy, because I am holy"? (1 Peter 1:16)

A growing segment of evangelicals are questioning the clarity of these truths and numerous others. Beneath the tip of the iceberg of waning commitment lies a growing mass of evangelicals with an eroded view of the inspiration of Scripture. The smoke screen is interpretation. How do we approach the interpretation of the Bible? Are we committed to its absolute inerrancy in the original autographs? Or is our preference simply to its broad authority? Our position will determine the hermeneutical principles we will use.

The Womb of Historical Drift

What triggers this slide toward nominality? Or, if we employ the title of Robert H. Bork's book, *Slouching Towards Gomorrah*, what steps led "an impressive young man without equal among the Israelites—a head taller than any of the others" (1 Samuel 9:2) to take his own life? (31:4-5). Consider this sequence of events in Saul's life:

- anointed king of Israel (10:1)
- faces opposition to his appointment (10:27)
- reaffirmed in his position (11:15)
- disobeyed God by offering the sacrifice (13:9-10)

- justified his action (13:11-12)
- broken relationship with son Jonathan (14:29)
- broken relationship with God—God does not answer him (14:37)
- failed to obey Samuel's instructions to completely destroy the Amalekites (15:7-16)
- became proud (15:17-19)
- broken relationship with Samuel, his mentor (15:35)
- rejected as king (15:35)
- Spirit of God departs (16:14)
- became jealous of David (18:9)
- was possessed by anger (20:30)
- consulted the Witch of Endor (chapter 28)
- committed suicide (31:4-6).

Moving to a New Testament analysis, James describes the spiritual spiral—temptation, lust, sin, spiritual suicide: "Each one is tempted when, by his own evil desire, he is dragged away and enticed. Then, after desire has conceived, it gives birth to sin; and sin, when it is full-grown, gives birth to death" (James 1:14-15). This embryonic process develops in the womb of the heart, the soul and the mind of the Christian. Temptation gains entry through the sensory gates of our lives. John summarizes them in three categories: "the lust of the flesh, the lust of the eyes, and the pride of life" (1 John 2:16, NKJV).

Why this focus on drift in the individual Christian? Are not church organizations the real concern? Answer: "Churches do not drift—only their leaders."

Technology in the last half-century has driven the speed of change off the charts. This exponential burst of change through the media has elevated the battle for our minds to unprecedented levels. No previous generation has experienced anything comparable. Commenting on the blatant display of nudity by the media, Billy Graham confessed for many of us: "I am shocked that I am no longer shocked!"

When temptation becomes full-blown sin, the Christian has two alternatives—confess and be cleansed or conceal and compromise. David chose confession. Saul followed compromise. Compromise feeds drift. The subsequent losses were as predictable and tragic for him as they are for any believer in any age:

- loss of personal relationship with God
- loss of communication through prayer
- loss of Bible reading and study
- loss of hearing the voice of God
- loss of faith
- loss of battle with self and sin
- loss of Christian lifestyle, e.g., personal, marriage, family, workplace, etc.
- loss of commitment to the church
- loss of spiritual life—death

The history of every embarrassing scenario of dead Christendom is replete with the tragic narratives of Christian leaders who allowed lust to give birth to sin, and sin to death. The good news is that this downward spiral to nominalism can be halted at any point. How? Simply through honest repentant prayer to a loving God who runs to embrace every prodigal: "Search me, O God, and know my heart; test me and know my anxious thoughts. See if there is any offensive way in me, and lead me in the way everlasting" (Psalm 139:23-24). "Keep your heart with all diligence, for out of it spring the issues of life" (Proverbs 4:23 NKJV).

Confession, repentance and cleansing are the very essence of renewal—the only antidote for nominalism.

~

Discussion Questions

1. "What the first generation rejects as sin, the second generation tolerates and the third generation approves." How does this relate to the three chairs? Share some examples.
2. How does God see generations? What's the key role of each generation in God's plan?
3. What is a "nominal Christian?" The major issues leading to nominalism are centered in the battle for the mind. Name them and check where you as leaders stand on each.

Good News

Personalizing Revival

" **D**raw a circle on the floor. Get inside the circle and pray: 'Lord, revive everything inside this circle' " (attributed to John Wesley).

"When we stop talking about the sins of others, and confess our own sin, then revival comes" (Corrie Ten Boom).

"Have mercy upon me, O God. . . . Cleanse me from my sin. . . . Create in me a clean heart. . . . Restore unto me the joy of thy salvation" (David, Psalm 51:1-12).

God was visiting Korea with revival in the 1940s. He chose to use a simple seven-step scriptural outline to lead many Christian leaders into personal renewal. An unassuming woman of God, Miss Aletta Jacobsz, received a special ministry helping Christian leaders, both missionaries and nationals, to recognize their need for such a renewal. People remember two things about Miss Jacobsz: 1) her obvious love for the Lord and 2) her simple method of bringing God's Word to bear on people's lives.

She was not satisfied with general confessions. When dealing with individual leaders, she would begin by handing them a pencil and paper. Her gentle yet persistent probing with a prominent Presbyterian missionary leader went like this:

Miss J: Have you considered Matthew 6:33: "Seek first the kingdom of God?"

Mr. X: Yes, I preach on it frequently.

Miss J: Are you willing to face this truth squarely and see if you are actually seeking God's will first in all things?

Mr. X: (after reflecting) Well, I suppose I am not seeking God first in everything. Yes, I will have to admit that I am not always putting Christ first in my life.

Miss J: Now, Mr. X, since you say you have preached this truth frequently, and you now recognize you are not fulfilling it in your life, what would you consider anyone, who, while urging others to do something is not doing it himself?

Mr. X: A hypocrite.

Miss J: Then how do you characterize yourself?

Mr. X: A hypocrite.

Miss J: Will you please write it down?

"I am a hypocrite," he wrote. Mr. X soon had a list of unconfessed sins that broke his heart. He was grateful, after repenting, to have a deep settled peace and forgiveness. As a missionary leader, he was then able to help others move from being nominal Christians to becoming normal Christians.[6]

"Christ loved the Church and gave Himself up for her to make her holy."

—The Apostle Paul

7

The Slippery Slope

Intentional Conditioning vs. Cognitive Defiance

TO TAKE A FIRM STAND on a slippery slope is tough. My roots are in Southern Ontario, Canada, a land of rolling hills with lots of wintry slopes. The memory of sitting helplessly in my truck as it slid backward downhill many years ago lives like yesterday in my mind.

Although meeting with increasing resistance in evangelical circles, the slippery slope analogy has never been more apropos. "Back to legalism" has become the inevitable retort to slippery slope warnings. Although I am very cognizant of the current evangelical aversion to anything negative, I am about to name some popular and seemingly innocent cultural practices which may seem trivial to some, but I will conclude with the all-important watershed issue of the Bible.

Lifestyle Issues

"Scratch to Win"

They come in multiple forms. Drop your business card in a jar at the restaurant. "Roll up the rim to win" at the donut shop. You can even win a car without the knowledge of having even consented to play. Our culture has overdosed on gaming—getting something for nothing. Some would never frequent a glitzy casino, but what about picking up a lottery ticket at the checkout counter of the local convenience store? According to a recent poll on 120 lifestyle questions of North American evangelicals, increasing numbers of us buy lottery tickets. Some churches and Christian organizations now accept government funding for community causes, fully aware that they are primarily from gaming revenue.

The issue here is conditioning. Las Vegas hotels now provide slot machines to entertain children while their parents gamble. This is intentional conditioning of the next generation. The news media manipulate their audiences to sell us their spin on current events. Conditioning is a bottom-line strategy of the marketing industry.

Early in my pre-ministry career as a salesman, I struggled with customers badgering me to buy raffle tickets. The causes were honorable—new hospitals, community centers, quilts for the needy, etc. One day, I was providentially directed to Proverbs and found this statement: "An inheritance quickly gained at the beginning will not be blessed at the end" (20:21; cp 13:11 and 28:20). Research done on winners of lotteries indicates that many end up living tragic lives. My response to my customers became: "That's a very good cause. Yes, I do want to support it. Here is the price of the ticket, but please keep the ticket."

Social Drinking

Temperance movements died around the mid-19th-century point. Today, breweries are the financial heavyweights in the promotion of professional sports. We are intrigued by their creative and expensive commercials. Governments thrive on their tax dollars. Liquor outlets are as convenient as the corner store. If evangelicals boycotted all restaurants that now serve liquor they would probably find themselves back home cooking Sunday dinners like previous generations.

We readily acknowledge that liquor is the major cause of highway accidents, a leading contributor to the breakup of marriages and the most common source of unhappy childhood memories. In Colombia, South America, where liquor is a major curse, they have this tragic saying: "We have to poison the parents to educate the children"; i.e., if parents do not become addicted to liquor, the government would not have the tax money to pay the teachers. North American culture differs little.

Among evangelicals, drinking socially has in many areas become acceptable. Two issues usually emerge. First, it is difficult to build a case of abstinence based on Scripture. However, there is an old book, *The Bible and Its Wines*, which describes the ancient system used to prevent the fermentation of grapes. The other argument for abstinence grows out of Paul's admonition that we should not become stumbling blocks for other Christians by our actions (Romans 14:13-18). This is reinforced by his exhortation to the Thessalonians: "Abstain from every form of evil" (1 Thessalonians 5:22, NKJV).

Entertainment

Twentieth-century technology spares no aspect of lifestyle. The vast realm of entertainment available with the advent of television has profoundly impacted the evangelical church. A mother attempting to explain to her daughter how movies have changed from her day expressed it this way: "In my youth, movies would end with intimate scenes of kissing and embracing. Today, your movies begin where ours ended, displaying every imaginable act of sexuality."

The powerful role of the media in the erosion of Judeo-Christian moral values has been muted in society and now is being muted in the church. The evangelical church is sending a mixed message to the next generation. Parents unconsciously allow their tolerance level to be nudged higher to accommodate more and more immoral content in their movie entertainment. As one mature Christian lady expressed it when questioned about the content of a movie she had seen: "Oh yes, there were some bad scenes, but you know, that's the way they are these days."

Pastors in their attempt at relevance resort to popular movies for sermon illustrations. Young people get a distorted message: "Immoral content is OK for older Christians, but harmful if you are a minor." These are the same evangelical parents who are now divorcing at a rate comparable to non-Christians. Our culture has lost its sense of shame.

Os Guinness reminds us that traditional evangelicalism "not only resisted worldly influences, but also stressed 'cognitive defiance' of the world spirit."[1] He notes that somewhere along the way evangelicals decided to make friends with the world. Our stance has been that we are "in the world" but not "of the world." He argues that many Christians have reversed the formula, i.e., becoming a part of the world, but not really in the world.

How has this happened? Unquestionably, one way has been by allowing cable television, VCRs, radio, Internet, etc., to infuse worldly values into our minds right in the privacy of our homes. And this has been happening to us while we find ourselves more and more isolated from the people in the world who need our message. "Evangelicals are now outdoing liberals as the supreme religious modernizers— compromisers—of today."[2]

Subtle Cultural Changes

Historical drift thrives on culture. Our culture, in the throes of exponential change, has turned up the heat on Christians. The commitment of our changeless Christ is to "conform us into His image." But our cultural milieu stubbornly pushes us into the world's mold. Both processes are slow, hidden and mutually exclusive.

How does culture change the behavioral patterns of evangelical Christians? This insight from a Christian anthropologist is timely: "The process of change goes on so subtly and so thoroughly, in every aspect of life, that a program without built-in mechanisms to cope with change may drift toward falsehood in every part of its program and ministry."[3]

Early in the 20th century, these adverse pressures were all laid at the feet of secular humanism and its Humanist Manifesto of 1933 which declared war on Christianity with its opening statement: "Humanists regard the universe as self-existing and not created." Today, similar attacks continue but under what is called "postmodernism." These assaults also advocate human self-determination, freedom of the individual to do what brings the greatest pleasure and personal fulfillment, but differ in that they give benign neglect to history, including the history of origins, i.e., the Bible, creation, etc.

The Desire to Accommodate

The desire to accommodate is more than a missionary question in a foreign culture. Every Christian must learn to accommodate, i.e., live cross-culturally and yet identify sufficiently to communicate the gospel effectively. The current focus on the North American segregation of generations for greater effectiveness in reaching each age group is commendable. However, the exegeting of the cultural values of each decade is akin to chasing the wind.

The critical question for the church continues to be: Which of these cultural values can the church address to reach them, and which must be challenged and become part of their repentance and turning from the world? The polarized answers from a previous generation are inadequate: All culture is bad—everything must go; or full identification—everything can be Christianized. Both are faulty. The former abandons us to our evangelical ghettos singing 18th-century hymns to ourselves. The latter leads to pragmatism, syncretism and ultimately nominalism.

The desire to accommodate is biblical. Paul promoted and practiced it: "I have become all things to all men so that by all possible means I might save some" (1 Corinthians 9:22). But what sounds like pragmatism is balanced by his nonnegotiable conviction that "the message of the cross is foolishness to those who are perishing, but to us who are being saved it is the power of God" (1:18).

To take a firm stand on this slippery slope, one foot must be set in biblical revelation, and the other must be pointing toward biblical relevance.

Shifting Values

A retired farmer, who survived the Great Depression, is now comfortably retired in the city. Having lived his life battling the elements to keep food on the table, he now finds that his values have changed drastically. One of the major issues that preoccupies him is how to keep the leaves out of his beautiful swimming pool.

Although high-tech North American change is perceived as explosive, it is deceitfully gradual. Even as we speak, our values are shifting on the slippery slope. Consider the following:

From work to leisure: "When we used to part ways with a Christian brother, we would admonish one another 'hang in there—work hard.' Today, I hear myself with a new line: 'Don't work too hard—take it easy' " (the confession of a post-boomer pastor).

The new psychology considers it politically incorrect to ask a new acquaintance, "And what is your work?" With a growing focus on leisure, one's work and one's character are mutually exclusive. Work is to be tolerated. Real life consists of weekends. Surveys reveal that most people don't enjoy their work. Bumper stickers attest to this: "I'm in no rush—I'm going to work."

From needs to wants: "I've had all my needs met and now I'm working on my wants." This was one Christian's testimonial on a promotional video for a multi-level sales scheme.

North Americans live with a dotted line between needs and wants. In the harsh realities of third-world countries, the dotted line becomes a solid line. They have few options. A Burmese pastor reports that some spouses must rotate their work schedules not only to care for the children but also to share the same work clothes.

Historically, and particularly in this century, each generation has anticipated and experienced a lifestyle higher than that of their parents. This economic trend, powered mainly by technology, has transferred scores of wants into needs. Given our fallen natures, and being at the mercy of consumerism, we will continue to rationalize our wants into needs.

"Fur coats are worn by beautiful animals and ugly people." A demonstrator's placard reminds us of how distorted the cultural mandate of Genesis has become in a rights-intoxicated society. Ironically, the rights movement has flourished in the Western world where Christianity has made its greatest impact on governments. But the postmodern person thrives on the insatiable demands of an unchallenged self-life.

All of these value shifts impact the leadership of the evangelical church. This one, in particular, is seen in the questions of ministerial candidates. Up front, straight from seminary, many ask, "What's in the financial package?" And once the answer is given, a second question follows: "Does that include all of the fringe benefits?" The young people obviously have forgotten that Christ, the Head of the Church—those who will employ them—refused to claim His rights (Philippians 2:5-11).

From commitment to happiness: "What is the difference between American society and evangelical Christian society? Not much. What is the difference between the average middle-class American and the average middle-class Christian? Not much."[4]

Who is this pessimist? His name is Edward Dayton, a business-man-turned-mission executive. His book is titled *What Ever Happened to Commitment?* Employers complain that employees give only a minimal commitment to their work. A coach wonders: "Where are the players who give 110 percent, who come early to practice and stay late and who don't believe in off seasons?"

A senior pastor laments the breakup of ten Christian marriages in his church over a three-year period. Despite his efforts to stop the ignoring of biblical principles and knowing how much it will bring hurt to their children, these couples willfully and skillfully walked away from their vows to God and their commitments to their spouses.

If commitment is the glue of relationships, our culture has become unglued. Happiness becomes the bottom line. If you are not happy with your job, quit! If your marriage falls short of the sexual satisfaction and happiness marketed on the tube, walk away from it! If your pastor does not hit a home run with every sermon, leave and find a church where the preacher bats 1000!

From toughness to softness: We often reach for missionary biographies of another century to illustrate toughness. Certainly William Carey of India is one of those who endured incredible losses in his family and opposition from the host culture. But we need not leave our continent or century to find outstanding examples of strong commitment, both secular and Christian. We need to be reminded that the 20th century has seen more Christian martyrs than all the previous centuries combined.

Twentieth-century missions have seen radical change. Many missionaries live in urban centers which, compared to the pioneer days, provide access to the basic amenities of life. Good local schools are now available for their children. But the remaining Unreached People Groups (UPGs) live in tough, dangerous or remote places. Will the products of our evangelical churches provide the raw material needed to pay the price of the Careys, Livingstones and early pioneers of a previous era? We are recruiting gifted young people, but they are a generation who have embraced many of the subtle value shifts in culture.

Summary

I believe it is obvious to all that our perspective has abandoned the long haul for the quick return. In 1994, the government of India officially honored William Carey. It took 200 years. Beyond his brilliant translation work, he impacted the society far beyond the Church. He was appalled at the horrible practice of *sati*, the burning of widows on the funeral pyres of their husbands. Under God, he saw that practice abolished in his day.

The Puritans of the 17th century were known for their godliness and passion to change society. They saw very little impact in the culture of their day, but they were committed to doing what was right even though they never lived to see the results. They were content with the knowledge that what they did was right, and that in God's timing the impact would come.

The biblical focus is on casting "your bread upon the waters, for after many days you will find it again" (Ecclesiastes 11:1). God thinks in generations. We think in days, weeks, months, years and sometimes in decades. The rapid revolution of communication systems has programmed us for instant responses. This expectation permeates every aspect of life, including the Christian church. If a thousand dollars was given last week for missions, the donor needs to know this week what it has accomplished.

The Bottom-Line Issue—
Our View of Scripture

God loves us the way we are. But, because He loves us, He does not want to leave us this way, but rather to conform us into Christlikeness. Many Christians—unconsciously eroded in their spiritual life and sliding on the slope—are oblivious to His plan. Only as they look into the mirror of God's Word, do they become awakened to their needs:

> For the word of God is living and active. Sharper than any double-edged sword, it penetrates even to dividing soul and spirit, joints and marrow; it judges the thoughts and attitudes of the heart. Nothing in all creation is hidden from God's sight. Everything is uncovered and laid bare before the eyes of him to whom we must give account. (Hebrews 4:12-13)

The Word of God faces three obstacles in accomplishing the work of penetrating and judging the thoughts and attitudes of Christians.

Biblical Illiteracy

We expect non-Christians to be biblically literate. The North American church, during the first half of this century, was privileged to work with a nonchurched society with a considerable residue of Bible knowledge. In the last fifty years, this is no longer true.

We should, however, still expect to find Bible literacy high among evangelicals. We pride ourselves in being people of the one Book. Today we have become people of many books. Something has happened to Bible memorization. The proliferation of English versions becomes a convenient excuse. (We could still choose a version. Thousands of junior high young people are doing just that through quizzing programs.) Serious Bible study classes have taken a hit. Adult electives in

Sunday school have been downloaded into small home groups. Although positive in some ways, in my observation many of these groups tend to focus on relational issues at the expense of serious Bible study. We have lost a chunk of in-depth indoctrination in the shift.

Relational Preaching

For the past generation the importance of preaching has diminished in the North American evangelical church. The causes are multiple, complex and not easily defined.

Corporate North America loves numbers and bigness. Numbers became the bottom line in late 20th-century church success. A couple of decades of pastors have paid a high price both in their marriages and ministries. The social sciences have become dominant in North American church growth philosophy. Pragmatism, the only American-born philosophy, has pushed aside theology.

With the decline in theology came the inevitable diminishing of the role of preaching. To fit the growth mode, it became relational, man-focused and felt need-oriented. This became particularly evident during the baby boomer focus in the 1970s.

On the heels of the boomer thrust came the revelation that we were living in a postmodern era, a mind-set with no place for history or absolute propositional truth. This has pushed the church even further toward relational theology.

How does this trend in preaching relate to our view of the Scriptures? Obviously, it impacts what transpires or fails to transpire Sunday mornings.

One of two scenarios plays out: Christians leave having seen a transcendent God who can meet all their felt needs and, more importantly, their core spiritual needs. Or they depart with a good feeling that a very gifted relational speaker hardwired into their felt needs and gave them some Jesus answers to try this week. When the latter happens, some would dare to say, "There's profanity in the pulpit!"[5]

Our people come to church having been bombarded all week by the superficiality of the news media, the business world of Wall Street or Bay Street, the professional sports hype, the public school systems and the multiple levels of government. Their church experience must be radically different. They must see and hear from the One Reality, the God of the universe. And where do you find Him? In the Bible. If they do not see Him Sunday morning, there is indeed profanity in the pulpit.

Have you ever wondered why the Bible has such a large Old Testament? It's there to show us who God is. Until we see who He is, we cannot experience Him.

Then we come into the New Testament and meet His Son, revealed in humanity. In Christ we have another dimension of God's self-revelation. The incarnate Son puts God into sandal leather. Jesus declares: "Anyone who has seen me has seen the Father" (John 14:9).

Absence of the Holy Spirit

Some church historians will no doubt dub the 20th century as "the century of the Holy Spirit." It opened with the 1904 Welsh revival when God again poured out His Spirit on the tiny country of Wales. This mighty moving spilled over into America. One of the most significant expressions was the Azusa Street meetings in 1906 which gave birth to Pentecostalism.

Then, two more charismatic waves swept over the church in that century: 1) the 1960 charismatic phenomenon of tongues which impacted many segments of the historical denominations, and 2) the signs and wonders movement of the 1980s which emerged from John Wimber's ministry at Fuller Seminary and became the Vineyard churches. As the millennium closed, several controversial renewal movements, some focusing on the slaying in the Spirit and other related phenomena, were swirling around North America and parts of Europe.

Most mainline evangelical churches have chosen to let the charismatic waves roll by, but the movement continues to expand independently of mainline evangelicalism. The Holy Spirit's ministry, apart from the mainstream Pentecostals, appears restricted in the majority of evangelical churches. The significant exception is the growing minority of churches and ministries committed to revival. The bulk of mainline evangelicals seems to be satisfied with a two-thirds-of-the-Trinity theology. This major oversight has been disastrous for large numbers of evangelicals.

We would go to the mat in defense of the orthodoxy of the Trinity. In so doing, we affirm the personhood of the Holy Spirit. Yet, in experience, most offer Him benign neglect at best. This sends a powerful nonverbal message to our people: The Holy Spirit is a force like wind and gravity—they are there whether you acknowledge them or not.

Let's consider a few of the Holy Spirit's roles:

- He was sent by Jesus to complete the work the Son began (John 14-16; Acts 1:1, 2, 8).
- He is the agent of the new birth (John 3:5-8).
- He played the lead role in the birth of the Church (Acts 2).
- He is the Lord of the Harvest (Matthew 9:37-38; Acts 13:1-3; 16:6-10).
- He is the key person in evangelism (John 16:8-11).
- He maintains an indispensable role with the Scriptures:
  "He [guides us] into all truth" (16:13).
  "He will testify about me" (15:26).
  He has the role of reminding the believer of the teachings of Christ (16:15).
  He had the lead role in the inspiration of the Old Testament Scriptures (2 Peter 1:20-21).

"Take . . . the sword of the Spirit, which is the word of God"
(Ephesians 6:17).

The anemic condition of biblical knowledge among mainline evangelicals is, in my opinion, in direct proportion to their ignoring of His
critical roles especially as they relate to the interpretation and application of the Scriptures.

Ironically, God is using the evangelical wing of the Church of England
to restore this truth to North American evangelicals. It is being delivered
in an unexpected package: They have combined good old relational skills
with food to attract non-Christians to see a video on the gospel, then interact around tables. They call it the Alpha Course.

Halfway through the three-month course, the group goes away for a
weekend retreat. Subject? The Holy Spirit. Little wonder that many
new Christians comment, "We never understood these things before,
but now we do." It's encouraging to find an evangelistic method which
invites the Holy Spirit, the Lord of the Harvest, back to do what only
He can do—"[convicting] the world of guilt in regard to sin and righteousness and judgment" (John 16:8).

The Watershed Issue: Our View of Scripture

I promised we would finish this slippery-slope discussion addressing
the watershed issue. I am convinced that for all who affirm the deity of
Christ, there is nothing more important than our absolute commitment
to the Scriptures.

Many lament the ongoing battles for the Bible. Personally, I rejoice
that we're still fighting for this Book. Many segments of Christendom
signed a truce with culture years ago. They now enjoy the serenity of
the ecclesiastical graveyard.

The war continues, but the battlefields change. There were the battles with kings and queens whose strategy was to burn Bibles. William
Tyndale, to whom we owe the English Bible, was held prisoner in a

dark, cold cell. He asked for two things from his captors—warmer clothing and his Hebrew Bible to pursue his work. He went to his death with a firm step and died with this prayer on his lips: "Lord, open the King of England's eyes."[6]

Three Significant Battles

At least three significant battles were waged in the 20th century. The 1920s featured the battle between the liberals and the fundamentalists. The essential doctrines of the Bible were at stake: "The deity of and virgin birth of Christ, the bodily resurrection of Christ, salvation through faith in His substitutionary sacrifice on the cross, the inerrancy of the Scriptures, and the visible return of Christ, in judgment and to set up His kingdom."[7] These became known as the "fundamentals of the Christian faith." The debate raged primarily in the seminaries. It resulted in several new seminaries and schools being established.

The second battle was waged at Fuller Theological Seminary in the 1960s and '70s over the question of the inerrancy of Scripture. A former professor of Fuller led the attack.[8] He argued that Fuller had compromised its historic commitment to inerrancy. After prolonged debate, in 1972 the seminary chose to adopt a position of the "authority of Scripture" rather than the "inerrancy of Scripture."[9]

This development at Fuller became the bridge to the third battleground for the battle for the Bible in the 1980s and '90s—hermeneutics—how Scripture should be interpreted. On the surface, the shift sounds innocuous. But when Paul Jewett, a long-term Fuller professor, published his book, *Man as Male and Female*, the significance of the shift in hermeneutics became quite apparent. In the interpretation of the difficult passages in Paul's writings on the question of the role of women in the home and church, he argued that one must remember that Paul was both a Jew and a Christian. "He was a rabbi of impeccable erudition who had become an ardent disciple of Jesus Christ. And his thinking about women—their place in life generally and in the Church specifically—reflects both his Jewish and his Christian experience."[10] He sees Paul as double-minded—and wrong. As a Jew he sees the woman as subordinate to the man (1 Corinthians 11:9). Yet as a Christian he sees man and woman as all one in Christ (Galatians 3:28). Which Paul do we follow?

This approach to Scripture began to emerge in other areas of theology. Some concluded that those who had never heard the gospel could be among the redeemed. Worst-case scenario—they would be annihilated. John Stott acknowledged that he could no longer believe that God would send someone who had never heard of Christ to an eternal hell, and that "eternal" does not necessarily mean eternal.[11]

This battle also moved from the realm of debate among theologians to the agenda of local church elders. Denominations, especially in the last two decades, grappled with the role of women in leadership. Some debated the role of women as elders, while others moved on to the ordination of women—issues which have little to do with women and everything to do with how we interpret Scripture. In all cases, the eye of the storm is centered on the interpretation of key passages. All believe they have a high view of Scripture. This again attests to how slippery the slope really is on this the most critical of all issues.

There are many related matters at stake which should give pause to all responsible evangelical leaders. Here are but a few of them: 1) sanctity of life questions, e.g., abortion, euthanasia, genetic engineering, bioethics, etc.; 2) sanctity of family issues, e.g., definition of marriage, grounds for divorce, right to remarry, family planning, etc.; 3) sanctity of sexuality matters, e.g., homosexual behavior, homosexual orientation and practice, etc.

The responsibility of leaders is to see sooner and see farther than those they lead. Where will decisions in these key areas lead the church? Recent church history of denominations, with few exceptions, reveals a dangerous sequence of debates on these slippery-slope issues. The tracking of denominational conferences over a decade shows an alarming pattern, i.e., the discussion on the ordination of women precedes the debate on the ordination of homosexuals within, in one case, about a ten-year span. They are very different issues, but what creates the sequence is the common approach to interpreting Scripture: If clear Scriptures prohibit it, focus on the obscure. If that is not possible, then declare the clear passages as culturally time and place specific.

Historically, on this critical issue of interpreting the Bible, the slippery slope has always taken the Church in one direction: The interpretation of the Scriptures becomes the exclusive right of the academic elite. For dark centuries, many were held in the grasp of the Roman Catholic Church. Even after the Protestant Reformation and the Gutenberg press, liberal theologians intimidated the churches under the guise of academia. In the current battle for the Bible, with its focus on hermeneutics, once again the everyday Christian feels disenfranchised when told by the academicians that the clear sense of the Bible on such basic issues as the roles of men and women is no longer true. Although there are numerous exceptions, the educated elite tend to muddle our understanding of Scripture.

Reinterpreting the clear passages by appealing to the obscure passages is not good scholarship. The use of such hermeneutical principles cannot be passed off as a true demonstration of the high view of Scripture.

~

Discussion Questions

1. According to a Barna poll of 150 lifestyle issues, including abortion and divorce, evangelicals differ little from non-Christians. Discuss some of the slippery slope lifestyle questions.
2. What's the difference between intentional conditioning and cognitive defiance?
3. In this context, what makes our interpretation of Scripture a "watershed question?"

Good News

Spurgeon's Downgrade

When I hear the name Charles Spurgeon it triggers two images—the prince of preachers and a mentor to students. But Charles Haddon Spurgeon (1834-1892) was also a churchman with a prophetic voice.

Just five years before his death, he began to publish articles on what he called "The Down Grade." His colleague, Robert Shindler, wrote the early articles which appeared in his monthly magazine, *The Sword and the Trowel*. It was Shindler's observation that every revival of true evangelical faith is followed within a generation or two by drift away from sound doctrine. He likened it to a downhill slope. Both Shindler and Spurgeon referred to this drift as "the down grade."

They were convinced that the Puritan fervor, which had so profoundly impacted the soul of England, had become dry, listless and apostate in its teaching. Churches were receiving into membership unregenerate people. Some were even hiring such persons as pastors. Shindler summarized his first article on the downgrade with this warning: "These facts furnish a lesson for the present times, when, as in some cases, it is all too plainly apparent men are willing to forego the old for the sake of the new. But commonly it is found in theology that that which is true is not new, and that which is new is not true."[12]

In his second article, Shindler named several Baptist churches perceived to be on the downgrade and identified the first step on the downgrade as an inadequate "faith in the divine inspiration of the sacred Scriptures." He also noted the correlation between Calvinistic doctrine and a high view of Scripture.[13] Some felt that Shindler was too pessimistic. Others expressed strong agreement and identified with his concerns about the trends in British evangelicalism.

Charles Spurgeon wrote the third article. This time, he was more militant in his critique of the churches: "A new religion has been initiated which is no more Christianity than chalk is cheese; and this religion, being destitute of moral honesty, pawns itself off as the old faith with slight improvements, and on this plea usurps pulpits which were erected for gospel preaching."[14]

For the first time, he suggested that it may be necessary for true believers to consider separating organizationally from those promoting a new theology. This shocked the evangelical world. Although counseled by some to soften his position, Spurgeon became even more confrontative in his next article. As the attacks against him became more personal, his responses became more specific:

> A chasm is opening between the men who believe their Bibles and the men who are prepared for an advance upon Scripture. Inspiration and speculation cannot long abide in peace. Compromise there can be none. We cannot hold the inspiration of the Word, and yet reject it; we cannot believe in the atonement and deny it; we cannot hold the doctrine of the fall and yet talk of the evolution of spiritual life from human nature; we cannot recognize the punishment of the impenitent and yet indulge the "larger hope." One way or the other we must go. Decision is the virtue of the hour.[15]

Spurgeon served notice that his church was withdrawing from the Baptist Union. When asked to reconsider, he countered with a request that the Union adopt an evangelical statement of faith. They refused. Five days later, they voted to accept his withdrawal, then took a vote to censure and condemn his actions. Only five of 100 members of the council supported Spurgeon. Even his brother voted against him. Close friends and some of his students from his Pastoral College also turned against him.

John MacArthur notes that "Spurgeon was the first evangelical with international influence to declare war on modernism."[16] Although the Evangelical Alliance supported Spurgeon, British evangelicalism in general did so with little fervor. The subsequent decline in British evangelicalism proved Spurgeon to be a true prophet. Only in the second half of the 20th century has there been a significant resurgence.

"Our first responsibility is not the evangelization of the world, but to be spiritually worthy to proclaim. It would be a tragedy to propagate a defective form of Christianity."

—A.W. Tozer

8

The Best Things in the Worst Times

Who Sets the Vertical?

I HAVE FOUND THAT THE AIRING of the historical drift theory often runs into a buzz saw of opposition. The perennial optimists particularly jump to the attack. "Look at the phenomenal growth of Christians in this century. Compare the status of missions in 1900 with the impressive figures with which we begin the 21st century. Why this concern that the church is drifting?"

They are right on. I know those statistics well. In the year A.D. 100, for every Christian there were 360 non-Christians. By 1900, it was down to 112 to one. Today it's about nine to one. That's progress! I'm on that bandwagon. But . . .

The Best of Times
and the Worst of Times

Responsible Christian leaders have always lived and led in a world of contrasts, often described as "the best of times and the worst of times." This glimpse from the 17th century was one of those times:

> Targeted in the aftermath of the Cromwellian civil war were the Anglicans who were tied closely to the king who had served as the head of the church. Cromwell emptied the monasteries, removed baptismal fonts from the churches, defamed the clergy and did everything in his power to disengage their place and influence in the culture. If you were an Anglican pastor, these were tough times to be in the religion business. In the face of such times there were some who were undaunted. An inspiring but little-known inscription hidden away in Harold Church, Staunton, England reads like this: "In the year of 1653, when all things sacred were throughout the nation destroyed or profaned, this church was built to the glory of God by Sir Robert Shirley, whose singular praise it was to have done the best things in the worst times."[1]

The leaders of Israel too were often called to lead in such times. One king served God for forty years, and the land prospered. Another followed, and everything went downhill—God judged His people. The psalmists let it all hang out, crying out in the agony of despair and often questioning God's love. But all but two psalms end on a note of praise and hope.

Then there is the cycle in Judges. The people sinned. God brought judgment. The people cried out. God raised up a judge. They repented. And God prospered them for thirty years. Habakkuk declares himself in one of those "bad times": "Though the fig tree does not bud and there are no grapes on the vines, though the olive crop fails and the fields produce no food, though there are no sheep in the pen and no cattle in the stalls, yet I will rejoice in the LORD, I will be joyful in God my Savior" (Habakkuk 3:17-18).

Paul rejoiced but was never satisfied. Writing to the Romans, he revels in the advance of the gospel. In fact, he assessed the situation in this way: "There is no more place for me to work in these regions" (Romans 15:23). His new plan was to visit Rome, but that was only in passing. He had his sights on Spain (15:24).

The New Testament worldview is a paradox. When you synthesize the teachings of Jesus and the epistles, two incompatible scenarios emerge. One is a future of judgment and destruction of this world system. The other, standing in sharp contrast, is a future of hope for all the redeemed. There is even a promise of a "new heaven and a new earth" (Revelation 21).

So what are we? Optimists or pessimists? Answer: The Christian leader must be both. Some would call it "biblical realism." That is where I stand. I rejoice in the growth of Christ's Church. I've studied it, seen it—and it's real. Christ's promise to build His Church causes me to rejoice daily with a keen sense of high privilege. Then His incredible commitment to "present her [the Church] to himself as a radiant church, without stain or wrinkle or any other blemish, but holy and blameless" (Ephesians 5:27) energizes me to contend for the purity of the Church in preparing Her for that glorious day. In so doing, we follow the great biblical tradition of the New Testament writers.

That's why I have pursued historical drift with a passion. I have probed its causes, but more importantly, I want to pursue the remedies. We need to seek God's provision for His needy people. After all, it's *His* Church. Holiness is *His* call.

Who Sets the Standard
for a Holy Church?

Multiplied numbers of books may be read which explain the characteristics of healthy churches. How do we define a healthy church? More importantly, what are the characteristics of a holy church? Historically, the Church Growth Movement has failed to address this question. In any diagnosis of church health, a basic question must be answered: Who sets the vertical? Who establishes the vertical scale for the healthy church chart? Terms such as "radiant . . . holy and blameless" aren't easily quantified (Ephesians 5:27).

Christ the Head

Who sets the vertical? Let's start with the Head of the Church, the Lord Jesus Christ. What do we learn from His two references to the Church? The first is Matthew 16:18: "And I tell you that you are Peter, and on this rock I will build my church, and the gates of Hades will not overcome it." Our Protestant understanding extracts two qualities from this text: 1) the Church's foundation is the confession that Jesus is "the Christ, the Son of the living God" (16:16); and 2) the Church is indestructible (16:18).

The second reference to the Church is Matthew 18:17: "If he refuses to listen to them, tell it to the church; and if he refuses to listen even to the church, treat him as you would a pagan or a tax collector." The context is the discipline of a believer. Again two principles emerge: 1) the Church is the final court of appeal, after individual confrontations have failed; and 2) failure to heed the Church leads to excommunication from the Church. By deduction, we also learn that the Church gathered has a high level of authority over the lives of her members. She speaks for God. She must be holy.

Christ's Standards for Church Members

Matthew 5:1-12 identifies personal characteristics of those who are part of Christ's body. Interestingly, this passage moves the focus from the corporate church to individual members. What are their qualities to be?

- poor in spirit (5:3)
- those who mourn (5:4)
- the meek (5:5)
- those who hunger and thirst for righteousness (5:6)
- the merciful (5:7)
- the pure in heart (5:8)
- the peacemakers (5:9)
- those persecuted because of righteousness (5:10)
- those insulted and falsely accused of evil (5:11)

Note its counterculture nature in each of these characteristics. Except for the possible exclusion of peacemakers, none of these are sought-after traits in the world system. Jesus repeatedly reminded His followers of the fact that His people were not of the world (John 15:18-19). So, what are His expectations? 1) That we live lives counterculture to this world system and 2) that we live as light and salt in this present world (Matthew 5:13-14).

Since this is our calling, how do churches—groups of believers—actually live this out in contemporary society? The churches of Revelation chapter 2 hold those answers.

The Church in Ephesus: Revelation 2:1-7

A respectable church with illustrious leadership, it was commended for its hard work. Their moral integrity was beyond reproach. Doctrinally they were intolerant of sin. But in His audit, Christ identified a major deficiency: "You have forsaken your first love" (2:4). A love relationship with Himself was a nonnegotiable.

The Church in Pergamum: Revelation 2:12-17

Although they lived "where Satan has his throne," they were affirmed for their uncompromising witness (2:13). Yet Christ censored them for their myopia. In their nearsightedness they had condoned heresy, i.e., the seductive teaching of Balaam and the eating of things sacrificed as taught by the Nicolaitans, both of which had led them into idolatry and immorality. Doctrinally sound and morally pure—that's what Christ was and is looking for.

The Church in Thyatira: Revelation 2:18-29

This church is commended for the essentials of love, faith, service and perseverance (2:19). They were even on the growing edge of these virtues, " . . . doing more than you did at first" (2:19). But they too tolerated unsound doctrine which promoted immorality (2:20-23). Christ warned them that He is the one who searches hearts (He knows even when nobody else knows) and that He will repay them according to their deeds (2:23). His second statement reinforces the fact that Christ's judgment ultimately will not be corporate, but individual—member by member.

The Church in Sardis: Revelation 3:1-6

Although they were commended for "a few people . . . who [had] not soiled their clothes" (3:4), Christ fingered their major flaw: "You have a reputation of being alive, but you are dead" (3:1). Apparently hypocrisy, meaning "to play a part on the stage," was totally unacceptable. The opposite, integrity—meaning that the outer and the inner are the same—must be true of all believers.

The Church in Laodicea: Revelation 3:14-22

For this church, located among the rich and famous, and renowned for its medical expertise, Christ has no words of commendation. With cutting words, He bites through the veneer of affluence and spiritual apathy. They are "lukewarm," then He adds, "I wish you were either one or the other," either hot or cold (3:15). But that isn't all. He rebukes their "self-righteousness" (3:17). Note that this is the only church where Christ positions Himself as an outsider: "Here I am! I stand at the door and knock. If anyone hears my voice and opens the

door, I will come in and eat with him, and he with me" (3:20).
White-hot devotion—that is what Christ is looking for.

A Model Church

We have already dismissed the myth of the "holy apostolic church of
the New Testament." To desire a New Testament church is asking for
some of the carnality of the Corinthian church, some of the divisive-
ness of the Philippian church and some of the legalism of the Galatian
churches.

Though no New Testament church was perfect, I submit Antioquia,
Syria, as the leading candidate. What catches my attention up front is
this statement: "The disciples were called Christians first at Antioch"
(Acts 11:26).

I understand that the Antioquians liked nicknames. One day, a Roman governor visited. He had a beard, so they quickly labeled him "the
goat." These same people were aware of a little band of religious zealots
who professed to follow a man they referred to as Christ. As they
watched His disciples' lifestyle and commitment, they nicknamed
them "Christians."

But there is more substance to my choice. Consider the following
characteristics of this healthy church:

- Lay people with church-growth eyes founded it. Initially
  some went to Antioch. Then a different group of unnamed
  lay persons "began to speak to Greeks also" (11:20). What
  happened? "The Lord's hand was with them, and a great
  number of people believed and turned to the Lord" (11:21).
  Churches with church-growth eyes evangelize the responsive and monitor the unresponsive.
- They discipled the new believers quickly and effectively.
  Barnabas, the great encourager, arrived from Jerusalem and
  "encouraged them all to remain true to the Lord with all
  their hearts" (11:23).

- They developed a strong, spiritual team ministry. To the founding laymen, Barnabas, "a good man, full of the Holy Spirit and faith" was added (11:24). He took a risk and recruited Saul, the former persecutor of the church. Result? More growth: They "taught great numbers of people" (11:26) who were then called Christians (11:26).

- They had compassion for the social needs of people beyond their church. Fellow believers in Judea were suffering from famine. Antioch responded. "The disciples, each according to his ability, decided to provide help for the brothers living in Judea" (11:29).

- They listened when the Lord of the harvest called asking for two missionaries. The Holy Spirit bypassed the mother church in Jerusalem and launched the missionary movement from Antioch. Note how it was done: "While they were worshiping the Lord and fasting, the Holy Spirit said, 'Set apart for me Barnabas and Saul for the work to which I have called them.' " The Holy Spirit did not speak to the two men, but to their church. The church's response was both spiritual and obedient: "So after they had fasted and prayed, they placed their hands on them and sent them off " (13:2-3). Any church would do well to measure their spirituality, strategy and core values against the church in Antioch.

Paul's Philosophy of Ministry

Paul's passion seemed equally focused on both the quantitative and qualitative aspects of the Church. In Ephesians 5:27, he describes the radiant, spotless, blameless and holy universal Church as the bride of Christ. A major part of his ministry was admonishing troubled local churches to become imitators of Christ. We catch a glimpse of his philosophy of ministry in Colossians 1:24-29. It helps us set the vertical in our ministry:

1) He was committed to suffering joyfully for the Church (1:24) This text has confounded the scholars, but Paul understood that the Church would only be completed as Christians paid the price of suffering to reach the last unreached peoples.

2) He was committed to serving selflessly as a servant of the Church (1:25-27) He had become a servant of the Church to proclaim God's word in its fullness, thus identifying himself with Christ who became a servant. He was also committed to continually proclaiming Christ and discipling believers into maturity in Christ (1:28), and to doing all this effortlessly through God's power not his (1:29). This fleshed-out ministry philosophy pushes the benchmark for Christian commitment considerably beyond current acceptable levels.

Peter's Plan for Productivity

In his last letter, Peter reminds us of our union with Christ and that our resources for living an effective and productive life are found through His divine power (2 Peter 1:3). Because of Christ's divine power and our knowledge of Him, "He has given us his very great and precious promises, so that through them you [we] may participate in the divine nature and escape the corruption in the world caused by evil desires" (1:4). What follows is a simple step-by-step approach to a growing Christian life:

- Add to your faith, goodness (virtue, excellence, resolution, and Christian energy)
- To goodness, knowledge (intelligence)
- To knowledge, self-control
- To self-control, perseverance (steadfastness, patience, endurance)
- To perseverance, godliness (piety)
- To godliness, brotherly kindness (affection)
- And to brotherly kindness, love (1:5-7)

This formula comes with a threefold guarantee: "For if you possess these qualities in increasing measure, they will keep you from being ineffective and unproductive in your knowledge of our Lord Jesus Christ" (1:8). "For if you will do these things, you will never fall, and you will receive a rich welcome into the eternal kingdom of our Lord and Savior Jesus Christ" (1:10-11).

These are only a few of the biblical criteria for measuring a normal level of Christian living and defining a healthy church.

What about the additional verticals that define the church that pleases God?

During the last half of the 20th century, the focus on church growth has produced a plethora of verticals. Most have been strong on quantitative measurements but weak on the qualitative aspect. Biblical models, it should be noted, are almost exclusively oriented to the quality of spiritual life. The possible exception would be the book of Acts where numbers are frequently mentioned and again in Revelation where terms such as "many peoples" and "multitudes" describe the gathering of the redeemed.

In recent years, I am happy to say, several new approaches to church growth have focused more on quality than quantity.

The Purpose-Driven Church

Rick Warren, the pastor of Saddleback Church in Lake Forest, California, believes that in order for a church to be healthy it must become a purpose-driven church built around the five New Testament purposes given to the church by Jesus:

- Love the Lord with all your heart.
- Love your neighbor as yourself.
- Go and make disciples.
- Baptize them.
- Teach them to obey.

Saddleback's Purpose Statement reads as follows: "To bring people to Jesus and membership into His family, develop them to Christlike maturity, and equip them to their ministry in the church and life mission in the world, in order to magnify God's name."

Only one of their five-fold strategy focuses on numerical growth:

- warmer through fellowship
- deeper through discipleship
- stronger through worship
- broader through ministry
- larger through evangelism.[2]

Natural Church Development

Christian A. Schwarz of Germany has surveyed 1,000 churches worldwide. He has been searching for a better answer to the basic question the Church Growth Movement has been asking for forty-five years: "What growth principles are true regardless of culture and theological persuasion?" Schwarz believes he has found the answer. It is based on the "biotic element," i.e., "the release of the 'all by itself' principle." Approaching the Church from the perspective of it being an organism versus an organization, he has identified eight quality characteristics which provide a diagnostic tool to profile the health of a church:

- empowering leadership
- gift-oriented ministry
- passionate spirituality
- functional structures
- inspiring worship services
- holistic small groups
- need-oriented evangelism
- loving relationships.

One component which appears to be missing is the evidence of a theology of missions.[3]

SonLife Ministries: Growing a Healthy Church

This ministry, under the leadership of Dann Spader, has grown out of the very effective SonLife Youth Ministry. It is based on a biblical understanding of Great Commission priorities as observed in the life of Christ. These have been summarized into three priorities: winning, building and equipping. Their mission is "to restore to the heart of the local church for Great Commission passion." Their strategy is "training leadership in Great Commission priorities resulting in healthy Christians with a balance of winning, building and equipping priorities."[4]

Summary

Who sets the vertical for the church that pleases God? Short answer: God. He has amplified and illustrated how that church should be: "Holy." How it should look: "Like His Son." How it should function: "Like salt and light." How it should serve: "Like Christ, selflessly, fearlessly."

God, not man, sets the vertical on the chart of the healthy church.

~

Discussion Questions

1. How do you understand the concept of "the best of times and the worst of times?"

2. Everyone wants a healthy church. Who sets the standard? What is the criteria for a biblically "healthy church?"
3. What is your church's GCQ (Great Commission Quotient)? (See pages 146-148.)
4. What steps could you take to increase it?

Good News

What Is Your GCQ?

The Church Growth Movement was conceived and delivered on a mission field. The concepts and strategies pioneered by Donald McGavran in the 1950s in India have impacted missions more than any other movement in the last half of this century. In the 1970s, it was popularized, promoted and pontificated into a methodology driven by the social sciences in North America.

Although large numbers of North American churches have bought into some aspects of this missions-born movement, missions-minded churches have often not been the outcome. Polls of what churches consider to be their top seven key activities consistently place missions sixth or last. Even those which focus strongly on the healthy aspect of a successful church often gloss over missions.

Robertson McQuilkin, missionary statesman, college/seminary professor and president asks the question of churches: "What is your GCQ (Great Commission Quotient)?" His test probes four aspects of church life to arrive at its GCQ.

The FIVE Factor

- How many baptisms of new believers did your church have last year? _____
- What percentage of the membership is that? _____

"Some years ago church growth analysts concluded that, in most communities in America, a church ought to have a five percent conversion growth rate each year—not transfer, not children of the church but baptisms of new believers."[5]

The TEN Factor

- What percentage of your staff have you sent as missionaries?

  _____

- What percentage of your church members is that?

  _____

(Antioch sent two of their staff, which was twenty percent [Acts 13:1-3].)

Calvary Church in Lancaster, Pennsylvania, has 1,800 members and has sent 180 missionaries, ten percent. "For a standard, I suggest . . . 10% as a gold medal performance. How is your church doing? _____ Is it time to set a faith goal and step up one percentage?"[6]

The FIFTY Factor

Norfolk Tabernacle Church has the policy that "seventy-five percent of its income [be] invested away from the home church. That's the only church I've seen that gave seventy-five percent, but many churches reach the fifty percent level and that seems appropriate—half for _us_ and half for _them_."[7]

- How is it at your place? _____ percent of total gift income is invested in missions. Would God be calling you to a ten percent increase?

The HUNDRED Factor

"Right up front I admit that I've never seen a church meet this standard, though I still believe it is a biblical one. . . . I remain convinced that 100% of true disciples ought to be involved in praying for the world and for those sent to reach that world . . . ."[8]

But Augusta First Presbyterian Church comes close. Twenty years ago there was no prayer for missions and little for anything else. They gave token support to one missionary, not from their church. The new pastor began leading his people to become a praying people. "Each Sunday night for an hour before the evening service—which is a packed house—hundreds gather in prayer bands to pray for the world and for their dozens of representatives in Asia, Europe, Africa, and South America."[9] There are many new believers. At a recent missions conference, thirty new volunteers stepped forward for career missionary service. They are giving over fifty percent of their total income to missions.

- What percentage of your people are praying regularly for your missionaries? _____
- How much prayer time each week does some group within the church or the church as whole devote to missions?

_____

"There you have it: 5-10-50-100. This need not be a formula for frustration and guilt, but rather a realistic gauge reminding us to raise our Great Commission Quotient."[10]

What is the GCQ of your church? _____

"Ministries often look for leadership skilled in public relations and in raising funds from large foundations. . . . All of this tends to treat God as a peeping Tom in economic affairs."

—Carl F.H. Henry (*Christianity Today*, January 1989)

Part IV

HISTORICAL DRIFT IMPEDED

Historical drift is the inherent tendency of human organizations to depart over time from their original beliefs, purposes and practices. John Wesley lamented it as the "eternal erosion of Christian virtues." He was pessimistic that any adequate answer could be found to impede drift. In the 18th century, he linked it with the acquisition of material wealth.

Although many if not most of us would be prone to reject his diagnosis as simplistic, we nevertheless recognize that economics has, without question, become the bottom line in every facet of 20th-century life. The North American evangelical church has become a mega financial player. One American church raised $31 million for its new complex.

However, before we summarily dismiss Wesley's analysis as irrelevant to our sophisticated times, let's recall the following interaction of

Christ with His disciples about riches. It was in the context of the rich young ruler:

> Then Jesus said to his disciples, "I tell you the truth, it is hard for a rich man to enter the kingdom of heaven. Again I tell you, it is easier for a camel to go through the eye of a needle than for a rich man to enter the kingdom of God."
> When the disciples heard this, they were greatly astonished and asked, "Who then can be saved?" (Matthew 19:23-25)

Jesus' statement on riches and kingdom membership has a universal ring to it. The reaction of the disciples adds credence to Wesley's view. Note their retort: "Who then can be saved?" They were thinking, "Don't you know, Master, that everyone is into materialism?"

Before continuing this examination of causes and cures, diagnoses and treatments, let me restate my theses regarding historical drift: "Although drift is inevitable in all social structures, including religious organizations, it can be curbed and even reversed through renewal and wise, godly and courageous leadership." Let me add these caveats:

- I am not advocating the eternal preservation of any human structure including churches and denominations.
- Not all organizations should be perpetuated indefinitely. Some should be given a timely and dignified burial.
- In the religious world, only those with a biblical mission and the integrity to deliver it should continue.

"The Bible says what God says through human writers without error."

—Final statement of the Chicago Statement on Inerrancy

9

Pitfalls, Passion and the Thin Edge of the Wedge

The Causes and Cures of Historical Drift

A RECENT EXPERIENCE GAVE ME PAUSE to reflect on the anatomy of historical drift. The setting was a dying denominational church in a small town. Fifteen elderly people, plus my wife and I, were present for the Sunday 11 a.m. worship. They were between pastors. The deacon who was to lead became sick. His backup was called away to an uncle's funeral. The deaconesses who took the morning service did a good job.

There are thousands of such churches around. What made this one special? History—personal history. I have known this church for fifty-five years. It was, at one time part of a two-point charge. At age eleven, I became a Christian through the children's ministry in the second church. Why had this church not closed its doors long ago? The other one had—thirty-five years earlier. What happened in this denomination that this church continued to struggle to survive for six decades?

There were no easy answers then, and there are no easy answers now. Sometimes it is demographics. Weak pastoral leadership could explain some chapters. Loss of spiritual leadership at the denominational level may be a major contributor. That denomination had, in the 1940s, experienced a major theological controversy. Their seminary became embroiled in the aftermath of the liberal/fundamentalist controversy of the 1920s which resulted in a split. This church had stayed with the denomination when others left protesting the inroads of liberalism. But I also remembered that there were other churches in the same denomination which were and are dynamic, growing and conservatively evangelical congregations.

The causes of drift are multiple and complex. First, let's analyze the obvious.

Causes: Surface Indicators

Surface symptoms can be traced to root or core causes. Those causes will lead us to tangible answers for impeding historical drift.

Failure of Leadership

Twentieth-century church historians will label the 1980s as "The Decade of the Rise and Fall of TV Evangelists." A fast-growing church in Dallas, Texas caught my attention during that period. The first assistant the senior pastor hired was a pastor of prayer. Their dynamic young senior pastor had put the tough question to David Yonggi Cho: "What's wrong with the American church?" Answer: "They won't pray. They'll give money. They'll build churches, but they won't pray." Armed with Cho's read on the American church, he had determined that his Church on the Rock would be a praying church.

I visited that church in the late '80s. The 5 a.m. prayer times were powerful. The elders' board consisted of the eighteen staff pastors. It appeared to be a dynamic church. Where is it today? Well, let's say that it should probably be renamed "The Church on the Rocks." The senior pastor is gone. The remnant has become four churches. Was their elder structure flawed? Perhaps. But bottom line, their leader failed.

The Bible leaves no doubt: God is always looking for leaders. It shouldn't surprise us that Satan also has Christian leaders at the top of his list—his hit list. Let's look at some of his favorite traps.

Money: "For the love of money is a root of all kinds of evil. Some people, eager for money, have wandered from the faith and pierced themselves with many griefs" (1 Timothy 6:10).

A cartoonist in Dallas greatly helped Billy Graham. As he was leaving Dallas after one of his early crusades, Billy looked at the leading daily. It featured himself leaving town clutching two large bags of money. Billy got the message and immediately took steps to incorporate and put himself on a salary.

Although money is technically amoral, it ensnares Christian leaders in two vulnerable areas. One is the temptation to buy into an opulent lifestyle which destroys their credibility with their people. The other is to manage their ministries following the principles of the corporate world: e.g., speaking fees, not unlike those of motivational speakers on the corporate circuit.

Chuck Swindoll questions this approach:

> Financial benefits come along with certain levels of ministry, and they can create ethical problems. People write and ask what I charge to do such-and-such. On only one occasion did I ever state a fee for speaking, and it led to a misunderstanding that took months to clear up. I got burned too badly from that situation. I decided I'd never state a fee again.[1]

The real cause of failure is not money, but the love of it—the obvious breaking of the tenth commandment—"you shall not covet." God's first answer is always repentance. However, God does honor the rich who, like Abraham, are generous. He also blessed Solomon and his temple as long as he was walking humbly with his God. But Jesus harshly rebuked the self-sufficiency of the Laodiceans who boasted, "[We] are rich; [we] have acquired wealth and do not need a thing" (Revelation 3:17). The core problem is not financial, but spiritual.

John Wesley's answer to the financial pitfall was simple: "When I receive money I get rid of it as quickly as possible before it can harm me."

R.G. LeTourneau, the American industrialist, decided to live on the tithe of his income and give the ninety percent to God's work.

Billy Graham chose to live on a modest salary. In over a half-century of ministry, he and his association modeled financial integrity while others crumbled around them.

Some have refused to market their ministry following the corporate pattern. Still others, to protect themselves from the lure of money, refuse to ask about salary when considering a career change. It makes it much easier to determine God's leading!

Wise Christian leaders, who recognize the hazards of affluence, will become proactive to impede drift. We can learn from those past and present who have done just that.

To regularly check their attitude to money, some leaders periodically decline salary increases. This is a helpful check of one's true motivation.

Sex. "But among you there must not be even a hint of sexual immorality, or of any kind of impurity, or of greed, because these are improper for God's holy people" (Ephesians 5:3).

The second major area of leadership failure is sex. How can this be? It is interesting and somewhat curious to note that Paul's letters to the churches reflect his constant concern for leaders in the two areas of money and sex.

In four decades of ministry, working with some of the most committed Christian leaders, pastors and missionaries, I have observed that moral and financial troubles are indeed the most frequent causes of failure. In one year I assisted in the recovery process of eight cases of moral failure in our small organization.

How can sex and money be the two major pitfalls of Christian leaders? A friend asked a Christian leader: "If Satan wanted to destroy your ministry what would he use?" He responded, "One thing I know he wouldn't use is my marriage because it's very strong." Almost predictably, this leader later committed adultery. An outstanding Christian leader wisely warned: "A strength left unprotected becomes a double danger."

The exponential growth of technology and its impact on the entertainment media has increased the moral failures of Christian leaders. Cyberspace and access to the Internet is taking its toll. Pastors on every side are falling victim to pornography, with chat rooms leading to addictions and illicit relationships.

There are two aspects of moral failure among Christian leaders that double the devastating impact on Christian organizations. The sin often remains covered for months, even years. When it emerges (and it always does), it is seldom David confessing, but rather Nathan pointing the finger. They are caught. This element of deception in leaders known for their integrity seems even more difficult to accept than the sinful act itself.

What is the core cause of all this? Desire—lust—temptation—sin—death. This second aspect of the failure/impact cause and effect is as old as Genesis and as current as pornography on the Internet: "Each one is tempted when, by his own evil desire, he is dragged away and enticed. Then, after desire has conceived, it gives birth to sin; and sin, when it is full-grown, gives birth to death" (James 1:14-15).

The good news is that God forgives the repentant sinner, but restoration to ministry is difficult. Integrity that has been built up over many years may be destroyed in five minutes through a moral lapse. The rebuilding of trust with those betrayed is slow at best.

Although more Christian organizations are implementing measures to protect their leaders, the leader is still primarily responsible. Accountability has become the evangelical antidote in this area. Certainly it has helped men to be more open and honest. But much more important is the individual's accountability to God. "Search me, O God, and know my heart; test me and know my anxious thoughts. See if there is any offensive way in me, and lead me in the way everlasting" (Psalm 139:23-24). It is possible that being in an accountability relationship with peers can subtly become a substitute for being honest with God.

Are there proactive steps organizations can take to ensure moral integrity in their leaders? I believe there are.

First, when hiring, *give more attention to the quality of the marriage relationship*. Tests such as the MSI (Marriage Satisfaction Inventory) can be part of the application process. It checks out the couple's communication level in eleven areas of their marriage. The corporate mind-set that only one spouse is hired is flawed, particularly in the special context of Christian ministry.

Secondly, in screening of the candidate, *lend more weight to their personal devotional life than their public ministry*. In the midst of the moral collapses in the 1980s, one mission executive revealed that, given the number of high-profile Christian leaders falling like flies, he determined that no matter where he was he would rise one hour before his departure time. In that hour, he got his body going, spent time in the Word and prayed through his prayer list.

Third, *provide the interviewees with an expectation of how to handle travel, hotels, etc.* Some organizations provide a traveling companion for their leader. Billy Graham never rides alone in a car with a woman other than his wife. He never enters a new hotel room for the first time alone.

Penchants of Clergy Leaders

There is another set of chronic tendencies that also may foster historical drift. I call them penchants. They are common to all.

The first penchant is to remain in a position beyond one's effectiveness. Oswald J. Sanders, in *Spiritual Leadership*, observes: "Many who have wielded great influence fall before the temptation to think that they are irreplaceable and that in the best interest of the work they should not relinquish office."[2]

This penchant extends well beyond the clergy. I once witnessed a special service to honor a man who had completed fifty consecutive years of service on a local church board. Apparently it had been a positive experience for the church. However, that is not always the case. Often longevity is ambivalently described as "being in the way a long time." The operative term in this discussion is not longevity but effectiveness.

A strong appeal against the system of limited tenure for Christian leaders can be made to the history of the Old Testament. In theocracy, lifetime appointments were common, apart from God's judgment. Organizations which lack the intestinal fortitude to submit their leadership to regular in-depth evaluations have to resort to constitutional regulations and bylaws. This, of course, ensures orderly change after the stipulated maximum length of service.

The second penchant is to get stranded at the top. "People tend to rise to their level of incompetence and remain there." This disturbing observation, as mentioned in an earlier chapter, is the thesis of Laurence J. Peter's book, *The Peter Principle*.[3] Although his focus is on secular corporations, Christian organizations face the same issue with one major difference—they do not have the luxury of creating additional vice-president roles at the top or implementing the more current practice of the "golden handshake."

So how does a church, denomination or enabling agency handle this critical question? We are very adept at moving leaders up the ladder, but stymied as to how to bring them back down graciously. Thank God for the Calebs who step forward with inspiring answers:

> Right Reverend Bishop, give me a new mountain. Let me take that struggling church plant meeting in the Elks Lodge, or that troubled church of 100 that is working hard at becoming a church of 200. Or maybe there's a short-term tough assignment overseas where a hoary head with a steady hand might be helpful for a while?

Unfortunately the more common scenario looks like this: Plateaued parish priests become bishops or superintendents. College presidents become parachurch executives with opportunity for overseas travel. Denominational leaders are given low-risk, high-profile interim pastorates to bridge them into retirement. And historical drift flourishes.

The third penchant of leaders is to buy into the corporate image. How does the Christian leader handle the make-believe world around us concocted on the fallacy that "life consists of the things that one possesses?" There's a human bent in all of us that gravitates toward the perks of corporate lifestyle. It hits me every time I board a full late-night commuter flight. As I trudge through business class and glance sideways at those big comfortable seats, I secretly pray for an unsolicited upgrade from the crowded seating in economy.

Obviously the flagship churches of North America can slip very comfortably into the corporate landscape. I am certainly not advocating doing Christian work in a second-class fashion, nor is it so much the outward expressions as the mind-set I am concerned about. Thankfully, due to the rapid growth of evangelicals, leadership of necessity must function to some extent as big business. This is not a criticism, but a warning of the potential pitfalls that come with affluence. We must be relevant without compromising revelation. That will always be a balancing act. In our reaction to the pith-helmet image, it is all too easy to slide uncritically into the opposite end of the spectrum. The critical question for the impeding of drift is much more than techniques and methodologies. The germane issue is: "Where is the real source of power?"

Today, more than in any previous generation, the media easily becomes the message. Computers, consultants, schooled experts, high profiles and professional programs become the easy answers and can unconsciously replace our reliance on God. If leadership does not regularly see God intervening in unmistakably divine ways, then we have relegated Him to a peeping Tom. Historical drift thrives on the subtle demise of the supernatural while the supernatural of the counter-kingdom lurks at every grocery checkout.

I recall with a smile my early attempt to use my newly acquired doctorate to gain some clout with the Seafarers' Union. I wrote a letter on behalf of my aging father to argue that he should qualify for a pension. I signed it Dr. Arnold Cook, D.Miss. In due time, they replied. "Dear Miss Arnold Cook," the letter began. "We are sorry to inform you that your father does not qualify for a pension."

Christian organizations can manage quite successfully on corporate principles. But will they survive the test of persecution? In China, we learned that much of what missionaries thought they had built, such as institutions, collapsed. What God chose to use instead was their testimony of a sacrificial life. Still today, the tougher biblical questions must be asked, "If North American Christians are asked to experience what their Chinese counterparts have, will they stand firm?" And, of course, there's the final test: Will our work pass the test of fire at the judgment seat of Christ? (1 Corinthians 3:9-15; 2 Corinthians 5:10).

The fourth penchant of leaders is to become power hungry. "Power corrupts and absolute power corrupts absolutely." Lord Acton could easily have included church history in this sweeping statement.

The power struggle began with the sin of the garden. Later, the promising reign of Saul was cut short by his hunger for power, and Peter had to respond harshly to a power-hungry Simon. Then, in the last century, there was Jim Jones who, intoxicated with power, led almost 1,000 persons to their death, and David Karesh, in Waco, Texas, took his followers to a fiery doom.

Authority and accountability become the critical issues. Currently in evangelicalism, denominations face a growing challenge in these two areas. C. Peter Wagner describes it as the "post-denominational era." In his book, *The New Apostolic Churches*, he profiles eighteen large churches. Many of these, such as Willow Creek Community Church, have developed an "association of churches." Churches can be associates and gain access to resources without the authority and accountability aspects of the traditional denomination. In Wagner's book, at least two of those highlighted are structured around the apostolic model, i.e., authority rests in a strong, high-profile leader, a modern-day apostle.[4]

These trends away from constituted authority and accountability are dangerous. Even the apostles in the first century submitted themselves to human authority. The first church council was composed of "apostles and elders" along with some "believers who belonged to the party of the Pharisees," and the "whole church" (Acts 15:1-29). The apostles were only a part of the decision-making process described in these terms: "It seemed good to the Holy Spirit and to us . . ." (15:28).

Although it is argued that associate member churches retain their local church authority, it is a subtle shift away from the additional level of denominational authority. Despite their weaknesses, denominations have served as a deterrent to power-hungry leaders. Some of the fallen leaders of the 1980s were only loosely tied to a denomination. When Jimmy Swaggart's denomination asked him to submit to their disciplinary policies, he withdrew his church from the denomination. With the advent of megachurches, many of which are members of denominations, the authority factor is being tested. Constituted authority, resting in the hands of spiritually and biblically committed ecclesiastical bodies, is a major factor in impeding historical drift.

There are, in addition to the four penchants already mentioned, several pressure points common to all leaders.

Presidents, directors and executives tend to dominate discussions on leadership. Is it possible that those at this level focus on the wrong people in the church context? The real truth is that local church elders or deacons, meeting on a Wednesday night, make many of the most critical decisions that can impede drift.

Local churches are God's first line of defense in His commitment to keeping His people from "the corruption in the world caused by evil desires" (2 Peter 1:4). Paul addressed his concerns to local churches. Local assemblies can walk away from denominations that drift from the Word of God. Some even vacate a building they financed and build another across town. This is the high cost of standing for truth.

The taproot of all pressure points facing church leaders is the danger of compromise. Compromise was originally a good word. In Middle English, it meant "a mutual promise to abide by an arbiter's decision." Webster defines it in its fallen state: "A concession to something derogatory or prejudicial, e.g., principles."[5]

Men and women of faith have always demonstrated the power of God's grace to stand firm in moments of severe testing. Abraham refused to buckle under pressure. He raised the knife to sacrifice his promised son (Genesis 22:10). Joseph refused to compromise his moral standards and fled from Potiphar's wife (39:7-12). Esther refused to hide her identity and laid her life on the line: "If I perish, I perish" (Esther 4:16). Martin Luther, facing the wrath of Rome, declared, "My conscience is captive to the Word of God. I will not recant anything; for to go against conscience is neither honest nor safe. Here I stand, I cannot do otherwise. God help me. Amen."[6]

There is a much less noble list, headed by our first parents, who chose compromise. The Abels, Lots, Jacobs, Samsons, Sauls followed them, as did the Judases, Peters and John Marks.

I don't want my name to be on that list.

Discussion Questions

1. The author restates his thesis on *historical drift*. How do you harmonize the idea that it is both "inevitable" and "reversible?"
2. What is your organization or church doing to protect your leaders from these pitfalls?
3. "*Historical Drift* thrives on the subtle demise of the supernatural." How is this related to the "thin edge of the wedge" concept?
4. How does the Hugheses' approach to ministry impede drift? (See pages 163-164).

Good News

Liberating Ministry from the Success Syndrome

K ent and Barbara Hughes entered ministry believing they could
be successful. This prospect was shared by all that knew this
gifted couple.

> As a promising young couple, they were put in the position of
> raising up a promising new church in a very promising com-
> munity. They did everything "right" and developed great ex-
> pectations. But for some reason the church never grew. Deep in
> a "dark night of the soul," Kent and Barbara reexamined their
> understanding of success—this time according to God's Word.
> They discovered exciting, and revolutionary, new concepts
> that ultimately freed them from the tyranny of their expecta-
> tion of success.[7]

Since the mid-20th century, the bar for ministerial success has been
bumped up significantly. With the focus on numerical church growth,
several decades of pastors have suffered. To discover how God defines
success constitutes a major step in the impedance of historical drift.

In their book, *Liberating Ministry from the Success Syndrome*, Kent and
Barbara share their journey in discovering true success from God's
perspective.

- Success is Faithfulness: As they searched the Scriptures,
  they found no place where it says that God's servants are
  called to be successful. Rather, He calls us to be faithful.
- Success is Service: The life of Jesus is all about service. They
  discovered that the ultimate expression of His servanthood

was the cross. They saw in Jesus, there hanging on the cross, the Servant par excellence, performing the ultimate service.

- Success is Loving: They experienced a new surge of freedom as they refreshed themselves in this truth. They committed themselves to loving God above all things, regardless of whatever happened in the rest of life.

- Success is Believing: They gradually experienced a revival of belief that "He is." This led them to the assurance that "he rewards those who earnestly seek him" (Hebrews 11:6).

- Success is Prayer: As they isolated prayer as another ingredient of true success, they were heartened. Although discouraged during the darkest times, they remained committed to prayer. Seeing it as a key success factor from God's perspective increased their commitment to prayer.

- Success is Holiness: They learned that to be accorded success in ministry, they had to pursue lives of holiness. This meant that they must follow the example of Job when he said, "I made a covenant with my eyes not to look lustfully at a girl" (Job 31:1). With God's power they believed they should not view anything that would pull them away from holiness into sensuality, whether in printed material, in the media or in life.

- Success is Attitude: Through the example of Paul and others, they became conscious of the importance that their mind-set played in their ministry. They discovered that an encouraging attitude and a positive attitude were foundational to a truly successful life.

"It is easier to look back into the past and smile on yesterday's accomplishments than it is to look ahead into the future and think about tomorrow's possibilities."

—Charles Swindoll

10

Taking a Firm Stand on the Slippery Slope

Accommodation: Historical Drift's Best Friend

"ACCOMMODATION" SOUNDS LIKE A COMMENDABLE commodity. How does Merriam-Webster define it?

1: to make fit, suitable, or congruous; 2: to bring into agreement or concord; 3: to furnish with something desired, needed, or suited; 4: a: to make room for; b: to hold without crowding or inconvenience; 5: to give consideration to: allow for, e.g., the special interests of various groups: to adapt oneself.[1]

Accommodation is the very essence of hospitality. It is the core characteristic of a gentleman. How has such an honorable concept become a bedfellow with such a deplorable process as historical drift?

165

The answer is found in probing the two sides of accommodation. It is all about conforming—an essential prerequisite for communication. But there is the dangerous aspect when as Christians we conform to the wrong pattern. Paul reminds us that we are to be "conformed to the likeness of his Son" (Romans 8:29). This term "conform" brings to mind Paul's strong exhortation in Romans 12:2: "Do not conform any longer to the pattern of this world, but be transformed by the renewing of your mind."

We must go to Scripture to discover what, where and how to walk this fine line between accommodation to the world and being conformed to the likeness of Christ. We can't have it both ways.

The Absolute Authority of Scripture

This will not appear as an agenda issue on any forum, but it should. Every decision made by any group relates directly to the prevailing view of the Bible held by the leaders around the table. It continues to be the watershed issue in evangelicalism.

Francis Schaeffer chose the term "accommodate" over "compromise" as he analyzed what has happened to the evangelical church.

> First, there has been accommodation on Scripture so that many who call themselves evangelicals hold a weakened view of the Bible and no longer affirm the truth of all the Bible teaches. . . . And second, there has been accommodation on the issues, with no clear stand being taken even on matters of life and death.[2]

Schaeffer, in his final book, *The Great Evangelical Disaster*, reiterates his lifelong thesis: "Here is the great evangelical disaster—the failure of the evangelical world to stand for truth as truth."[3] For this reason, I use the absolute authority of Scripture for faith and life in an attempt at clarity.

I am very concerned with the hermeneutical principles employed by the authority-of-Scripture evangelicals. My definition continues to include "the inerrancy of the Scriptures as given in the original manuscripts." Most definitions of evangelicals no longer include the term "inerrancy." More important than the terms, however, is the actual interpreting of the Bible and applying its principles to the church and culture of our day.

Hermeneutics and accommodation are inseparably linked. Weak principles of interpretation pave the way for accommodation to culture affecting many critical aspects of evangelicalism. We will now consider four areas.

The Sanctity of Life

The biblical and ethical position that holds human life to be sacrosanct has been under attack for some time. Pro-choice and pro-life battles have split hospital boards and politicians for decades. The challenge to the sanctity of life issue as it relates to the unborn has moved logically to the fate of the born. If human life can be taken before birth, why can it not be taken after birth?

Euthanasia, although practiced clandestinely by doctors for many years, has moved from the privacy of hospital wards to the political agenda of world governments. Some countries such as the Netherlands have approved ultra-liberal pro-euthanasia policies, while North American state and provincial governments have struggled to convict doctors involved in assisted suicides.

Historical drift thrives on the thin-edge-of-the-wedge principle, i.e., accommodation in the initial aspect of a controversial issue leads to further accommodation on more critical questions. Even the evangelical consensus on abortion, i.e., that it is allowed in situations where the life of the mother is endangered or a pregnancy results from rape or incest, sets a dangerous precedent.

As we move into the third millennium, sanctity of life is facing an even more complex challenge. The cloning technology that gave us Dolly the sheep is rapidly moving toward the possibility of cloning humans. Biogenetics as a science has become a burgeoning industry. Although human beings cannot be patented, their 60,000 genes can be. The possibility of the ultimate shopping experience is just around the corner—shopping for your dream child, choosing the preferred genetic combination.

How will church boards handle such sanctity of life decisions? They will have to make tough decisions with names attached, e.g., it's the chairman of the elders board whose daughter wants an abortion. How they counsel their colleague on this difficult decision will condition their vote on euthanasia and bioengineering questions later.

The Sanctity of Marriage

Marriage is God's first institution. It precedes civil law. Marriage is the most intimate—and difficult—of all human relationships. It creates a new social unit described as the forming of "one flesh" (Genesis 2:24). "One" is indivisible.

Jesus, underlining the one-flesh principle, also spoke to the permanent nature of marriage. "What God has joined together, let man not separate" (Matthew 19:6). He saw divorce as an aberrant concession to unbelievers, not the church (19:4-12). For the encouragement of governments, being pressured to recognize the union of same sex couples as marriage, here is Jesus' definition of marriage: "At the beginning the Creator 'made them male and female,' and said, 'For this reason a man will leave his father and mother and be united to his wife, and the two will become one flesh' " (Matthew 19:4-5).

Why this strong admonition regarding marriage? I obviously feel strongly about the cultural accommodation on this issue. Divorce and remarriage are quickly becoming the norm, not the exception, in Western culture. One hundred years ago, our governments supported marriage. Even liberal mainline churches had a healthy respect for the permanency of marriage. Today, governments and liberal churches approve same-sex marriages. This leaves only the evangelical church in defense of God's special institution—and half of them are backing away!

In the latter part of the 1900s, many evangelical churches contributed to rather than becoming a deterrent and impedance to the rapid drift toward divorce. Churches bought heavily into what is known as "the evangelical consensus on divorce and remarriage," i.e., divorce is wrong, but it happens. The church must handle it. If the divorce occurred on "biblical grounds" (i.e., marital unfaithfulness of a spouse), then probably the innocent party could remarry.

Essentially this consensus is constructed on the very shaky interpretation of the exception clause found only in Matthew's Gospel: "except for marital unfaithfulness" (5:32; 19:9). Matthew was addressing the Jews. As seen in the engagement of Joseph and Mary, divorce could break an engagement (1:18-19).

Heth and Wenham, in their scholarly study on Jesus and divorce, challenge this conclusion. They conclude that the evangelical consensus is based more on the teachings of Erasmus in the 16th century than the teachings of Jesus.[4] I believe that the evangelical church has contributed to the rise of divorce. How has it happened?

- by buying into the evangelical consensus contrary to the clarity of Scripture.
- by performing remarriages contrary to the clear teaching of Jesus in Mark and Luke, not to mention the sociological factor of the high failure percentages of second marriages.

- by inadequate premarital counseling. Couples tend to prepare themselves for a wedding but receive limited help in their preparation for a life-long union.
- by failing to provide postmarital checkups and developing marriage lay mentors.
- by hiring as pastors divorced and remarried personnel. In a respected American denomination, two-thirds of the pastors in one district have been divorced.
- by electing as elders divorced and remarried men.[5]

On the positive side, how can local church leadership impede accommodation in this area? Short answer: Reverse your policy in the six areas above.

Consider the powerful nonverbal message leadership sends to lay people every Sunday morning, many of whom are wrestling with the decision whether to keep trying to save their marriage or to walk away from it. If they sit under the ministry of leaders who have been divorced and remarried, they could easily conclude: "If my spiritual leaders have done it, I guess it's OK for me."

The converse is equally true and powerful—integrity in the pulpit sends a strong exhortation to find God's answer for restoring troubled marriages. I have observed several high-profile senior pastors who, after years of remarrying couples, have revisited the teaching of Jesus and changed their positions. One such pastor based his decision on a review of the gospels: "I have recently come to the conclusion that the exception clause in Matthew 5:32 and 19:9 is not intended to provide a loophole for divorce and remarriage when one of the partners commits adultery."[6] To the credit of his church leadership, they supported him in this critical decision.

This is drift impedance where the rubber meets the road, allowing the clarity of Scripture to speak boldly into culture. When marriages of leaders fail, drift in laity prevails. Conversely, a strong marriage in the pulpit strengthens weak marriages in the pew.

The Sanctity of Sexuality

Homosexuality has become the Trojan horse of Western culture. While this movement has tenaciously been pushing the envelope for gay rights, many other subcultures have also been covertly accommodated into the mainstream of society.

What is the clear teaching of Scripture regarding sexuality in general and homosexuality in particular? It is

- that God created man, in two genders male and female (Genesis 1:27).
- that God established marriage as the union of a man and woman (2:24).
- that God created human sexuality and sanctioned it as good (1:31; 2:25).
- that God condemned sexual relations between same-sex partners (Leviticus 18:22; Romans 1:24).
- that God set down specific guidelines for sexual relationships (Leviticus 18).

God describes nineteen sexual relationships which are detestable and incur His judgment (18:6-24). Among them is this clear statement prohibiting homosexuality: "Do not lie with a man as one lies with a woman; that is detestable" (18:22). How do Bible-believing Christians justify homosexual practices? Let's look at two of their arguments:

The first is the complexity of the issue and a weakened view of Scripture. A liberal bishop debating this question argued that he took the Bible very seriously, but insisted there was no way a book, written thousands of years ago, could speak specifically to such a complex issue as homosexuality in the 20th century. This argument dismisses the clear and specific Bible references condemning homosexuality as place and time specific. End of discussion.

The second pro-homosexuality argument is the smoke screen of the sexual orientation argument. Sexual orientation has become the politically correct terminology of our day. Some evangelicals have adopted it to justify their natural attraction to those of the same sex. They argue that they must claim God's power to resist sexual temptation just as others do who are heterosexually oriented. Such are the thin-edge-of-the-wedge challenges to accommodation in the most pervasive issues in our culture.

The Gender Debate

Since women left their homes to shore up the work force during World War II, the question of roles has become a front-burner issue. Women fight the glass ceiling in a male-dominated corporate world. At conferences, denominations one by one vigorously debate the role of women in the church and frequently leave fractured. Some would dismiss it as strictly a cultural matter. Others are equally convinced of its hermeneutical nature.

Among the latter, two distinct schools have emerged. The egalitarian position is that women had full equality at creation, there are no role limitations, the fall created an illegitimate hierarchical system, the hierarchical system was abolished as redemption was achieved, therefore, all church offices and all ministries are open to qualified persons of both sexes.

The complementarians believe that women and men were created equal in essence, but given distinction in roles (e.g., male headship in marriage), that at the fall distortions in the relationship between men and women were introduced and that in redemption Christ aims at removing the distortions introduced by the curse. Finally, they believe that, in the church, men are elders, deacons can be qualified men or women (deaconesses) and all non-elder ministries are open to qualified women and men.

How then does a local church board handle this culturally and ecclesiastically sensitive question? I again argue for a view of Scripture that begins with the question: "What appears to be the clear pattern in the Bible?" In our academic sophistication we easily forget that the Scriptures were written for the ordinary believer. The vast majority of Bible readers worldwide have no access to commentaries, seminaries nor even a formally trained pastor. But they do have the Holy Spirit to illuminate their understanding.

A broad sweep of the Bible identifies the following scenario:

- God is referred to as male.
- Woman was created from man.
- Male leadership was the pattern in the Old Testament.
- Jesus chose twelve disciples who were men.
- Paul named church elders who were men.
- Women served in many areas of ministry.

How then should leadership lead? I believe we must be guided by two major principles: First, we must accept the clear and timeless teaching of the Word of God on these contentious issues. Second, we must understand where culture is pressuring us to accommodate in these areas, then make a decision to the right.

I am told that the tendency of propellor-driven aircraft in takeoff is to veer left. Experienced pilots steer right to go straight. Historical drift could be significantly impeded if church leaders at every level would steer a little to the right to go straight in these controversial areas.

~

Discussion Questions

1. What does the term "accommodation" mean?
2. Why did Francis Schaeffer see it as negative for Christians?

3. What are the three critical areas where Christians tend to accommodate to the world? Are these issues in your church?
4. Should more Christian leaders speak out like Joseph Wright (see
   pages 175-176)? In what situations?

Good News

More Than They Bargained For

**State regulators got more than they bargained
for in 1999 when they asked local minister
Joe Wright to bless the new session in prayer.**

W hen a minister, Joe Wright, was asked to open the new session
of the Kansas Senate, everyone was expecting the usual politically correct generalities, but what they heard instead was a stirring
prayer, passionately calling our country to repentance and righteousness.

The response was immediate. A number of legislators walked out
during the prayer in protest. In six short weeks, the Central Christian
Church had logged more than 5,000 phone calls with only forty-seven
of those calls responding negatively.

Heavenly Father, we come before You today to ask Your forgiveness and to seek Your direction and guidance.

We know Your Word says, "Woe on those who call evil
good," but that's exactly what we have done.

We have lost our spiritual equilibrium and reversed our values.

We confess that:

- We have ridiculed the absolute truth of Your Word and
called it pluralism.
- We have worshiped other gods and called it multi-
culturalism.
- We have endorsed perversion and called it an alternative
lifestyle.
- We have exploited the poor and called it the lottery.

- We have neglected the needy and called it self-preservation.
- We have rewarded laziness and called it welfare.
- We have killed our unborn children and called it a choice.
- We have shot abortionists and called it justifiable.
- We have neglected to discipline our children and called it building self-esteem.
- We have abused power and called it political savvy.
- We have coveted our neighbor's possessions and called it ambition.
- We have polluted the air with profanity and pornography and called it freedom of expression.
- We have ridiculed the time-honored values of our forefathers and called it enlightenment.

Search us, O God, and know our hearts today, cleanse us from every sin and set us free. Guide and bless these men and women who have been sent to direct us to the center of Your will. I ask it in the name of Your Son, Living Savior, Jesus Christ. Amen.[7]

(Commentator Paul Harvey aired the prayer on *The Rest of the Story* on the radio and received a larger response to this program than any other he had ever aired.)

"If I have seen further than others, it is only because I have stood on the shoulders of giants."

—Isaac Newton (*Bartlett's Familiar Quotations*, p. 379.)

11

Built-to-Last Movements

Champion Impeders of Historical Drift

THE FLAMBOYANT U.S. SECRETARY OF STATE, Henry Kissinger, periodically staged his entry for critical meetings with the State Department. Arriving late, he would appear, arms full of files and journals, which he proceeded to methodically spread out. Then, following a dramatic pause as his eyes scanned the room, he would say: "Ladies and gentlemen, the decisions we make today in this room will determine the destiny of this world."

That old adage still stands: "Decisions determine destiny."

Biblical Precedents

Old Testament theocracy was blessed with no board meetings—well, maybe one—the report of the twelve spies returning from their

177

survey trip into Canaan (not a great example!). The majority report was accurate: "The people who live there are powerful, and the cities are fortified and very large" (Numbers 13:26-33). This report was technically correct, but theologically wrong. What was their major oversight in the majority report? God's ability to intervene.

Now, listen to the minority report: "Then Caleb silenced the people before Moses and said, 'We should go up and take possession of the land, for we can certainly do it. . . . And do not be afraid of the people of the land, because we will swallow them up. Their protection is gone, but the LORD is with us' " (13:30; 14:9).

At that point, God joins the discussion and overrules the majority report of the pessimists. He informs them that they will not be entering the land and proceeds to single out the participants in the negative report and judges them by death through a plague (14:37). Then He names the leadership team for the conquest of the land—the minority report people—Joshua and Caleb.

In Old Testament times, the decisions that determined the destiny of God's people were made by individuals—kings, judges and other appointed leaders.

In the New Testament, particularly in the book of Acts, there appears to be some experimentation with democracy, e.g., the proposal by Peter that they find a replacement for Judas. Matthias was chosen by drawing lots, then promptly disappears (Acts 1:15-26). The choosing of the seven deacons (6:1-6) was initiated by the apostles, then shared with "all the disciples." The most formal democratic gathering was the Jerusalem Council (15:1-35). Their historic decision is a wonderful example of the incredible ramifications of a group decision (15:19-21). The door to take the gospel to all peoples was swung wide open by a unanimous decision superintended by the Holy Spirit (15:28). World evangelization was launched.

The question becomes: How then and on what basis should decisions be made that will impede drift and preserve built-to-last ministries?

A Business Perspective

I want to revisit the study *Built to Last*, done at the Stanford University Graduate School of Business. Jerry I. Porras and James C. Collins, the authors, identified four concepts which they believe were the key factors in the long-term success of eighteen corporations with an average age of 100 years.

- "Their leaders were clock builders not time tellers." Telling the time is most helpful, but how much better it is to replace yourself with clocks to tell the time.
- "They avoided the tyranny of the 'or' and discovered the genius of the 'and.' " They refused to get trapped in either/or decisions, carefully guarded their core business and added some new initiatives.
- "They preserved the 'core' but stimulated progress elsewhere." Their core values were few but clearly defined apart from methods.
- "They sought consistent alignment throughout the company." They recognized that certain procedures and policies were productive and were determined to maintain them.[1]

A Church Perspective

Are these success factors transferable to the Christian world? It occurs to me that Christian leaders, of all people, given our two-world view, should be passionate about building to last. However, we are unique in that we bring to the table a distinct understanding of what "lasting" means. "For we must all appear before the judgment seat of Christ, that each one may receive what is due him for the things done while in the body, whether good or bad" (2 Corinthians 5:10).

Every Christian organization must balance its unswerving alignment with God's revelation with its commitment to communication through relevance. Decisions in this sensitive area of balance will determine the effective lasting ability—endurance—of our movements. Whenever Christian leaders lose the sensitive balance of revelation and relevance, historical drift revives.

Before drinking too deeply from the well of business acumen, let's review those values that set the Church apart from the corporate world.

- The Church is essentially an organism compared to a corporate organization.
- Economic profit is bottom-line in the marketplace. This was not Christ's intention for His Church, although many are moving in that direction.
- In the marketplace, the client is sovereign. A drugstore clerk does not attempt to dissuade an unmarried teen from buying condoms. But in the Church, members are counseled as to which service or class would serve them best.
- The end justifies the means (within the parameters of the law): manipulation, appeals to sensuality, subtle conditioning of perspective clients, etc. These are fair game in the marketplace. But such maneuvering in the Church should be labeled "lack of integrity."

Building "to-Last" Organizations

I am writing this book on the eve of a new millennium, a timely vantage point indeed for reviewing 20th-century Christian movements. A few rooted in the 19th century have entered the 21st with amazing vigor while others, approaching their 75th birthday, continue strongly in the tradition of Caleb, asking God for new and challenging mountains. What can we learn from these movements? What significant decisions have their leaders made? How have they impeded historical drift? What biblical principles have they applied?

The selection of case studies for this section has been difficult. I have decided to limit the criteria as follows:

- primarily those founded in the 20th century
- some from the 19th century which continue strong
- those which are seventy years and older
- those representing varied ministries.

Salute to Fundamentalism

We will look first at one which continues to serve with spiritual vitality well beyond its centennial. In my early research, it became apparent that many extant vibrant ministries were founded in the 1920s or shortly thereafter. The reasons for this trend should be obvious for the historically literate. That was the decade of the fundamentalist/modernist battle for the Bible. Although many end-of-the-century evangelicals react negatively to the label "fundamentalist," we need to understand its origin.

The intellectual challenges to Christianity in Europe arrived in the United States in the 19th century. Robert G. Ingersoll (1833-1899), son of an evangelist, led the charge. As an enthusiastic Darwinian, he believed the Old Testament sanctioned evil. In addition, the popular higher criticism of German scholarship was eroding the credibility of the Scriptures. Many Christians defected to Unitarianism.

By the turn of the century, a strong reactionary group emerged in one segment of the church. D.L. Moody died in 1899, but his impact continued with R.A. Torrey into the 20th century. Dispensationalism blossomed with the publishing of the Scofield Bible in 1909. These all fed into a movement parallel to the birth of the Pentecostal phenomenon in the first decade of the century.

After World War I, the conservative, noncharismatic Christians became aligned with what became the Fundamentalist Movement. During the 1920s they took their stand against the Modernists. Five fundamental Christian doctrines were at the eye of the storm:

- the deity and virgin birth of Christ
- the bodily resurrection of Christ
- salvation only through faith in His substitutionary sacrifice on the cross
- the inerrancy of the Scriptures
- the visible return of Christ in judgment to set up His kingdom.

Granted that the term "fundamentalist" has subsequently accumulated some negative connotations, let us salute those valiant Christian leaders who took their stand for these core truths. These same five doctrinal statements would become the platform from which Christian leaders such as Carl F. Henry, Charles Fuller, Harold Ockenga and Billy Graham would launch evangelicalism in the 1940s.

Healthy Geriatrics

Like people, some organizations age more rapidly than others. Physical tests are available to establish your "real age." Criteria include speed of walking a mile, flexibility of limbs, health history, number of sit-ups per minute, etc. These are only valid if the designer of the criteria is professionally competent.

Who is the competent authority who sets the biblical test for Christian movements? Obviously, from this writer's perspective, that authority rests with Christ, the Head of the Church. He's adamantly committed to building His Church (Matthew 16:18). When she is completed, He will "present her to himself as a radiant church, without stain or wrinkle or any other blemish, but holy and blameless" (Ephesians 5:27).

The finished product will reflect His expectations. During His ministry He clearly identified the characteristics which would mark His Church and kingdom:

- She would be radiant, glorious, pure, without stain, wrinkle or blemish; holy and blameless (Ephesians 5:27).
- She would confess Jesus to be "the Christ, the Son of the living God" (Matthew 16:16).
- She would faithfully hold to the authority of God's Word versus the traditions of men (15:6).
- She would joyfully carry out Christ's commission to the world (28:16-20).
- She would demonstrate His character as expressed in the beatitudes: humble, broken, meek, hungry for righteousness, merciful, pure, peaceable and willing to suffer (5:3-11).
- She would maintain a love relationship with Him, e.g., the church in Ephesus (Revelation 2:1-7).
- She would be doctrinally sound and morally pure, e.g., the church in Pergamum (2:12-17).
- She would be known for integrity, e.g. the church of Sardis (3:1-6).
- She would be marked by a white-hot devotion, e.g., the church in Laodicea (3:15).

In summary, God's movements would confess Christ as Lord, preach Christ, live in holiness, hold tenaciously to His Word, joyfully carry out His Great Commission, love Christ supremely, maintain sound doctrine, be known for their integrity and good works and have a passion for Christ's glory in all things.

The question then becomes: What are the geriatric movements alive today that embody these qualities, and what have been their secrets to holding to their core values? We will examine three.

Moody Bible Institute (MBI): 1886-present

Dwight L. Moody, a man with a fifth-grade education, founded one of the first three North American Bible institutes. Although preeminently known as an evangelist, he became one of the outstanding educators of his day and the main promoter of the Sunday school movement. In 1879, he established a school for girls and initiated another one for boys in 1881. He also became a strong supporter of the YMCA. In 1886, he founded the Chicago Evangelistic Society which became the Moody Bible Institute.

Its purpose statement reads as follows: "Moody Bible Institute exists for the education and training of Christian workers, including teachers, ministers, missionaries, and musicians, who may competently and effectively proclaim the gospel of Jesus Christ."

Over 50,000 have attended MBI since 1886. As of 1999, nearly 6,000 have become missionaries, and 2,400 graduates serve in 108 countries. In addition, some 5,000 Moody graduates minister in local churches as full-time staff members. Another 5,000 are married to full-time workers, and 12,000 more are vocationally associated with church-related organizations.

Even a cursory glance at this institution reveals that it has resisted at least three normal changes. The first is its name, Moody Bible Institute. All of its counterparts replaced "institute" with "college" several decades ago. Most have also dropped "Bible" to allow for broader exposure. The third is its location. While others have moved to suburbia and established new campuses, Moody remains in the inner city of Chicago.[2]

What has been its secret to preserving the core? How has it continued its effectiveness yet remained faithful to its mission for more than 114 years? My answer is not based on in-depth research, but is taken rather from the context of comparative observations of similar institutions.

One of its major secrets to preserving the core is "through strong boards of trustees." This has resulted in carefully chosen presidents. The board has also been careful to maintain continuity between administrations. On at least one occasion, it assigned the out-going president to serve as a one-man search committee to find his successor. I have been unable to confirm another policy of their board (it may be one of those unwritten traditions transmitted orally), but it is this: It assumes that during the tenure of a president there has been some slight drift to the left. Therefore, it seeks a successor who is just a little to the right of his predecessor as a corrective measure to maintain the course.

The answer to the effectiveness/faithfulness question is "through a concise but critically focused doctrinal statement." The MBI doctrinal statement contains only five articles. They cover God, the Bible, Jesus Christ, man and the Church. The most extensive article describes the person and work of Christ.

The third answer is "through preserving its core values while strategically adding programs." Two examples at MBI would be the addition of an aviation program and, in 1996, a graduate studies program.

Columbia International University (CIU): 1923-present

In 1917, a woman by the name of Emily Dick, who had a burden for textile workers in South Carolina, visited Moody Bible Institute. Upon her return to the South, she shared her dream for a similar school in the South with her prayer group. Six years later, God directed R.C. McQuilkin to accept their invitation to become the first president. He served from 1923 to 1952.

Today, CIU is situated on 400 acres in the state capital and is the parent company which encompasses Columbia Biblical Seminary and Graduate School of Missions, Columbia Bible College, Ben Lippen Schools and radio stations WMHK and WRCM.

What commends CIU to this select group of built-to-last organizations? The answer: "A history of change and rapid growth while remaining unchanged at their core. Over their long history only four presidents have led the organization. Under the aggressive leadership of Robertson McQuilkin, 1968-1990, son of the founder, there were major changes both in the growth of the campus and the expansion of programs.[3]

Joy Ridderhof, a member of the first graduating class, returned for the fiftieth anniversary. "I have discovered here," she reported, "the same CBC . . . that I knew fifty years ago. The message is the same, the doctrine is the same, the atmosphere, the standards are the same, and everything is just like it was. God's blessing and presence are so wonderful." She paused, then added, "In fact, I think it's better."[4]

What has been the secret of preserving the core at CIU?

The answer has many facets. Obviously, it is the strong commitment of each president to the core values of the organization, i.e., deeper-life teaching and world evangelization. The school's memorable motto— "To Know Him and Make Him Known"—boldly declares that it is not into time telling but is concentrating on clock making.

It also has managed to preserve the core while aggressively adding other programs such as a Christian school in 1940 and the Graduate School of Missions in 1947. In addition, there has been a strong and unique commitment to the core value of financing by prayer and faith. It has constantly set faith goals for the funding of new programs and buildings, and its basic approach to realizing those goals was prayer.

It has also maintained continuity and consistent alignment to the core through strong presidents—only five in seventy-seven years. Their sixth president was installed in March, 2000. The Board of Trustees has carefully and prayerfully appointed each one. The following aspects of the board have contributed significantly to continuity and alignment:

- It is a twenty-four-member board which is self-perpetuating.
- It has strong commitment to prayer and days of prayer, especially in times of searching for a new president.
- It is guided by a Statement of Faith which cannot be changed based on the founding charter.
- It meets three times a year for closer communication with the president.
- It has taken action in recent years to abolish tenure for professors and replaced it with a system of multiple-year contracts after the initial six years of service.

The Peoples Church: 1928-present

"With your poor health you could never stand the rigors of a foreign field." This response of the Presbyterian Church of Canada to a young seminary graduate proved providential. As God redirected him, Oswald Smith, a missionary evangelist, founded the Peoples Church in Toronto. Before dying at age ninety-six, God enabled him to preach 12,000 sermons in eighty countries. He also wrote thirty-five books and more than 100 hymns.

Over its seventy-two-year history to date, only three senior pastors have led Peoples Church. Peoples is known as one of the great missionary churches of the 20th century. With that century now closed, it is still internationally known as "a church which puts missions first." Throughout its history, it has steadfastly held to its core value of missions.

This one factor commends Peoples to this select group of built-to-last organizations. How has it preserved the core amid the proliferation of church models and church-growth philosophies? The profile of its three pastors, including the length of each ministry, suggests some answers.

Oswald J. Smith (1928-1958)

The founding pastor of what was initially called the Cosmopolitan Tabernacle explained what the church would be:

> A permanent evangelistic center, standing preeminently for the conversion of souls, the edification of believers and world-wide evangelism, emphasizing especially the four great essentials, viz., Salvation, Deeper Life, Foreign Missions and our Lord's Return, endeavoring by every means to get the Message out to the Christless masses both at home and abroad.[5]

Although the essentials were technically four in number, missions quickly became and remains to this day the central core value. After two years of renting prestigious Massey Hall in Toronto, the congregation moved into larger facilities in a church and began with a week of meetings. Each night Smith preached on missions. Many were converted. His explanation was simply: "When a church puts first things first, God moves."[6]

Oswald J. Smith's consistent use of his favorite mottoes reinforced the core value of the church:

- Why should anyone hear the gospel twice before everyone has heard it once?
- You must go or send a substitute.
- The light that shines the farthest shines the brightest nearest home.
- The supreme task of the Church is the evangelization of the world.
- Give according to your income lest God makes your income according to your giving.
- The church that ceases to be evangelistic will soon cease to be evangelical.[7]

Paul Brainard Smith (1959-1993)

Church history appears to be of two opinions with reference to the effectiveness of leadership passed down from father to son. In theological circles in Europe, the sons of evangelical pastors often became the liberal theologians of the next generation. Not so at Peoples Church. Paul Smith inherited his father's evangelistic fervor. Following graduation from McMaster University, he became an evangelist with Youth for Christ and rather reluctantly assumed the role of senior pastor in 1959.

Paul bought strongly into his father's counsel, "Never let your people get bored." He continued the tradition of exciting services with a constant diet of high-profile speakers. Upon assuming leadership at Peoples Church, Paul echoed his father's vision for missions.

Under Paul Smith the missionary ministry not only continued but was accelerated. Annual giving through the faith promise surpassed 2 million dollars in 1988. But the new leader realized the world was changing. While preserving the core of Peoples Church, he became an aggressive agent for change:

- He moved the church from the inner city to the emerging new city center, 1961.
- He lifted the profile of Sunday school, which grew to 1900, to minister to the whole family.
- In response to the secularization of the public school system, he opened a Christian school in 1971.
- To expand the impact of the church for world missions, he established the first nationally televised evangelical church in Canada in 1972.

John D. Hull: 1993-Present

Can you imagine the challenge of leading a sixty-five-year-old church which has been pastored by Oswald Smith followed by his son Paul Smith and your name is not Smith? John Hull's incredible task was further compounded by arriving during a period of severe financial instability due to a failed relocation project.

Hull clearly enunciated his three primary convictions of pastoral ministry: 1) the authority of Scripture, inspired, inerrant and illuminating; 2) the dynamic of preaching: expositional, exegetical, exact, applicable and relevant, and 3) evangelization of the world, a natural result of scriptural authority and dynamic preaching.[8]

While establishing a new church in Atlanta, Hull had invited Paul Smith to speak at his missions conference. Smith returned the favor. It was then that Hull became the heir apparent in Smith's mind.

Wisely, Hull believed that to equip a church for the future one must have an appreciation for its past. He became an ardent student of Peoples' history. At every opportunity he affirmed his predecessors, the Smith family. On the final Sunday morning of a missionary conven-

tion, just before collecting the faith promises, he played an audio re-
cording of Oswald Smith praying for the future of Peoples Church.

Hull strongly endorses the original core values of the church and, although new to Canada, reads Canadian culture well. He believes "the
church must penetrate the culture with leadership that will become involved in the major public communities of Canada—the courts, the
media, the school, the arts, the marketplace."[9]

Under Hull's leadership, the Peoples Church congregation has been
well positioned to address the challenge of the new millennium. They
have reaffirmed their mission and have realigned their strategy to be
relevant to their local responsibilities without diminishing their passion for world missions.

What commends Peoples to the built-to-last organizations? Answer:
preservation of the core. Peoples Church has held closely to the vision
of its founder. In review, here are the salient factors that God has used:

- continuity of leadership: three pastors who have passionately owned the same vision of world evangelization as the
  supreme task of the church.
- modified democracy: under the first two pastors, Peoples
  Church had a unique approach to church government:
  —no membership and a large number of elders—as high as
    200 under Paul Smith.
  —two pastors who were "benevolent autocrats" with differ-
    ent leadership styles; e.g., Oswald had the managerial
    style of a pioneer with an explosive strategy. Paul's style
    was that of the conqueror, the nonconformist and creative
    leader who expanded the ministry.
  —an expectation that at least half of church income should
    be spent outside the church.[10]

Summary

The overview of these three ministries has been at best a needle biopsy. I also have initial research on eighteen other Christian organizations which time and space do not allow for here. The fact is that educational institutions and independent churches, given their monolithic structures, more readily facilitate analysis.

In my brief sampling of these three case studies, I have become intrigued at the high level of correlation of these leaders:

- They were all clock makers.
- They established organizations that outlived the founder by generations.
- They embraced the genius of the "and" by adding new initiatives without eroding the core.
- They all consistently aligned the organization with its core ideology.

In contrast to these three successful organizations, a fourth case study is found in Appendix I. It outlines the demise of The United Church of Canada, the largest Protestant denomination in Canada. It's a classic study in historical drift over a relatively brief period of seventy-five years.

What am I saying? Can we learn from non-Christian professors of a Graduate School of Business? Indirectly, yes. I see these men as scientists who have studied God's creation and discovered little by little the God we know through the Scriptures. Their success principles could be documented from the strategy of Moses, Jesus or Paul.

What I'm saying is that the three organizations we have briefly examined are exemplary as effective impeders of historical drift. Many more could be profiled. Decisions do determine destiny. Because of the wise decisions of their leaders, these movements continue to enjoy God's blessings into the second and third generations.

Let me again reiterate: Organizations don't drift, only the people who lead them. God repeatedly demonstrates this truth throughout the Old and New Testaments—and even today.

~

Discussion Questions

1. How do built-to-last corporations differ from built-to-last churches?
2. What are the five fundamental Christian doctrines from the 1920s? Are they still essential for today?
3. What core values do Moody Bible Institute, Colombia International University and Peoples Church hold in common?
4. Judge Paul Pressler (see pages 193-194) paid a high price for his role in reversing drift in his denomination. Is his methodology transferable to other organizations?

Good News

A Hill on Which to Die

W hat was so special about the annual meeting of the Southern Baptist Convention (SBC) in the Georgia Dome in 1999? This huge Protestant denomination representing 40,000 churches with 15 million members meets every year. Each year they elect a president. In many ways, this is an honorary position and part-time.

However, the president does have one role that gives him far-reaching influence in the denomination—he appoints the Committee on Committees. This committee nominates members of the Committee on Nominations. Then this Committee nominates members of the governing boards of all twelve SBC agencies and institutions, e.g., seminaries, etc.

So why was the Georgia conference so important? It marked the 20th anniversary of the conservative leadership resurgence in the Southern Baptist Convention. For the last twenty years it has been electing conservative presidents. Because of their power to nominate key committees, they have seen their six seminaries, which were drifting into liberalism in 1979, turned back to conservatism in 1999.

The book *A Hill on Which to Die* is the story of Judge Paul Pressler. He has been the key player, humanly speaking, in seeing the conservative resurgence in the Southern Baptist Convention over the past two decades.

Even as a college student, Pressler became concerned about liberalism. His first encounter was in a local church to which he tried to transfer his membership. Later, he was exposed to neo-orthodoxy and liberalism in his classes at Princeton and special lectures with Union Seminary professors. He eventually became a state judge and legislator. His concern for his church grew, and he began to document signs of liberalism.

In 1967, he met a seminarian, Paige Patterson, at New Orleans Baptist Seminary. Patterson shared his concerns. He became a pastor, then the head of a Bible college. At the 1999 meeting of the SBC he was elected by acclamation to serve a second term as president of the convention.

In 1975, Bill Powell, a former SBC executive, explained to Pressler how the SBC system worked. A vision of renewal through denominational leadership was born in his heart. With the help of Paige Patterson, he dedicated the next few years to recruiting like-minded leaders.

The vision has been realized. But at what cost? Many nasty confrontations. Accusations of political maneuvering and abuse of power. Harsh criticism from the denominational press. Churches which have jumped ship. Threatenings to form another denomination.

In leadership, we must choose the hills on which to die. Paul Pressler believed that the saving of his denomination from liberalism was a worthwhile hill for him and his family. It seems that in this imperfect world we cannot always marry truth and unity. In fact, without our forefathers, who paid the price of division in their stand for truth, we would not enjoy a true gospel as evangelicals today.[11]

"Shall we modify the truth in doctrine or practice to gain more adherents? Or shall we preserve the truth in doctrine and practice and take the consequences?"

—A.W. Tozer, *Rut, Rot or Revival*, p. 165

12

Truth or Unity?

The Unpopular Challenge of Impeders

IT WAS THE SPRING OF 1997. Evangelical unity took a major hit when *WORLD* magazine broke a story that split the ranks. It revealed that Zondervan Publishing, in conjunction with the International Bible Society (IBS), planned to print a gender inclusive version of the NIV. Although this new version was available in the United Kingdom, it had never been printed in North America. However, under ecumenical auspices, a New Revised Standard Version using gender-inclusive language has been marketed in North America for several years.

Opposition to a new NIV erupted quickly from such influential organizations as the Southern Baptist Convention, the Assemblies of God, the Presbyterian Church of America and Focus on the Family. As the pressure mounted, Zondervan quickly recognized they were caught in the crossfire between two factions of North American evangelicalism. Both IBS and Zondervan grossly miscalculated the depths

195

to which the gender issue was dividing evangelicals. Their rapid withdrawal of the marketing plan sent a disturbing reminder to evangelical consumers as to what drives some publishers. Theology? No. Economics? Yes.

To their credit, the two sides conducted several joint sessions, seeking some middle ground on hermeneutic principles for translation. This vigorous interaction boldly underlined the tension between embracing both truth and unity. Two questions: Can the responsible Christian leader always embrace both? If it is not always possible, how does the leader choose?

We immediately recall Jesus who perfectly embodied both virtues. He was the Truth, and He prayed that future believers would "be brought to complete unity to let the world know" that God also had sent Him and loved all who believed in Him (John 17:23). In His vigorous defense of truth, Christ obviously had not bought fully into organizational unity in the 20th-century ecumenical sense. He reserved His most caustic rebuke for the religious leaders of His day. Jesus became physically violent only twice. The Gospels record two occasions when the money changers were driven out of the temple. On the first, it appears He personally used a whip on them (2:13-17).

This raises two more questions about unity: "What level of unity did Christ teach and model?" and "How much liberty do we—denominations, churches, enabling ministries, etc.—have to minister independently?" Did Jesus endorse dissident groups?

Catholicism has its orders, but early in its history, Protestantism broke into denominations. Both are forms of division. Jesus' prayer for unity is well known, but He made another statement which appears to provide some degree of flexibility within a broader range of unity: " 'Master,' said John, 'we saw a man driving out demons in your name and we tried to stop him, because he was not one of us.' 'Do not stop him,' Jesus said, 'for whoever is not against you is for you' " (Luke 9:49-50). Through this answer, He seems to approve, at least in principle, organizational separation which supports the same truth.

Paul's Perspective

Paul, too, as an overseer of scattered churches, had a perspective on unity and truth. Hear his admonition to the Corinthians: "I appeal to you, brothers, in the name of our Lord Jesus Christ, that all of you agree with one another so that there may be no divisions among you and that you may be perfectly united in mind and thought" (1 Corinthians 1:10).

He also reminds the Philippians that since they are "united with Christ" they should be "like-minded" (Philippians 2:1-2). And his concern for unity is seen in his admonition to Euodia and Syntyche "to agree with each other" (Philippians 4:2). He singles out contentious persons as a special concern. First, back in Corinth, there were contentions and divisions in the context of the role of women (1 Corinthians 11:16). Even in the coming together for the Lord's Supper there were divisions (schisms) (11:18). In this context, he makes an interesting comment: "No doubt there have to be differences [*hairesis*—heresies] among you to show which of you have God's approval" (11:19).

So what was Paul's perspective on holding both truth and unity? Perhaps his personal conflict with Barnabas best reflects his understanding. "Barnabas wanted to take John, also called Mark, with them, but Paul did not think it wise to take him, because he had deserted them. . . . They had such a sharp disagreement that they parted company" (Acts 15:37-39). Note that this disagreement was not about truth in the doctrinal sense. Rather, it was related to choice of personnel.

Who was right? In retrospect, perhaps both. Paul believed Mark needed to prove himself before making another trip. Barnabas agreed, but felt the place to do it was on another missionary journey with himself and Paul. Mark resurfaces at the end of Paul's life, apparently having redeemed himself. "Get Mark and bring him with you, because he is helpful to me in my ministry" (2 Timothy 4:11).

In his teaching on the gifts, Paul speaks both to the unity of the body and to the diversity of spiritual gifts, e.g., "There are differences of ministries, but the same Lord. And there are diversities of activities, but it is the same God who works all in all" (1 Corinthians 12:5-6, NKJV).

Standing for doctrinal truth will place us in situations where we will be perceived as breaking Christian unity. Paul's statement to the Romans gives us his guideline for such instances: "If it is possible, as far as it depends on you, live at peace with everyone" (Romans 12:18).

A Glimpse at Church History

How has this uneasy marriage of truth and unity played out over history? Consider these hypothetical questions:

- Would Christianity have survived the heresies of the second century if Christian leaders had failed to stand for truth and ensured that the theological nonnegotiables were entrenched in the Apostles Creed?
- Would the action of Emperor Constantine to make Christianity the state church in the fourth century have been even more disastrous if Christian leaders had failed to confront Arius and his denial of the deity of Christ?
- Would Islam have exterminated Christianity in the Dark Ages (476-1000) if Christian monasteries had not risked becoming missionary and taking the gospel to England and Ireland?
- Would the Protestant Reformation have happened if two brave men, John Hus, a Czech, and John Wycliffe, an Englishman, had not prepared the way by raising their voices for truth and urging their people and governments to question the corrupt teaching and practice of the Church of Rome?
- Would the Protestant Reformation have been born if a lonely monk had not broken rank with his colleagues and

risked his life by nailing his theses to the Wittenberg church door?

- Would England have become the spiritual giant for missions if John Wesley had not withdrawn from the Church of England to take the gospel to the common man?
- Would the World Council of Churches (1948) have evolved from one of the streams of the Edinburgh International Missionary Conference (1910) if Francis Schaeffer had been there to insist on the absolute authority of Scripture?
- Would North American evangelicals have become a powerful movement in the 20th century if fundamentalist leaders had remained silent in the 1920s when the modernists were attacking the fundamental truths of Christianity?
- Will evangelicals move into the new millennium with God's blessing without some courageous leaders risking evangelical unity and calling us back to the absolute authority of Scripture and the foundational doctrines of historic evangelicalism?

If we persist in pursuing broad and greater unity in a day of theological erosion we will do so by ignoring the strong warning from church history. We have been privileged to be the recipients of a true gospel in the incredible 20th century. May we never forget the debt we owe to the courageous leaders of previous generations. Many paid a high price for choosing truth over unity. It cost some their lives.

Contemporary Reformers

Prophetic voices are speaking up:

- David Wells laments the loss of truth and virtue in the evangelical church.

- Josh McDowell reminds us that the moral standards of churched young people vary little from those of the un-churched.
- R.C. Sproul feels uncomfortable being called an evangelical due to doctrinal erosion. He would like to be known as a "historic evangelical" or a "classic reformer."
- George Barna believes that very early in the new millennium either revival will have come to North America, or we will have anarchy.

A New Battle for the Bible

The war continues, but the battleground keeps changing. Certainly, it has shifted from inerrancy in the 1970s to hermeneutics in the '80s and '90s. The venue change could be anticipated. In the '60s and '70s, we were still very much in the Modern Era mentality. Technical debates such as the inerrancy of Scriptures were still in vogue. But in the Post Modernity era of the '80s and '90s and in the new millennium, we are told that apologetics is out—experience is in. "Don't waste your time explaining the authority of the Bible to non-Christians. Get them into the Gospel of John. Let them 'taste and see that it is good.' Let them discover the authenticity of the Word through experience."

This thinking, which may well be valid for evangelism, has left the question of hermeneutics in limbo, suffering from benign neglect. Everyone is doing what is right in his own eyes. When the question is raised in a denominational setting, the divergent approaches to interpreting the Scriptures quickly become evident.

The New Evangelical Divide

Although it has emerged gradually, the current hermeneutical battle has fractured evangelicalism. In my opinion, this division became

public with the 1972 Fuller Theological seminary's decision to officially change their position from "inerrancy" to the "authority" of
Scripture. Fuller was not only the largest North American Seminary at
the time, but was also renowned for its avant-garde positions in the
fields of theology, psychology and world mission. Since the School of
World Mission has attracted hundreds of national church leaders from
around the world, Fuller's "progressive" position on Scripture has
been disseminated worldwide.

From its beginning in the 1970s, this same approach to Scripture
was adopted by the Willow Creek Community Church in South Chicago. Through their popular leadership conferences and growing association of churches networking with contacts in seventy countries, this
approach to the Bible has been effectively although probably not intentionally marketed. A former professor at Wheaton College, Gilbert
Bilezikian, was part of the founding group of Willow Creek and has become their resident theologian.

His book, *Beyond Sex Roles,* has become a classic presentation of the
egalitarian position on women in leadership. In the preface, he shares
three anecdotal experiences which influenced him to examine the
question of women's role in leadership. First, he became aware of a
very gifted woman who was an assistant to an incompetent man in an
institution of higher learning. Eventually the man was released, and
the skilled assistant replaced him. She and the organization flourished
under her leadership.

The second experience was related to his family. Due to extenuating
circumstances, Bilezikian had to be overseas away from his family for a
year. In his absence, his wife did a magnificent job of managing the
home and doubling as both mother and father. Upon his return, he felt
that he could not again install himself as the chief decision-maker or be
in a supervisory role with his wife.

The third circumstance that forced him to grapple with the women
in leadership question was in the context of his church, Willow Creek.
Due to its rapid growth, with many new Christians, they had difficulty

finding enough men to serve as elders. During a three-year study, they concluded that women could be elders.[1]

Squarely on the other side of the divide is a very new organization. Its genesis dates back to 1994. A group of leading evangelical scholars met with some conservative Catholic theologians. Since the challenges of postmodernity centered around defending the sanctity of life and family and marriage, evangelicals and Catholics found themselves more and more standing shoulder to shoulder. The agenda for the historical meeting was to move this dialogue to a deeper level of theology. Was there also a basis for collaboration beyond the mutual social concerns?

An accord was drafted. Initially it was signed by a group of high profile evangelicals including J.I. Packer, Bill Bright, Os Guinness, Pat Robertson, Charles Colson, et. al. The document became known as ECT (Evangelicals and Catholics Together). It immediately drew fire from other quarters of evangelicalism initially attributed to the fundamentalist camp. But it became quickly apparent that high profile theologians, especially of the Reformed tradition, were alarmed by what they perceived as a compromise to the very heart of Protestantism—the truth of justification by faith. One succinct retort was: "The one missing word in the ECT accord was 'alone.' " Although later revisions were made to the document, the strong reaction contributed to the founding of ACE, The Alliance of Confessing Evangelicals. What were their concerns?

- Evangelical churches today are increasingly dominated by the spirit of this age.
- The term "evangelical" has become so inclusive as to have lost its meaning.
- The confessional *solas* (literally, "only things") of the Protestant Reformation are being lost.

These concerns led to The Cambridge Declaration. This document affirms five nonnegotiable truths, central to the Bible, which the participants believe are being eroded in modern-day evangelicalism:

- *Sola Scriptura* (Only Scripture)—The Erosion of Authority: "The evangelical church today has separated Scripture from its authoritative function. . . . We affirm the inerrant Scripture to be the sole source of written divine revelation, which alone can bind the conscience."

- *Solus Christus* (Only Christ)—The Erosion of Christ-centered Faith: "The result is a loss of absolute values, permissive individualism, and substitution of wholeness for holiness, recovery for repentance, intuition for truth, feeling for belief, chance for providence, and immediate gratification for enduring hope. . . . We affirm that our salvation is accomplished by the mediatorial work of the historical Christ alone."

- *Sola Gratia* (Only Grace)—The Erosion of the Gospel: "Unwarranted confidence in human ability is a product of fallen human nature. This false confidence now fills the evangelical world; from the self-esteem gospel, to the health and wealth gospel, from those who have transformed the gospel into a product to be sold, and sinners into consumers who want to buy, to others who treat Christian faith as being true simply because it works. . . . God's grace in Christ is not merely necessary but is the sole efficient cause of salvation."

- *Sola Fide* (Only Faith)—The Erosion of the Chief Article: "This is the article by which the church stands or falls. Today this article is often ignored, distorted or sometimes even denied by leaders, scholars and pastors who claim to be evangelical. . . . We affirm that justification is by grace alone through faith alone because of Christ alone. In justification

Christ's righteousness is imputed to us as the only possible
satisfaction of God's perfect justice."

- *Soli Deo Gloria* (Only God's Glory)—The Erosion of God-
centered Worship: "The loss of God's centrality in the life of
today's church is common and lamentable. It is this loss that
allows us to transform worship into entertainment. . . . We
reaffirm that because salvation is of God and has been accomplished by God, it is for God's glory and that we must
glorify Him always. We must live our entire lives before the
face of God, under the authority of God and for His glory
alone."[2]

The Mission Statement of the Alliance of Confessing Evangelicals is
as follows:

ACE exists to call the church, amidst our dying culture, to repent of its worldliness, to recover and confess the truth of
God's Word as did the Reformers, and to see that truth embodied in doctrine, worship and life.

It is becoming evident that Christians in this new millennium will
have to choose between at least two brands of evangelicalism which
will no doubt come to be viewed as the Evangelical Left and the Evangelical Right.

Postmodern thinking is impacting every facet of evangelicalism.
Worship must be more entertaining. Preaching must be more relevant
and practical. Churches must be user-friendly. Evangelism must connect with felt needs. Present approaches to propositional truth must be
replaced. How and when we talk about the Bible must be rethought.
Finally, theology and doctrine must be downplayed.

While evangelicalism has become preoccupied with all of the above,
theology has been relegated to benign neglect. However, theological
vacuums nurture new brands of theology. Millard Erickson in his

book, *The Evangelical Left: Countering Post-conservative Evangelical Theology,* analyzes what he identifies as a new school of theologians. He traces evangelicalism over the centuries, concentrating on the 20th century. As he traces the context of the emerging post-conservative theologians today, he identifies the crisis in Fuller Seminary in 1962.

December 1, 1962 became known as "Black Saturday." Daniel Fuller, the son of Charles Fuller, the founder, chose to address the faculty on the topic of inerrancy. "He contended that there were errors in the Bible that could not be accounted for as copyists' errors."[3] This threw the seminary into a decade of chaos, culminating in 1972 when they altered their statement on Scripture.

Richard Quebedeaux published two books in the '70s: *The Young Evangelicals,* 1974, and *The Worldly Evangelicals,* in 1978. In his books he notes a shift in evangelicals in both their doctrine and lifestyle. James Davison Hunter, in *Evangelicalism: The Coming Generation,* 1987, comments further on the young evangelicals. He shares this observation: "For what one finds is a brand of theology that for generations had been considered 'modernistic' being advocated by theologians who vigorously defend their right to use the name evangelical."[4]

Roger Olson, in his May 1995 article, "Post-conservative Evangelicals Greet the Postmodern Age," comments that there are significant changes in evangelicalism. Traditionally the terms "evangelical" and "theologically conservative" have been synonymous. This new brand of evangelicals, such as Bernard Ramm, Clark Pinnock, Stanley Grenz and James McClendon, is "shedding theological conservatism."[5]

Summary

Discerning leaders down in the trenches of evangelical denominationalism are struggling. At many levels, the term "evangelicalism" is still a helpful monolithic term. People continue to abandon mainline churches in their retreat from lifestyle forms of liberalism. They are thankful to find evangelical churches. This is positive. But the historical drift, which these people have abandoned, is occurring among us incrementally. It has become even more intangible and subtle with this new emerging middle group—the post-conservatives, the evangelical left, the young evangelicals.

Few, it seems, are cognizant of this widening division in evangelicalism. Or is it that few want to acknowledge it? Emerging discussions on this matter are often quickly brushed aside by the admonition, "Let's not get tangled up in these doctrinal issues. Let's focus on what unites us."

It's tough and unpopular to take a firm stand on the slippery slope. It's much easier to champion unity, peace and truth. But responsible leaders, who would be God's impeders of historical drift, must count the cost and choose to pay the price. Two things are sure. If we don't, we will lose the next generation. If we do, our children and grandchildren will rise up and call us blessed.

~

Discussion Questions

1. Is it ever right to choose truth over unity? What are the biblical and historical examples?
2. What do you understand to be the new battle for the Bible?
3. Is the author's concept of a "new evangelical divide" valid? If so, where do you see yourself as a leader?
4. Which fork in the road would you want your church or organization to take?

Good News

Recovering Our Lost Confession

C harles Spurgeon's late 1880s doctrinal shift warning to his Baptist Union fell on deaf ears. Since they had no written doctrinal statement, they wrote off his concern as being vague accusations. They were adamantly opposed to Spurgeon's proposal that they adopt an evangelical statement of faith. "No creed but Christ" was the popular sentiment.

Some Christian organizations have embedded instructions in their founding documents that the statement of faith can never be changed. I am of two minds on this. Doctrinal statements are usually crafted when cultural issues challenge the belief system. Therefore, I believe there are times when a revision of the statement of faith would be in order. But there is danger in reworking such a significant document. For instance, statements written in a time of widespread renewal reflect that renewal in the points relevant to the work of the Holy Spirit. In a time of no revival, those points may be rewritten and adjusted to the current level of experience.

James Montgomery Boice, in his column, "On My Mind," addresses the critical matter of recovering a lost confession. In the 1950s and early '60s, evangelicals sensed the need to develop doctrinal statements as they took their stand against modernism. Boice comments that these served well since the evangelicals signing them believed much more than a National Association of Evangelicals (NAE) type statement included. However, today the situation is different. That deeper dimension of Bible and theology is no longer present. Boice argues that we need to recover "a new, robust, God-centered theology, which alone will be able to stand against the onslaughts of the postmodern age."[6]

One person who led his institution in a recovery of its past statements of faith is R. Albert Mohler, Jr., president of Southern Baptist

Seminary in Louisville, Kentucky. He insisted that his professors affirm the seminary's "Abstract of Principles" and by that policy alone turned the school from what had been drift toward liberalism to a strong new reformation conservatism.[7]

The United Church of Canada (UCC), founded in 1925 has strayed from its roots. The architects of the Union developed twenty Articles of Faith which were biblical and solidly evangelical. Over their relatively brief history, the UCC leadership has departed radically from these twenty articles. In recent years, several renewal movements have emerged. Some have withdrawn; others remain within the church. One which left chose to adopt as their statement of faith the original twenty articles.

This is literally "recovering our lost confessions."

"Men of Issachar, who understood the times and knew what Israel should do." (1 Chronicles 12:32)

13

Having Done All, Stand

Wanted: Historical Drift Impeders

STANDING FIRM FOR TRUTH. How does that challenge strike you? For some it may conjure up a negative image of a dogmatic insensitive Christian who prides himself in "speaking the truth even though it hurts." I like to recall the picture of Stephen, the first Christian martyr. He stood for truth in a tough situation. He would be considered a failure today—the people rejected both the message and the messenger. In fact, they stoned the messenger.

Two aspects of the Acts account greatly encourage me. First, the response from heaven: As he (Stephen) looked up into heaven, he saw "the glory of God" and "Jesus standing" (not sitting) at the right hand of God. Jesus, the Head of the Church, stood up to welcome the first martyr (Acts 7:55-56)! I am also profoundly impacted by his attitude toward the people who rejected him and the truth. "While they were stoning him, Stephen prayed . . . , 'Lord, do not hold this sin against them' " (Acts 7:59-60). From whom did he learn to pray like that?

Standing for truth is both an individual and corporate responsibility. Paul addressed the majority of his letters to churches, i.e., the Corinthians, Galatians, Ephesians, Philippians, Colossians and the Thessalonians. Others, such as the pastoral epistles, he addressed to individual leaders such as Timothy and Titus.

We have addressed the critical role of Christian leaders. This is important since organizations don't drift, only the individuals who lead them. But individuals work in teams. For this reason we now shift our focus to the corporate function of Christian leaders. Two somewhat worn-out axioms merit repetition: "Organizations are only as good as the people who lead them," and "Decisions determine destiny."

Where are the decision-making bodies that can impede historical drift? Let me suggest several venues.

The Local Church Business Meeting

Contrary to popular belief, this is the most critical decision-making body. It may be called the elders' board, board of deacons or simply the governing board. Whatever the label, these boards are the power brokers. On their shoulders rest not only the destiny of the local assembly but also, ultimately, the future of the denomination and evangelicalism within their country.

How so? They are not necessarily the preachers or teachers. No, but as an elected body, along with their pastor, they are the first line of defense against a post-Christian culture. The pressure for local churches to compromise on lifestyle issues comes through church members and their struggle with sin. The church must often make difficult decisions with far-reaching ramifications.

God's passion throughout history has been for His people. In the Old Testament, He had His chosen people, Israel. Under the New Covenant, He has His Church, the "called-out ones." Of necessity, the Bible focuses on leaders primarily because the spiritual welfare of God's people is inseparably tied to their leadership.

He has further revealed His zeal for the *laos* (the common people, laity) by insisting that His revelation be always accessible to them. His Son came as an ordinary man. As such, "the common people heard him gladly" (Mark 12:37, KJV). The New Testament was written in the language of ordinary people, *koine* (common) Greek.

It has been well said, "Truth is safest in the hands of God's people"—lay people. Some professional leaders protest saying, "There is nothing more dangerous than a Christian alone with his Bible." But they have overlooked the key person. The Holy Spirit superintended the writing of Scripture and dwells in every Christian to illuminate his understanding of the Bible. Who reacts first when historical drift begins to erode the faithful preaching of God's Word in a local church? Not the district bishop. Not the national denominational office. No, it is the ordinary Spirit-taught lay people who at some point begin to vote with their feet in search for another church.

By virtue of being God's chosen depository for truth, the local church board becomes Satan's preferred target. As such, truth in local churches can be subtly hijacked. Consider this typical small church scenario: The daughter of an affluent and influential elder wants to be married in her parents' church which has a center aisle. The father insists that his pastor perform the marriage. There are just two problems: The daughter, who is a Christian, is marrying a non-Christian. She is also two months pregnant. Will the church board support their pastor in his decision to not perform the marriage? Will they compromise and allow the church to be used but with an outside minister? Or will they stand firm and risk losing the elder and his support?

Local Church Discipline

It was John Calvin who believed that true churches demonstrate three characteristics: They revere the Word of God, they celebrate the Lord's Supper and they observe church discipline.[1]

The recent escalation of the rights movement in society makes litigation accessible to all. This new pressure can intimidate churches when facing situations where church discipline needs to be applied. One local church, after prayer and careful deliberation, placed under discipline a high-profile leader. Their practice was to allow the person being disciplined to speak after the action had been read to the congregation. In his response, he announced his plan to sue the church for 2 million dollars. Over several weeks, in answer to prayer, God intervened, and the man withdrew his court action. Drift experienced a major setback in that church.

The challenge to accommodate culture hits the local church first. Jesus Himself outlined the process of applying discipline. In Matthew 18:15-17 and First Corinthians 3:5-11, there are seven steps: 1) go to the person involved; 2) take a witness; 3) tell it to the church; 4) do not eat with that person; 5) do not associate with that person; 6) expel that person from the fellowship; and 7) deliver that person over to Satan.[2]

K. Neill Foster, in his book *Binding and Loosing*, expands on the final step:

> Commentators regularly refer to First Corinthians 5:5 as an example of Paul exercising the disciplinary authority of binding and loosing. Zwingli also relates binding to this passage. H.A. Ironside likewise refers to First Corinthians 5:5 as an example of binding and loosing: "In First Corinthians 5, [Paul] was binding [the offender's] sin upon him until he should repent. When in Second Corinthians 5:5-11, he instructed the assembly to forgive the man upon evidence of his repentance, he was loosing him."[3]

Foster notes further:

> But what is seldom addressed, or even recognized, is that this action of binding and loosing in the context of church disci-

pline is not merely exercising a judgment of discipline or excommunication, but it involves a binding, supernatural transaction. The offender is literally bound over to Satan.[4]

G. Campbell Morgan saw an eighth step: once the person is considered a "pagan," begin again the process of redeeming him or her.

Before the practice of abortion became routine in North American culture, one local church was forced to deal with it. A Christian medical student attempted to abort his child that his fiancée was carrying. She died in the process. His church dealt with it sensitively, providing support to the families, but also openly exercising discipline with the young man. In retrospect, the leadership of the church believed that by dealing with this situation with grace and biblical discipline, the practice of abortion was publicly judged by God. And, as in the case of the apostolic church, "Great fear seized the whole church and all who heard about these events" (Acts 5:11).

In Paul's letter, he strongly endorses one-on-one discipline. He reminds Timothy that the role of Scripture is that of "rebuking, correcting and training in righteousness" (2 Timothy 3:16). As leaders, in view of the coming judgment, we are to "correct, rebuke and encourage" (4:2). He adds that in those cases where believers refuse correction, a further step in discipline is to be followed: "Keep away from every brother who is idle and does not live according to the teaching" (2 Thessalonians 3:6).

K. Neill Foster believes "that historical drift can be impeded if we are willing to develop a practical theology of exhorting one another carefully and lovingly and if we are willing to initiate the principles of conflict resolution, i.e., follow the steps of Matthew 18 in which we first speak privately, then with witnesses, and finally, when necessary, tell the church."[5]

New Testament church discipline in both its personal and corporate dimensions is undoubtedly the most effective method of impeding historical drift. Paul employed the personal aspect when he confronted

Peter for his hypocrisy related to the critical racial issue of Jews and Gentiles (Galatians 2:11-13). Peter responded positively. And Christ, in His audit of seven relatively young local churches, addressed church discipline at the corporate level.

Denominational Councils

Is there New Testament precedence for the networking of churches for decision-making? I believe there is. The Jerusalem Council immediately comes to mind (Acts 15:1-35). Leaders, elders, apostles and prophets from various regions such as Antioch assembled in Jerusalem. Their historic decision to permit Gentiles to become Christians without conforming to Jewish ceremonial laws became binding on all the churches although their letter was specifically addressed to the Gentile believers (15:23).

How important are such decisions? Can you imagine Christianity without this Jerusalem mandate? It released the gospel to the entire non-Jewish world. It became the *magna carta* of the Christian faith. But not all subsequent church councils have left such a noble heritage. In A.D. 325, the Nicene Creed, authorized by the Council of Nice, condemned the heretical teachings of Arius which attacked the deity of Christ. In A.D. 381, the Council of Constantine formally made Christianity the state church, which opened the door to nominalism. Another council impeded historical drift by standing tall for the core of Christianity, the deity of Christ. A generation later, still another rolled out the welcome mat to historical drift that once again fast-forwarded the Church into nominalism and the Dark Ages.

Church conferences continue as both a blessing and bane for the church. Our strong commitment to the democratic process has greatly limited our ability to impede the drift process. However, here are two significant denominational case studies that engender hope. They have not only defended their position of biblical inerrancy, but also have seen the drift toward liberalism reversed in their seminaries. In both cases, one of the many significant results has been a renewed thrust for world evangelization. I will expand on this exciting development at the close of Chapter 18, but briefly, here are their stories.

The Southern Baptist Convention

In 1925, the Southern Baptist Convention approved a comprehensive statement of faith. The article concerning the Scriptures clearly stated that the entire Bible is free from error, and it rejected limited infallibility.

Although this statement has been periodically affirmed over the years, it continues to be the eye of the storm in North America's largest denomination. In what has been dubbed the "holy war," the battle lines have been drawn primarily between the conservatives and the moderates. (To the right and left respectively are also the fundamentalists and the liberals).

During the last twenty years of the 20th century, the conservatives have slowly but surely gained control of the national convention, and since 1979, they have been able to consistently elect conservative presidents. Their term of office is for one year, but they can be reelected for a maximum of two consecutive years. The president's executive powers are limited in the Baptist context of strong local church autonomy. However, his executive jurisdiction grants him power to nominate members for the Committee on Committees which, in turn, nominates members to all other committees that oversee the SBC agencies, including the training institutions.

The impact on the 15 million-member denomination is incredible. In just twenty years, the drift toward liberalism in their six seminaries was reversed. This renewal in leadership has profoundly impacted their mission boards. The North American Interfaith Witness Division launched the Mormon thrust at their 1998 convention held in Salt Lake City. A powerful renewal ministry, directed by Henry T.

Blackaby, coauthor of the widely used *Experiencing God Bible Study*, is a significant part of the Home Mission Board of SBC.[6]

Although layman Judge Paul Pressler played a significant role, this is an unusual example of corporate denominational leadership not only impeding historical drift but also reversing it, especially in their schools.

The Lutheran Missouri Synod

During essentially the same period, one of the three largest Lutheran bodies in the United States, the Missouri Synod, was involved in its own holy war. Again, the battlefield was the inerrancy of Scripture.

Every tradition comes to this pivotal question differently. Lutherans naturally look to the teachings of Martin Luther for their benchmark. Luther believed the Bible to be the true Word of God and strongly supported *sola scriptura*. Ironically, the Roman Catholic Church held the Bible to be infallible, as did Luther. The major difference was that they added to it and made the church the only authoritative interpreter of it.

From its founding, the Missouri Synod had held to an inerrant Scripture. But not until 1932 did they adopt a "Brief Statement" of its doctrinal position. The first article addresses their commitment to Scripture. The following is but part of a lengthy paragraph:

> Since the Holy Scriptures are the Word of God, it goes without saying that they contain no errors or contradictions, but that they in all their parts and words are the infallible truth, also in those parts which treat of historical, geographical, and other secular matters, John 10:35.[7]

This section became the focus of debate that ultimately divided the Missouri Synod. The definition of the critical phrase "the Word of God" split the denomination.

The controversy became centered in Concordia Seminary. Just as a strong conservative president was named to lead the denomination, the neoliberals negotiated the appointment of their candidate to head the seminary. The new seminary president championed the historical-critical method of interpretation. This methodology denies the transcendence in the history of Jesus, e.g., His miracles, the temptation story, the narrative of His baptism, etc. It became apparent that the denomination was being split between the laity and conservative clergy on one hand and the strong liberal element in the seminary and headquarters personnel on the other.

The conservatives won the day. The liberals responded by establishing their "Seminary in Exile" (Seminex) in 1974. One hundred thousand members left, forming a new church, which has now merged with the Evangelical Lutheran Church in America. Historical drift again was impeded by a denomination standing for Scripture but paying the high cost of fractured relationships. The long-term dividends of their stand for the absolute authority of all Scripture is found in the vignette at the end of this chapter.

In the Boardrooms

Can the decisions of councils and conferences be separated from the decisions of boardrooms? Probably not. A tougher question: Can the decisions of boards be free of political maneuvers? Politics is simply the "science of government"—a need wherever there are people.

The following is Churchill's evaluation on the subject: "Democracy is the worst form of government, but it is the best we can find." Christianity has seldom addressed the obvious question in the New Testament: "How do we explain the very limited democratic form in the Apostolic Church?" Was it a form of modified theocracy? The recent focus on New Apostolic Churches may be a reaction to the downside of democracy in the church context.

Were there any political decisions in the book of Acts? Philip Teng, in his little book, *The Crises of the Apostolic Church,*[8] suggests that the Holy Spirit sovereignly orchestrated every crisis to move the Church ahead. Often the intervention was strictly spiritual, e.g., when the believers were overcome by fear, God filled them with the Holy Spirit, and "they spoke the word of God boldly" and the Church moved aggressively forward (Acts 4:29-31). However, later, when dissension among the widows erupted, the apostles took a good political action: They appointed deacons to address the issue. Again, the Holy Spirit advanced the Church. "So the word of God spread. The number of disciples in Jerusalem increased rapidly" (6:1-7).

"Do you know of any Christian organization which has coped effectively with historical drift?" I asked a church historian professor. He quickly named a centenarian Christian school.

Next question: "How did they do it?"

"In two ways," he replied, "through their strong boards and their choosing of their presidents."

Although unpopular in our day, there is much to be said for strong, self-generating boards. A number of the built-to-last organizations appear to have successfully used such boards. If boards are to be effective in the maintaining of core values and consistent alignment with mission and vision, there must be greater continuity in board membership.

Strong boards can be powerful deterrents to historical drift. Some local denominational church boards can enact bylaws which can be more conservative than the denominational regulations in such critical areas as qualification of elders, marriage, divorce, etc. Some would argue that local churches are less prone to drift than are denominations. Certainly a number of large independent community churches would support that thesis. Conversely, a denomination which is effective in impeding drift can serve local churches as a positive outside prophetic voice.

The Holy Spirit is the greatest of all impeders of drift. He is sovereign yet confined to working through Christians. We are His body, His office. To the degree that the Holy Spirit, the master impeder and reverser of drift, controls us will we be effective in our role as leaders.

The Most Powerful Committee

Off to the side of the boardroom meets the most powerful of all committees, the nominating committee. When they do their work thoroughly, their nominations, in crass marketing terms, control the high ground. We have seen the effectiveness of the nominating process in the SBC turnaround.

There is another dimension to impeding drift and even rolling it back. I refer to the handling of corporate sin in an aging organization. Church and denominational boards can assume responsibility for the corporate sins of the past.

One church, led by the new senior pastor, took the congregation back thirty-five years to its beginnings. They identified times and issues where leadership had failed the church. As the current leadership team, they assumed responsibility for the past. In the midst of a sermon one Sunday morning, they asked for forgiveness and received it from the congregation. One ten-year-old, observing this unusual moment, asked his mother, "Is this revival? They are confessing their sins." Such radical action frees a congregation to move unshackled into the future under an open heaven of God's blessing. Historical drift was rolled back that Sunday morning.

Publishing Houses and Bookstores

The 1999 Christian Booksellers' Association Convention in Dallas drew more than 13,000 delegates. One of them, Diana Frazier, ob-

served that "music was big and WWJD stuff keeps growing." The spectrum of books was broad—all the way from R.C. Sproul on holiness to
Kenneth Copeland on managing your mutual funds. At the end of the
day, she mused: "I'm struck by what I didn't really see: theology. You
know, books on Christianity at a Christian Bookseller's Convention.
Now I know those titles are there, but they aren't prominent."[9]

Bookstores have become more than books. Some could be seen as
thriving on "holy hardware." A quick survey of most Christian bookstores would strongly suggest that they are driven more by consumerism than theology. How-to books, appealing to the quick-fix mentality
of our culture, continue to dominate.

In a crowded basement, with an obscure address in the heart of a
large city, functions The Reformation Book Services. The philosophy
of the owner/manager/clerk/bookkeeper is simple and clearly reflected
in this memo attached to his list of books:

> The materials listed here if carefully taken account of will help
> the minister of the gospel, the concerned pastor, rescue theol-
> ogy from those who have made it a mere academic exercise and
> divorced it from the living force it should be in the life of the
> churches. They cover a wide range of thought and are chosen
> not because they represent any one particular theology but for
> their provocative value and their practical thrust. They have a
> solid biblical content, but the reader will find it necessary to
> agree and disagree quite strongly, but that is the way to learn.
> This kind of theology is not dry as dust material but vibrant
> with life. The kind that brings the life of God to the souls of
> men.[10]

Publishing houses play an increasingly significant role as evangelicalism fragments. *Christianity Today*, founded as a bulwark of evangelical theology in 1959, has evolved, in the words of David Wells, into a
"Christian newsmagazine."[11] Another Christian magazine, *WORLD*,

with a radically different theological bent from *Christianity Today*, blew the whistle on Zondervan's quiet plan to market a gender-inclusive edition of the New International Version of the Bible. In the resulting confrontation between publishers, Bible Society and various evangelical denominations and agencies, theology won a rare victory over economics.

Denominational publishers can play either a positive or negative role in their church's struggle to remain conservative. Their choice of authors makes a powerful statement. Their proactive recruiting of high profile writers on critical issues can shape the soul of the denomination. They also speak loudly by their silence in choosing not to publish or market certain books.

One author, Ajith Fernando, from Sri Lanka, writing on the controversial topic of the lostness of man, was surprised to have his manuscript rejected by a respected evangelical publisher. Other evangelical publishers are known to thrive by dancing on the edges of orthodoxy.

Christian Publications, founded in 1883, is one of the oldest publishing houses in North America. It predates by four years the official founding date of its parent denomination, The Christian and Missionary Alliance. How well have they maintained evangelical orthodoxy and resisted historical drift? Their mission statement answers this question:

> The purpose of Christian Publications, Inc., is to propagate the gospel of Jesus Christ, as outlined in The Christian and Missionary Alliance statement of faith, particularly the message of Jesus Christ, Our Savior, Sanctifier, Healer and Coming King, to the Alliance constituency, as well as to the broader evangelical community worldwide and to unbelievers. This is done in active cooperation with other Alliance publishing houses around the world. It does so by evangelistic, deeper life and other publishing, by direct distribution to customers, by oper-

ation of its own retail stores, by distribution through other retail stores and by all legitimate and advisable means.[12]

Its sentiments are further expressed in this statement (abbreviated
here) which has been included in their catalogs:

> "We publish what we believe in, not what we believe will
> make money." So said retiring American Association of Uni-
> versity Press president, Collin Day, director of the University
> of Michigan Press. The comment is particularly unusual be-
> cause of its source—not a conservative denominational pub-
> lisher, but the head of a secular university press.
>
> The directors of Christian Publications reflect that senti-
> ment. In a day when many publishers . . . lean toward the de-
> scriptive side of the prescriptive/descriptive construct, some
> prescriptive publishers still exist.
>
> Over a century ago, Christian Publications . . . focused on a
> Bible-centered message. In the words of the founder, Albert B.
> Simpson, it was: Christ, our Savior; Christ, our Sanctifier;
> Christ, our Healer and Christ, our Coming King. That focus
> endures. . . . The essential message thrust remains: We publish
> what we believe. We believe what we publish. We are prescrip-
> tive publishers.
>
> We take seriously the motto which appears on the front
> cover of our catalog: "Faithful, Biblical Publishing Since
> 1883."

The Halls of Academia

The jury is still out on the role that academic institutions play in the
history of the Church. Are they the great defenders of the faith, or are
they frequent contributors to historical drift? There are persuasive

case studies supporting both schools of thinking. One thing is sure, they are subject to the same evaluation grid as other organizations; i.e., "They are only as good as the people who run them." This has been vividly illustrated in recent seminary-centered denominational controversies over the Bible.

By the very nature of their role, denominational schools particularly find themselves at the eye of theological storms. They must walk the tightrope between academic freedom and loyalty to the denomination's theological positions. Historically, the critical issue has been the position on Scripture. The denominational schools are under the constant scrutiny of pastors, some even alumni, who now wear the practitioner's hat and look back at academia with a jaundiced eye. "Are those ivory-tower professors actually in touch with the real world?"

One denomination with a large missionary outreach reacted strongly when two of its seminary professors became enamored with a Roman Catholic concept then called "implicit faith." (Today it would be called "universalistic inclusivism.") After several years of wrenching theological controversy, the church adjusted a statement in its policy manual and repudiated implicit Christianity as a form of universalism.

Professors, who of necessity must think in the world of theories, concepts and philosophies, need an accountability structure as do all Christian leaders. Some institutions do better at providing this than others. Leadership with a healthy respect for historical drift proactively and personally assists each faculty member to assess any shift in his or her theological positions. The most common approach is to require each faculty member to re-sign the Statement of Faith prior to renewing his or her contract.

Some take it a step further. The president actually sits with each faculty member and interacts on the current theological issues of the day. Some seminaries in the SBC, such as Southwestern in Fort Worth, Texas, now ask faculty to sign a pledge "to teach in accordance with the updated 'Baptist Faith and Message' statement."[13]

On the other side of the ledger, academic policies such as tenure for faculty members have made the monitoring of evangelical orthodoxy more difficult. James Collins, one of the authors of *Built to Last*, makes this interesting observation regarding academic tenure in the secular world: "It was initially introduced to protect professors and guarantee their freedom to think. Today it has become a policy that protects academic professors whether they think or not."[14]

Accreditation associations, such as the Association of Accreditation of Bible Colleges (AABC), have been necessary and helpful. But the danger always exists that in the push for the good-housekeeping seal of academic respectability conservative positions can be compromised.

In his plenary address to the 1998 conference of the Evangelical Theological Society (ETS), Norman Geisler, the president of ETS, shared some counsel for evangelical scholars:

- Avoid unorthodox conclusions while doing exegesis.
- Avoid the illicit desire to become a famous scholar.
- Avoid dancing on the edges; i.e., do not flirt with the latest critical methodology.
- Do not trade orthodoxy for academic respectability.
- Reject any methodology inconsistent with the Bible or good reason.
- Always choose Lordship over scholarship.
- Do not allow sincerity to be a test for orthodoxy.[15]

How can academia impede historical drift? In addition to the above, Geisler answers with a very helpful illustration from aviation:

Steer right to go straight. According to aerodynamic experts, when a propeller-driven airplane takes off, it naturally veers to the left unless it is steered to the right. Based on my observations of evangelical institutions and leaders over the past half-century, it appears to me that the same principle applies. The only way to keep on a straight orthodox path is to keep turning to the right. Churches, schools and even evangelical scholarship will naturally go left unless they are deliberately turned to the right. The prevailing winds of doctrine blow against us, and if we are to resist them then we must have a firm grip on the wheel of the good ship evangelicalism and steer it to the right.[16]

Statements of Faith, if used as the major document for the screening of new workers, can impede historical drift. Most statements simply state their beliefs in an affirmative manner. Recently, some seminaries are strengthening their position by placing an addendum after the affirmative statement to articulate what their statement is *not* saying.

A consortium of seminaries has developed the following four-point statement which new members are asked to sign as part of the application procedure:

- The absolute trustworthiness, inerrancy, infallibility of the Scriptures. We do not agree with current attempts to restrict and limit inspiration to matters of religion and faith only. Insofar as Scripture speaks on anything, it speaks truthfully.
- The sovereignty of God as defined in classical Calvinism and Arminianism expresses our understanding of God's rule. Thus we do not agree with current attempts to define God in terms of process, openness or lack of knowledge of the future.
- The necessity for individuals to respond in faith to the gospel within history in order to receive God's gift of salvation remains imperative. Thus we do not agree with current attempts to suggest that there will be postmortem salvation or that general revelation is salvific or that universalism is taught within Scripture.
- The future of believers and nonbelievers will be eternal existence. For believers this will be with God in heaven and

blessing; for the nonbeliever this will be with Satan and his angels in hell and judgment. We do not agree with recent attempts to argue for conditional immortality.[17]

Summary

Undoubtedly there are many additional venues for impeding historical drift. For some readers, many of these activities may appear defensive and even negative. Others may think we have dwelt too long on the power and might of man versus the power of the Spirit.

In the Good News vignette which follows, two denominations which were forced to fight for their survival now are thriving. The dark times of fighting for truth are behind them. Today, they enjoy a season of exciting growth. They are now able to address God's heart agenda—world evangelization—with renewed strength.

We have shared many testimonies of godly and courageous leaders who have taken a firm stand on the slippery slope to impede the downward momentum of historical drift. This is basic New Testament Christianity. We are light to penetrate the darkness. This is our offense. But we are also salt to preserve this world from self-destruction. This is our defensive role.

We have emphasized that churches don't drift, only their leaders. Often, as Christian leaders, we accommodate culture to the point of becoming trapped on a drifting ship. The good news is this: We need not go down with a drifting Christian ministry. As an individual, perhaps surrounded by colleagues who are adrift, God offers you the seventh heaven. The Spirit of God loves to reverse our direction. He can put us on that ascending pathway (drift in reverse) that Peter speaks of: "Add to your faith, goodness, knowledge, self-control, perseverance, godliness, brotherly kindness and love." Notice the two promises: He will make you effective and fruitful, and He will welcome you into eternity (2 Peter 1:8-10).

We have considered a variety of venues for impeding drift. But I have saved the best for the last. God in His graciousness visits His people in extraordinary ways from time to time. And He's about to do it again. This will be impedance at God's best. Read on!

~

Discussion Questions

1. "Decisions determine destiny." Is this a valid statement? Why?
2. In a denominational context, at what level are the most effective drift-impeding decisions made? Local church or denominational offices?
3. What was the common battle that both the Southern Baptist Convention and the Lutheran Church—Missouri Synod fought (see pages 228-230)?
4. Is there any correlation between winning that battle and God's blessing on these groups today in their renewed missionary strength?

Good News

New Blessings on Old Denominations

This Good News section focuses on two aging denominations which have managed to impede historical drift successfully. I find these stories particularly encouraging. Although they paid a high price to hold to the truth, they are now reaping an abundant harvest in their worldwide ministries.

The Southern Baptist Convention

The oldest of the SBC churches is the First Baptist Church in Charleston, South Carolina. In fact, it predates the founding of the SBC denomination which took place in 1845. Their struggle for unity over Scripture in recent decades is well known. It has taken its toll. For the first time in their history, the denomination reported a decrease in their membership and number of churches in 1999. But in several other areas, less tangible but ultimately more important, they are experiencing new blessing.

One of those areas is missions. The major restructuring began with a name change. The Foreign Mission Board is now the International Board. More important than the new name is their new focus: "To target the final frontiers and the unreached people groups (UPG)."

What difference has this restructuring made? Missionaries have been liberated from excessive administrative detail and internal organization. Following Henry Blackaby's emphasis in *Experiencing God* on discovering where God is working, they believe less structure will allow their missionaries to adjust quickly to where the Holy Spirit is working.

This commitment to revitalization has significantly impacted the American church. Missionaries have been empowered to mobilize the sending church. Short-term volunteers have increased from 10,000 in 1995 to 15,000 in 1997. They expect to see a major increase in those appointed as missionaries. Churches want more personal involvement. Giving to missions has increased dramatically, but not in what flows through the denominational office. Much of the increase is direct giving—local church to mission field. This, of course, makes denominational leaders nervous. But it's the wave of this new day.[18]

Lutheran Church, Missouri Synod (LCMS)

Recent history in the LCMS parallels that of the Southern Baptists. The 1960s and 1970s were turbulent times. Again, the eye of the storm was the inerrancy of Scripture. The result was also similar. The conservative wing prevailed—but not without a major split in 1974 when 100,000 members left along with most of the seminary faculty.

There was good news in the '90s. During that decade, they opened twenty new mission fields. Their long-term volunteers increased by 300 percent. Their budget increased from $12.6 million to $28 million between 1991 and 1998. The LCMS considered themselves strongly committed to world evangelization, but the dramatic increase in funding of their missionary enterprise caught them by surprise. By far the greatest increase came through direct giving, i.e., gifts from individuals or churches to a specific cause such as a missionary, project or team increased by 600 percent.

What is LCMS doing right? Their leaders choose to give credit to the Holy Spirit. But on the human plane, four words summarize their new direction:

- Decentralize: "They have opened a seat at the table to the congregation, . . . recognizing that people today are no longer willing to 'just give their money.' "[19]
- Spawn: They have become intentional advocates for birthing new mission societies that link with LCMS World Mission.

These have increased from twenty-two to fifty-five affiliated agencies in the last three years.

- Invest: They believe this is a generation of passionate evangelicals "who are willing to stand, in tangible, monetary ways, behind the causes that they believe are reflective of Scripture."[20] Congregations are given multiple options of participation. They have infiltrated their Sunday school curriculum with mission vision.

- Partner: They intentionally link stronger congregations with smaller new ones. The churches see the denomination in a new way. This empowering of local churches in missions can lead in some unexpected directions, e.g., one group of churches chose to form a partnership with a group of Sudanese churches to address a refugee need.[21]

God has promised to honor those who address His agenda. These denominations took a very unpopular stand for the integrity of the Word of God. There was a price. I believe there is a direct link between their rising to that challenge and God's fresh blessing on them today as they address God's heart for the unreached peoples of the world.

"My critics said after the crusade in Los Angeles that I set the church back fifty years. My response: I'm disappointed. I wanted to set it back 2,000 years."

—Billy Graham, Lecture at Fuller Seminary, 1974

Part V

HISTORICAL DRIFT REVERSED

It's Saturday night. Sunday is coming. Pastor Jack has experienced a rough week. He's still recovering from the death of his mother. The church is into another building project which means more administrative detail. Earlier in the week he heard rumors of growing discontent among a group of his people. He has pastored this church for fourteen years. God has given good growth. It is now a congregation of 2,000. But Pastor Jack somehow feels God has much more for his people.

Two years ago, he announced that on Sunday evenings for the next two years they would simply gather and pray for a visitation of God. He's amazed how many are coming. In fact, Sam, an evangelist friend of many years, is coming to speak tomorrow night at the prayer time.

As Jack and his wife visit with Sam, they discuss the Sunday services. Then Jack shares about his rough week and confesses that frankly he's beat. He wonders out loud if Sam would like to take the morning message also. Sam gladly accepts.

It's Father's Day morning. A good crowd is present. Sam is having trouble getting through his message because he's excited about the altar call. He keeps telling the people "Folks, God is going to move this morning. God is going to move this morning." Jack's thinking, *Yeah sure, Sam. We've been praying for revival for two and a half years.*

Before Sam even gives the formal invitation, half of the congregation is streaming forward. Jack watches in amazement as his people meet God. He realizes that yes, God is answering their prayers. Soon he's at the microphone saying, "Folks, this is it. The Lord is here." Little does Jack know that the excitement is just beginning.

God loves to surprise us with His extraordinary visits. Call it renewal or revival, what's important is God's unusual presence. Definitions for revival abound. Here's mine: Revival is a special moment when God comes down. His Word comes alive. Sin is revealed. Confessions are made. Forgiveness is sought and received. Broken relationships are healed. Restitutions are made. Joy flows like a river. New power is released.

On very special occasions, the revival breaks out beyond the church. Society in general becomes God-conscious as Christians begin living what they profess. Evangelism is spontaneous. Thousands are swept into the kingdom. This evangelistic dimension has sometimes been termed "an awakening."

Why These Times?

The short answer is the theme of this book: because historical drift is reality. The Church is more an organism than an organization. As such, God has designed it for spiritual renewal. Thank God for godly leaders who stand for truth and become effective impeders of historical drift day by day. But there are those *kairos* moments when God comes down.

What are the biblical bases for such expectations? My thesis rests squarely on two clear expressions of God's promised visitation among His people, one in each Testament.

The Old Testament promise is found in Second Chronicles 7:14: " . . . if my people, who are called by my name, will humble themselves and pray and seek my face and turn from their wicked ways, then will I hear from heaven and will forgive their sin and will heal their land."

God Shows Up

The setting is interesting. Solomon has just completed the dedication of the temple. And God showed up! He sent fire from heaven to consume the sacrifices. The people responded in powerful worship (2 Chronicles 7:1-10). Then God appeared to Solomon that same night with an unexpected reminder: Tough days are ahead—days of drought, locusts and plagues—but spiritual refreshing will also come.

God also shows up in the New Testament in Acts 2:1-41: "When the Day of Pentecost came" (Acts 2:1). Pentecost was an historical event. It came as a major fulfillment of Joel's prophecy (Joel 2:28-32). Pentecost literally means "fiftieth"—fifty days after the opening of the harvest season. It was also fifty days after the resurrection. God chose Pentecost as the birthday of His Church. But Pentecost was more than a birthday—it was a mega-revival. What better way for God to launch His Church on her amazing assignment to carry out His Son's great commission than with a mighty moving of the Holy Spirit in revival?

Author Erroll Hulse sees in Pentecost four basic essentials that characterize all revivals:

- The sense of God's nearness and especially an awareness of His holiness and majesty. At Pentecost everyone was filled with awe (Acts 2:43). A realization of the holiness of God is also one of the hallmarks of revival.

- A greatly intensified work of the Holy Spirit in conviction of sin and granting of repentance and faith.
- A marvelous increase in the numbers added to the church.
- Powerful preaching of the gospel.[1]

I believe there is good evidence that many elements of Pentecost are an integral part of God's commitment to revive His Church through the centuries. Peter, in the house of Cornelius, witnessed a similar outpouring of the Holy Spirit among Gentiles. Upon seeing the same manifestations as at Pentecost, Peter said: "Can anyone keep these people from being baptized with water? They have received the Holy Spirit just as we have" (10:47). Still later, when Peter went to Jerusalem to describe and defend what happened with the Gentiles, he explained: "As I began to speak, the Holy Spirit came on them as he had come on us at the beginning" (11:15).

In the prophecy of Joel 2:28-32, Pentecost was the first and most significant installment of this far-sweeping prophecy. But the house of Cornelius was another—the Pentecost of the Gentiles. The term "last days" in Joel's prophecy bridges the birth of the Church to the return of Christ. Over the centuries until today, the Holy Spirit has continued to pour out His Spirit in special seasons of renewal.

Revivals? Awakenings?

These terms can be confusing. Some use "awakening" to refer to "revival." I prefer to separate them. The distinction relates to the sphere of spiritual impact. Peter reminds us that God's corrective hand of judgment must "begin with the family of God" (1 Peter 4:17). Revival is God's method of bringing His people to repentance and restoration. The sphere of revival is the Church—God's people.

Although visitations always begin with God's people, some move beyond the Church to impact non-Christians. "Awakening" was coined to describe the societal impact of revivals in the 18th and 19th centuries, usually referred to as three in number.[2] A powerful conviction of sin came upon nonbelievers in their workplaces and on the streets. Universities were impacted. Thousands were converted.

Historian J.R. Green states:

> The Evangelical Awakening changed, after a time, the whole tone of English society. The church was restored to new life and activity. Religion carried to the hearts of the people a fresh spirit of moral zeal, while it purified our literature and our manners. A new philanthropy reformed our prisons, infused clemency and wisdom into our penal laws, abolished the slave trade, and gave the first impulse to popular education.[3]

Revivals can reverse historical drift and snatch churches back from the brink of nominalism. Spiritual vitality will be restored. Awakenings will restore standards of morality in decadent societies. History attests to these miracles. Why then does this amazing provision of God suffer from benign neglect in today's Church?

"You can learn how to live with the 'roof off' in your relationship with God and the 'walls down' in your relationship with others."

—Nancy Leigh DeMoss

14

Experiencing God

Revival: Impedance at Its Best

REVIVAL FALLS INTO THE CATEGORY of motherhood issues like prayer, humility, missions and evangelism. But, perhaps surprisingly to some, the opponents of revival are legion. Chief among them, of course, is Satan. In fact, it is difficult to separate his influence from all the *respectable* antagonists of renewal. What do we know about his diabolical agenda?

Well, we know he's been a deceiver from the beginning in the garden (Genesis 3:1-7). His basic strategy is to question God's Word; e.g., "Did God really say, 'You must not eat from any tree in the garden'?" Applying his strategy to revival, he would question: "Did God really say, 'Not by might, nor by power, but by my Spirit'?" (Zechariah 4:6). "Jesus didn't really tell the Ephesians, 'You have forsaken your first love?' did He?" (Revelation 2:4).

In his temptation of Jesus, Satan offered Him "all the kingdoms of the world" without the suffering the cross would demand (Matthew 4:8). He is a master tempter. Later, he used Peter to tempt Christ to once again bypass the cross (Matthew 16:22-23). This satanic strategy makes sense when we understand that revival takes the Christian back to the cross, and it involves death to self followed by the fullness of the Spirit. Satan would love to dupe us into a spiritual experience that avoids the cross. Beware. Pseudo forms of revival abound.

There is much that Satan doesn't know. He didn't know that when he used Judas to betray Christ he facilitated God's plan for world redemption and his own ultimate destruction (1 John 3:8). But he did know two things about Paul—that if he kept him powerless, bound by self and sin (Romans 7:7-24), he would never be a threat to his dark kingdom. Satan also knew that if Paul was set free from self and empowered by the Holy Spirit he would charge into Asia Minor and literally tear down his strongholds. That's why Satan works overtime to keep Christians away from genuine revivals.

The Self-Life

"I do not understand what I do. For what I want to do I do not do, but what I hate I do. . . . For I have the desire to do what is good, but I cannot carry it out. . . . So I find this law at work: When I want to do good, evil is right there with me" (7:15-21).

Who is this speaking here? A non-Christian? Some believe that this is Paul speaking during his pre-conversion state. However, the immediate context links this pitiful lament to Paul already having a new nature but struggling with the issue of full surrender (7:25). Throughout his letters he exhorts believers, using an assortment of terms, about this inner battle with self:

- "Get rid of the old yeast . . ." (1 Corinthians 5:7).
- "Live by the Spirit, and you will not gratify the desires of the sinful nature" (Galatians 5:16).
- "Put off your old self, which is being corrupted by its deceitful desires" (Ephesians 4:22).

- "You have taken off your old self with its practices" (Colossians 3:9).

Regarding self, A.W. Tozer noted: "Every man with moral intelligence must be aware of the curse that afflicts him inwardly; he must be conscious of the thing we call *ego*, by the Bible called *flesh* or *self*, but by whatever name called, a cruel master and a deadly foe."[4]

Self is a vital issue in the theology of revival. David Needham describes the struggle as an

> intense battle. At times, an overwhelming battle. Our flesh is constantly receiving independent "meaning possibilities" from its vast, computerized brain reservoir. It is also almost incessantly bombarded with counterfeit meanings from the world and the devil. So we war. (Galatians 5:17)[5]

Whatever the source of the conflict, God's answer to self is death—death to self—what I call making your second trip to the cross. Christ modeled death to self (Philippians 2:6-11); He taught it (John 12:24); He asked His followers to deny themselves (Luke 9:23). Paul also testifies to God's provision for dying to self: "I have been crucified with Christ and I no longer live, but Christ lives in me. The life I live in the body, I live by faith in the Son of God, who loved me and gave himself for me" (Galatians 2:20).

Revival starts with death to self. Resistance to revival teaching should not surprise us. The self-life, left unchallenged, explains the nominal level of the evangelical church. But those who make the second trip to the cross and experience the filling of the Spirit are released for true worship and powerful witness.

Church Leaders

Senior pastors are rightfully described as the "conduit to the hearts of their people." Leadership, like natural birth, must be headfirst. What the pastor models, what he prioritizes, what he teaches—all send a powerful message to his people. This is also true in the essential areas of prayer and revival which are inseparable in God's economy.

I was doing the final interview for two missionary candidate couples. Since our previous interview, they both had served two years in the same church. I asked each couple independently my stock question: "Tell me, what do you believe today more emphatically than you did two years ago?" Each gave the same answer: "The importance of the truths of the deeper life, death to self and the fullness of the Holy Spirit."

I was curious. "Why?" I asked.

The same basic response came from each couple.

"Because for the past two years we have worked with Christians who were struggling in their spiritual lives. They desperately needed this truth. And secondly, our senior pastor not only preached this truth, but regularly called his people to experience death to self and the filling of the Holy Spirit."

Few evangelical leaders would openly confess to a lack of commitment to renewal. But even in denominations with rich heritages of revival and a well-developed theology of renewal, pastors rarely preach or teach or lead their people in renewal. Such leaders become barriers to revival as they designate it as unimportant by benign neglect. They say nothing negative, but their silence shouts down revival as being irrelevant for our day. They send two dangerous messages to their people: First, that the dominant theme of God's Book—that He is constantly calling His people back to Himself—is no longer valid today. The second covert message is that our cozy, comfortable and cultured North American Christianity is normal Christianity.

What's Important in Academia?

Donald McGavran, in his passion for the growth of the church worldwide, provided a strong platform for revival. He invited J. Edwin Orr to join the faculty at the School of World Mission. Having given his life to researching revivals throughout the world, Orr now had the opportunity to teach revival to missionaries and national leaders from around the world. His extensive research combined with a passion for his subject impacted two decades of international leaders until his death in 1987.

But that was then, and this is now. What's important in the world of academia today?

Ninety-five Christian universities, colleges and seminaries promoted their institutions in the October 5th, 1998 edition of *Christianity Today*. Assuming that they utilize this costly space to highlight their strengths, here is what they consider important: counseling, psychology, theology, tradition, Christian education and music. None of the ninety-five made reference to missions or cross-cultural studies. Only five mention renewal. Just two made reference to Spiritual Life Formation.

What kind of workers will the new millennium need?

True Christianity remains always only one slim generation from extinction. The tendency is for the fire to go out. Nominalism becomes the growing edge of Christianity unless frequent times of renewal are experienced. Denominations, even those planting new churches, are dismayed by the growing number of closures. If Christianity is to have a future into the 21st century, it will need an army of leaders who have been revitalized through revival and who have a passion to preach it and teach it to the next generation.

Missions that continue to send missionaries armed for spiritual warfare but uninitiated in revival are derelict in their duty. One of two justifiable reasons for missionaries to continue working with an established national church is to see national workers raised up as evangelists to the church with a message of revival.

Two of the plenary speakers at the 1998 Evangelical Theological Society addressed the theme: "Training the Next Generation of Evangelical Pastors and Missionaries." John Piper, formerly a professor at Bethel Seminary, chose to bypass the expected theological discourse to focus exclusively on the spiritual preparation of workers. His thesis: "The greatest need of the pastorate and the greatest need of missionaries in every generation, including this one and the next, is to know God better than we know anything, to delight in God more than in anything else."[6]

It is becoming apparent in our broken society that the most important criterion for the Christian leader is brokenness of spirit. A spirit of brokenness is the very essence of revival. My expanded expectation of revival defines it as "a time when God comes down. When the Word comes alive. When sin is revealed. Where brokenness abounds. Where confessions are made. Where forgiveness is granted and broken relationships are restored."

In our present culture, we refer to brokenness in terms of human relationships. There's the brokenness which people bring to our churches, e.g., broken marriages, broken families, broken health, broken hearts, etc. Then there's the spiritual brokenness that commends us to God: "A broken and a contrite heart, O God, you will not despise" (Psalm 51:17).

This is our greatest need, prayerfully exemplified by Bob Pierce, founder of Samaritan's Purse: "O God break my heart with that which breaks Your heart." Professional counseling can be helpful in dealing with brokenness, but the counselor must have more than empathy. He or she must be prepared to lead the person into an experience with God in a fresh encounter with the Holy Spirit. The gates of hell cannot prevail against those who have a restored relationship with Christ, a renewed passion for God's glory and a spirit of brokenness for lost people.

Discussion Questions

1. How does an "organism" differ from an "organization?" Which is the church?
2. How does the author distinguish "revivals" from "awakenings?" Have you seen, heard or experienced either one? Describe.
3. Based upon the author's description of the three potential opponents to revival, where does your church or organization stand? Does that stance need to change?
4. Nancy Leigh DeMoss outlines in detail the meaning of brokenness on pages 244-246. What new insights can we learn from the outline of her message?

Good News

The Heart That God Revives

God did some amazing things at the Campus Crusade for Christ U.S. Staff Conference in July, 1995, and met our staff in a special way. Nancy Leigh DeMoss gave [a] message Monday morning. Following her invitation at the end of her talk, many staff were moved to make confessions before the thousands of assembled staff. For many hours throughout that day and the next two days, hundreds came forward to a public microphone and confessed their hurts and shortcomings. Some have called it the beginning of a greater revival, a renewal or stirring of God's Spirit.[7]

What was the message that produced such a powerful response? Brokenness. Her question: "What kind of heart does God revive?" Answer: "The sacrifices of God are a broken spirit; a broken and contrite heart, O God, you will not despise" (Psalm 51:17).

She contrasted the lives of David and Saul, the publican and the Pharisee, the sinner woman and Simon the Pharisee, and the prodigal son and the elder brother. She listed the characteristics of two kinds of people (the following is an abbreviated version):

Proud and Unbroken People	*Broken People*
Focus on the failure of others	Overwhelmed with their own spiritual need
Look down on others	Esteem all others better than self
Independent; have a self-sufficient spirit	Dependent spirit; recognize other's needs

Proud and Unbroken People	*Broken People*
Maintain control; must have their way	Surrender control
Have to prove that they are right	Willing to yield the right to be right
Claim rights	Yield rights
Have a demanding spirit	Have a giving spirit
Self-protective of time, rights, reputation	Are self-denying
Desire to be served	Motivated to serve others
Desire to be a success	Desire to make others successful
Desire for self-advancement	Desire to promote others
Driven to be recognized and appreciated	Sense of unworthiness; thrilled to be used
Wounded when overlooked	Rejoice when others are lifted up
Think of what they can do for God	Know they have nothing to offer to God
Confident in how much they know	Humbled by how much they have to learn
Are self-conscious	Have no concern with self at all
Keep people at arms' length	Willing to take the risk of loving intimately
Are quick to blame others	Can see where they were wrong
Are defensive when criticized	Receive criticism with a humble, open heart
Are concerned about being respectable	Are concerned with being real

Proud and Unbroken People	*Broken People*
Are concerned about what others think	Know all that matters is what God knows
Work to maintain an image and reputation	Die to own reputation
Have a hard time saying "I was wrong"	Quick to admit fault and ask for forgiveness

The following six questions will probe our hearts even deeper:

1. Do I truly yearn to have the kind of heart that God can revive? Do I desire to be a broken person?

2. In the list of Proud versus Broken People, how do I compare? In which column do I fall for each comparison?

3. What needs to be changed about my life? In what areas do I need to allow God to work?

4. Is there anyone with whom I need to be reconciled, whom I need to forgive, from whom I need to ask forgiveness?

5. Is there a sin that needs to be confessed? (Private sins should be confessed privately. Public sins should be confessed publicly.) Who has been affected by my sin?

6. Is there any sin that I need to make right (make restitution)?[8]

"My people have committed two sins: They have forsaken me, the spring of living water, and have dug their own cisterns, broken cisterns that cannot hold water."

—Jeremiah 2:13

15

The Subtlety of Substitutes

Why All the Fuss about Historical Drift?

THE EVANGELICAL CHURCH IN NORTH AMERICA has become high profile. We've bought heavily into the numbers game and other equally competitive exercises. This feeds unhealthy comparisons about which the Scriptures clearly warn: "When we measure ourselves by ourselves and compare ourselves with ourselves, we are not wise" (see 2 Corinthians 10:12).

Our more recent pattern of sitting at the feet of the megachurches during the annual leadership conferences gives us a popular but faulty benchmark for biblical comparison. Often these comparisons encourage us: "We're not doing so great, but certainly better than the other evangelical church in our suburb." There's just one slight problem: Both churches may, in fact, be in the danger zone on the slippery slope of historical drift. A Spanish saying expresses it well: "The comparing of yourself with others is the comfort of the stupid."

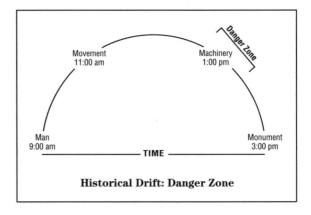

Historical Drift: Danger Zone

Figure 11: Historical Drift: Danger Zone

A Chinese house church leader paid a month-long visit to evangelical churches in America. When asked what his observations were of our churches, he graciously but pointedly responded: "I am amazed at how much you have been able to do in America without God!"

A.W. Tozer, in the 1950s, often compared the North American church with the New Testament church. One of his startling statements was: "Take away the Holy Spirit from the New Testament church and ninety-five percent of what was happening would cease. Take away the Holy Spirit from today's church, and ninety-five percent would continue."

As I observed the archeological digs in Israel, I noted in particular the remnants of cisterns. They were obviously commonplace in Jewish homes. Cisterns were necessary to store water. We had them on our farm when I was growing up (and I'm not Jewish!). They were prone to crack and leak. These memories remind me of the prophet Jeremiah and his lament for God's wayward people:

Has a nation ever changed its gods? (Yet they are not gods at all.) But my people have exchanged their Glory for worthless idols. Be appalled at this, O heavens, and shudder with great horror, declares the LORD. My people have committed two sins: They have forsaken me, the spring of living water, and have dug their own cisterns, broken cisterns that cannot hold water. (Jeremiah 2:11-13)

What were their sins? They exchanged their glory for worthless idols, and they substituted their broken cisterns for God, the spring of living water.

Substitutes

How does the North American church manage nicely without revival? One word—substitutes. What do our broken cisterns look like in this new millennium? Here's but a partial list.

Endless Technology for the Supernatural

Historians will no doubt dub the 20th century as "the great century of technical advance." We are being propelled into the future riding the wave of exponential expansion of cyberspace. But who can be against technology? Certainly not we comfort-driven North Americans! The startling truth is that technology has done a number on our churches and on us.

Richard Swenson, medical doctor-turned-researcher, documents the exponential rate of change and its negative impact on our lives in his books *Margin* and *Overload*. He argues that change has destroyed our margins for living in four critical areas: emotional, physical, financial and time reserves.[1] In his most recent book, *Hurtling Toward Oblivion*, he sees this relentless pressure culminating in the end-time teaching of the New Testament.[2]

Another author has described our pressurized lifestyle in these terms: "This is the age of the half-read page, the quick hash and the mad dash, the bright lights with the nerves tight. The plane's hot with a brief stop. The lamp tan in a brief span. The big shot in a good spot and the brain strain and the heart pain, and the catnaps and the spring snaps and the fun's done."[3]

Technology and Techniques

The evangelical church has been duped by these trends, and the North American version of the Church Growth Movement has unwittingly been a major contributor. In nontechnical third-world societies, church leaders are cast upon God as their only answer. But not so in our sophisticated Western world. For our every need, technology offers several answers. If one program gimmick fails, just plug in another. God used to be able to corner Christian workers into situations where God was the only way out. The corners have vanished, and God is relegated to being a spectator.

One leader comments: "In this day of computers, consultants, and schooled experts, the 'mechanics' of doing business appear to be substituting for reliance on God."[4]

Guiltless Evangelism for Radical Repentance

Evangelism should be a sign of spiritual health, but several decades of easy-believism evangelistic methods have contributed to growing nominalism. New believers are prone to buy into Christianity at the level of commitment they observe in their first church.

Even churches professing a strong commitment to the fullness of the Spirit can fall for this substitute. We may unconsciously soft-pedal lordship at conversion, assuming that we will address it later at the filling of the Holy Spirit. George Verwer, director of Operation Mobilization, has this timely word of counsel: "Don't be afraid to put too much into salvation. There will be plenty left for sanctification."

The Holy Spirit is actively involved in genuine conversions. We are born again by the Spirit (Galatians 4:23). He's the key person in any evangelistic team. Jesus sent Him expressly to "convict the world of guilt in regard to sin and righteousness and judgment" (John 16:8). By the way, who concocted the heresy that all guilt is bad?

Self-Fulfilling Missions for God's Glory

For several decades, members of the "me" generation have become our missionaries. Many, unfortunately, do not last a year. Why? The answer is a common response: "Our expectation of fulfillment was not met." I have interviewed young pastoral couples interested in missions. When I probed their motivation, they frequently replied: "We think it would be good for us as a family, and we want our children to experience the mission field." At least three essential elements are missing in their response: the call of God, the passion for the lost and the glory of God.

Therapeutic Prayer for Brokenness

Could prayer become a substitute for revival? Short answer: Yes. I am greatly encouraged by the growing worldwide prayer movement, but let's recall God's first agenda item in the classic passage on revival: humble yourself, then pray (2 Chronicles 7:14). A.W. Tozer asks, "Is prayer enough for revival?" His answer: Only if it is mixed with brokenness and humility. Otherwise, he notes, "the prayer meeting room becomes a wailing wall and the lights burn long, and still the rains tarry."[5]

Church Growth for Church Health

The Church Growth Movement in the 1960s and 1970s rescued Western missions from their colonial tendencies and released the young churches to become responsible masters of their own destiny. But when introduced to North America in the pragmatism of the 1970s, it rapidly turned into a movement that made numbers a god.

This has translated into an inordinate passion for quantity versus quality.

Several new movements are, at the time of this writing, seeking to reverse this trend. SonLife Ministries, with a strong commitment to planting healthy churches, is a welcome voice. Another group, Natural Church Development, is based in Germany. I am encouraged by the new emphasis on healthy churches, but God's ultimate answer for healthy churches—a sweeping revival—continues to escape the technicians. In all of this growth promotion and pseudo progress, God has gotten some credit but little glory!

Christian Counseling for the Cross

The 20th century has been called the century of psychology. Evangelicals have bought deeply into this behavioral science. It has been a mixed love affair. Who could oppose an emphasis on self-worth and self-image? With due respect to those well-intentioned Christian counselors who apply biblical truth well, much of Christian counseling could be described by Vance Havner's comment: "We are operating a secondhand repair shop for the 'old Adam.' "

Skilled and godly counselors are special gifts to the Church. Their primary task is to help their clientele identify where the cross needs to be applied and the power of the Holy Spirit appropriated in their lives.

Profanity for Preaching

The craze to be seeker sensitive on Sunday morning has dumbed down biblical, prophetic preaching to skillfully honed talks which intentionally zero in on felt needs. Preaching has gone manward.

Ironically, this shift occurs immediately following thirty minutes of worship which has been Godward. John Piper raises the obvious question: "Why, after a half-hour of singing Godward worship choruses, does a preacher stand up and preach manward?" Piper analyzes it this way:

The preacher knows that, unlike the choruses where the lyrics carry the music, he has no such help. So he simply discovers how people are wired. He knows the hot buttons are pain, stress, intimacy, success, family and marriage, etc. He skillfully selects some biblical verses, mixes in some pop psychology along with some relevant illustrations, and he connects with his people's psyche.[6]

Result? God's people head into another week with some good self-help ideas, but they never connected with the one reality of the universe—God. Without the knowledge of who God is and the great doctrines that flow out of His nature, His people will never sense their need of renewal. The preacher failed to introduce them to God, the One who can meet all their felt needs, but more importantly their core spiritual needs. Any message that is not God-centered is superficial—profane.

Self-Serving for Selfless Giving

Church historians, with intrigue, will analyze the giving patterns of 20th-century Christians. They will be shocked by the radical shift from the early faith missions' policies of not making their needs known to the solicitation of support through direct mail.

Planned giving has become a major industry. Christian stewardship conferences focus specifically on techniques for successful fundraising. The name-it-and-claim-it movement has given a divine twist to fund-raising. The factor of charitable receipts for donations has evolved into the most significant extra-biblical motivation in the history of the church. Historians will puzzle over how it seemed possible to give to yourself and receive a taxable receipt!

Then there is the magic month of December. Not only do merchants make half of their year's sales in December, but Christian charities also live or die by year-end giving. All of this is in sharp contrast to the widow's mite, a reminder that motivation supercedes amount, and the uncomfortable admonition of Christ: "But when you give to the needy, do not let your left hand know what your right hand is doing" (Matthew 6:3). This constitutes a strong reminder of the private nature of true giving in contrast to the public, even competitive, methods of today.

Nothing we do as Christians becomes a more deceptive substitute for revival than our giving. A.B. Simpson preached a sermon on seven kinds of giving. He relegated four of them to the category of self-serving. He questioned giving for buying a church organ as true giving because it was for the donor's benefit; even supporting the pastor, who is hired to serve the donor's family, fell into that category.

In our day, Simpson would scrutinize our motivation in December giving when we must decide between giving more to our government or to our church and ourselves. He commended systematic and what he called "fair giving"—giving as much to God as to ourselves. But the seventh form of giving he described as "the heroic way, the self-sacrificing way, giving more than you can, giving until it hurts, and then giving until it does not hurt."[7] It was giving beyond ourselves, independent of personal kickbacks.

All of the above is typical of the evangelical churches I know, serve, attend, visit and love. All of the above appear acceptable, even good, on the surface. They all have tempted me, and I confess to being duped more than once. However, they represent the broken cisterns that superficially satiate genuine hunger for God, the visitation of the Spirit and the Word of God that judges the thoughts and attitudes of the heart.

From God's perspective, we have fallen victim to the delusion of the Laodicean church—deception: "We say we are rich and need nothing." Yet Christ describes us as "wretched, pitiful, poor, blind and naked." Out of love He appeals to us to "be earnest and repent" of our lukewarmness and self-sufficiency (Revelation 3:15-19).

It is interesting—and convicting—to note that all of these substitutes have at least one thing in common: They accommodate the self-life. We are never more creative than when we want to pamper and protect self. God's answer is the crucifixion of self and His provision for selfless living through the resurrection power of the Spirit. This is the real answer to historical drift.

The lyrics of Ron Owens' song expresses our prayer well:

> Lord, we've replaced Your glory with man-made
>   pageantry,
>   we're good at imitating wind and fire.
> We try to recreate, Lord, what only You can do;
>   we substitute our programs for Your power.
> Lord, we've dug our cisterns and tried to keep
>   them full
>   with new and better methods every day.
> In seeking for success, Lord, we'll go to any means
>   except to seek Your face, except to pray.[8]

Summary

So, how is the evangelical church doing so well without revival? Answer: We're getting by by replacing the supernatural with substitutes which appear to be serving quite well, but which can never pass the faith on to the next generation. We have compared ourselves with ourselves in the mirror of North American evangelicalism, and apparently our response is, "We're satisfied with man-made pageantry and imitating wind and fire." The God of the "living waters" continues to call us to repent and be restored through revival.

Here's the tragic bottom line: We who are His glory have turned to worthless idols. Whenever Christians are satisfied with substitutes, historical drift becomes even more subtle.

~

Discussion Questions

1. How do you respond to Tozer's statement: "Take away the Holy Spirit from the New Testament church and ninety-five percent of what is happening would stop. Take away the Holy Spirit from today's church and ninety-five percent would continue?"
2. Technology is always a mixed blessing. Discuss how we can harness it without allowing it to become a substitute for the supernatural.
3. How can you address the church's subtle satisfaction with substitutes?

Good News

Grace Hospital

G*race Hospital? What a strange topic for a message at a revival confer-ence,* I thought as I read the program. *The speaker must be a hospi-tal administrator!*

But as Al Henson began to speak, I quickly discovered he was the long-term pastor of The Lighthouse Church in Antioch, Tennessee. Although his ecclesiastical tradition was not known for a revival focus, God renewed him, and his church also experienced renewal.

I sensed, as he shared what God had done, that this church was marked by the supernatural. As their pastor, Henson was not dependent on the broken cisterns so prevalent in evangelicalism. Nor was he into man-made pageantry. Rather, he was leading his people to the Christ, the spring of living water.

What gave me this impression? Answer: Three simple experiences from their church life.

The first is centered on Grace Hospital. Every second Monday evening, a special service known as Grace Hospital is held at the church. It is primarily for new believers, but is open to all who have been victims of abuse. They sit around tables. Following a brief worship time, pastor Al introduces these hurting people to the God of justice—His commandments, His wrath against sin and His judgment of sin. He addresses questions such as: Why did God have to deal with sin in His creation? Why did He vent His wrath on His own Son?

After forty minutes of teaching, he then shares the grace of God—His love, His mercy, His forgiveness, His gift of salvation, His power to heal their brokenness. Then the people are encouraged to share their needs. A mature Christian is at each table prepared to assist individuals to receive God's grace in salvation and healing.

At the conference, I heard the testimony from two who had come through Grace Hospital. One woman, who had been abused for over twenty years, shared her testimony publicly for the first time. Pastor Al stood by her side. A young man later gave his testimony at a men only session.

In their city of Antioch, the word is out about Grace Hospital. The buzz on the street is: "Hurting people get help at The Lighthouse Church." Even the local social services department now refers people to Grace Hospital.

The second experience Pastor Al shared with us concerned prayer. Between Sunday school and the morning service, the church is prepared for worship. A group of about seventy-five men enter the sanctuary and spend fifteen minutes in united prayer. More than a powerful prayer statement to the congregation, it clears the heavenlies for the communication of God's Word.

And third, in keeping with their commitment to become a house of prayer, Al said they were considering a radical restructuring of their Sunday school. Every age level would have an intentional focus on learning to pray—from the preschooler sessions to the adult electives. The goal? Everyone, every Sunday, will be taught how to be committed to and effective in prayer.

How does a congregation know if it is running on broken cisterns or living water? It seems the answer is simple. How much do they depend on God through prayer alone? Every church has cosmetic and ceremonial prayer, but those who depend on the spring of living water live and die by corporate congregational prayer.[9]

"Oh, Lord, send us the old revival, without the defects; but if this cannot be, send it with *all* the defects. We must have the revival!"

—John Wesley, quoted in *Another Wave of Revival*

16

Wildfire or Real Fire?

Defining a Genuine Revival

IT GOES WITHOUT SAYING THAT we have all heard of revivals. Some revival enthusiasts tend to longingly recall the Great Awakenings of the 18th and 19th centuries. Such a practice begs the question: "Has anything happened since?" And, if it has, where did it happen, when did it happen and what happened? My intention is not to postulate a definitive criteria for genuine revival. Such an attempt is hazardous, but leaders must be discerning.

I found two bookends from Scripture—both related to spiritual experience—which are helpful in evaluating such religious phenomena and coming to a conclusion as to what constitutes a genuine revival. The first bookend is a biblical warning which speaks to all efforts to evaluate, pronounce on or discern between phenomena.

The Unpardonable Sin (Matthew 12:22-37)

In Matthew chapter 12, in the context of His healing a demon-possessed man who was blind and mute, Christ refers to the unpardonable sin (12:22). The Pharisees had been accusing Him of casting out demons through Beelzebub, the prince of demons (12:24). But Jesus countered with the "divided kingdom" argument: "Every kingdom divided against itself will be ruined, and every city or household divided against itself will not stand" (12:25), including Satan's kingdom (12:26-29). Immediately following this interaction, Jesus addresses the issue of "blasphemy against the Spirit" (12:30-32).

Theologians have vigorously debated this question. Personally, the intentional link between the Pharisees' accusation that Jesus had acted through the power of Satan and His declaration that blasphemy against the Spirit is unforgivable has always served as a strong check in my spirit. Whatever view we hold of the unforgivable sin, the context of this passage connects it with attributing to Satan that which is of God. This is the first bookend: how we distinguish what is of God and what is not.

Testing the Spirits (1 John 4:1-8)

The second bookend deals with the discerning of spirits included in the list of spiritual gifts in First Corinthians 12:10. Like most spiritual gifts, it is a special anointing for a specific area of ministry in which every Christian has some ability: i.e., we all have a measure of faith, but there is the gift of faith. We all can lay hands on the sick and pray for healing, but there is the gift of healings. Every Christian is admonished to be discerning, but there is the special ability to discern between spirits.

Under the title, "Biblical Signs of the True Spirit's Work," one scholar outlines the following criteria for judging what is of God and what is not, based on First John 4:1-8. The manifestation or working of the Holy Spirit will:

- exalt the true Christ: "By this you know the Spirit of God: every spirit that confesses that Jesus Christ has come in the flesh is of God, and every spirit that does not confess . . . Jesus . . . is not from God" (4:2-3, NKJV).
- oppose Satan's interests: "You are of God, little children, and have overcome them, because He who is in you is greater than he who is in the world. They are of the world. Therefore they speak as of the world, and the world hears them" (4:4-5, NKJV).
- elevate truth: "We know the spirit of truth and the spirit of error" (4:6, NKJV).
- result in love for God and others: "[The one] who does not love does not know God, for God is love" (4:8, NKJV).[1]

Matthew 12 and First John 4 are the bookends for my criteria in identifying some of the special visitations of God in the past century.

Upstreaming Revivals of the 20th Century

Let's first take a look at some of the obvious and unusual manifestations of God during the 20th century. This is not an exhaustive attempt by any means. Happily, that is not possible with a God who is always at work. But rather, it is an overview of places where God has manifested His presence and power to renew His people.

Texas (1999)

A student-led Passion Conference was held January 1-4 at the Fort Worth Convention Center. A sold-out crowd of 11,000 attended, double the 1998 figure. Attendees were encouraged to make a lifestyle decision based on the "268 Declaration" (inspired by Isaiah 26:8). It consisted of five points in which they committed themselves to be a part of a "generation that lives for the glory of [God's] name."[2]

Bethel College, Minneapolis (1997)

The voluntary Sunday night student-led meeting, known as Bethel's Vespers, doubled in only two years to 1,700. Estimates indicate that nearly half of the attendees came from the University of Minnesota and Northwestern College, plus some high schoolers.[3]

Wheaton College (1995)

In 1995, Wheaton's World Christian Fellowship (WCF) hosted a group of Howard Payne College students who had experienced a visitation from God. WCF, as a follow-up, initiated five days to seek God for a spiritual outpouring. Meetings lasted until two and three in the morning. Students awaiting the cleansing opportunity of public confession formed long lines. Reconciliations were commonplace. Crowds of 1,800 forced them to find larger facilities. Wheaton sent teams of students to other campuses to share God's blessing.[4]

The Father's Day Outpouring: Pensacola, Florida (1995)

141,000 decisions for Christ were recorded; 2.6 million people have attended; 1,600 watch on closed-circuit TV in overflow facilities; regional conferences called "Awake America" have been hosted and a School of Ministry established.[5]

The Toronto Blessing (1994)

Its influence spread to an estimated 50,000 churches worldwide; more than 20,000 people have professed to making first-time commitments to Christ; an estimated 2.8 million people have visited the Toronto church (now called the Toronto Airport Christian Fellowship); more than 7,000 people of various denominations in the United Kingdom have been impacted.[6]

Hope College, Holland, Michigan (early 1990s)

Hope College could have been called post-evangelical in the early 1990s. Voluntary chapel for a student body of 2,500 had dwindled to an attendance of twenty to forty. Today 800 to 1,000 fervent worshipers make their way to the chapel four times a week. Following the Sunday evening meeting, it is not uncommon for seventy-five percent of them to remain for praise well into the night.[7]

Western Canada (1971)

Two years of prayer preceded the Sutera Twins meetings in Saskatoon, Saskatchewan in 1971. People crowded the altar confessing sin. Reconciliations of families and marriages occurred. Many churches joined in. Crowds grew to 3,000 in the city's civic auditorium. Lay teams spread the flame of revival far beyond the province.[8]

Solomon Islands (1970)

There had been an earlier revival in 1936. Nationals and missionaries prayed for revival for a year. A letter was sent to 300 churches urging them to pray daily. Revival broke out in a congregation of 600. They moved to a location which held 2,000. A team of nationals touched by revival crisscrossed the island of Malaita. Many of the people threw their fetishes into the sea.[9]

Asbury College, Wilmore, Kentucky (1970)

It was a regular Tuesday morning chapel service. The assigned speaker chose to simply share what God had done in his life. He encouraged others to share. A senior shocked them with his confession. The unusual chapel service concluded 185 hours later. By the end of the summer, 130 campuses were touched, and teams visited five continents.[10]

Scotland (1949)

The churches in the Hebrides were almost empty. A group of men led by a minister prayed three nights a week for revival. After five months they began confessing their sin. God's power descended. Conviction of sin struck people everywhere. Within two days the drinking house was permanently closed. Nearly every young person aged twelve to twenty was converted in that town within forty-eight hours.[11]

Congo (1929, now The Republic of Congo)

Christians were returning to their pagan practices. The missionaries prayed with fasting for two years. The glory of God came and flooded the countryside. Thousands responded with confession and repentance, extending for hundreds of kilometers in all directions. Thirty-three years later, aspects of the revival continued that ignited a generation of African pastors.[13]

Burma (1916, now Myanmar)

James Fraser was discouraged in his attempt to reach the Lisu tribe who worshiped demons and ate vile food. He prayed and made one last trip to their villages. He planned to abandon the tribe if no interest was shown. In the first home, the family asked if they could turn from demon worship. Calls came from other villages wanting to turn to God. In a short period, 20,000 of the Lisu became Christians.[14]

Korea (1907)

Missionaries were facing difficult years just prior to World War I. Revival came through a teacher from South Africa, Miss Aletta Jacobsz. She asked them to write out their sins. She then would lead them through repentance and restoration. Many missionaries, including Jonathan Goforth, were revived and soon scattered due to the war. During Goforth's last term, his ministry was marked by revival in China.[12]

Azusa Street (1906)

The afterglow of the Welsh revival impacted the greater Los Angeles area. Evan Roberts was praying for California. Revival fires were kindled in Pasadena. A group of students in Topeka, Kansas had spoken in tongues. These streams merged into a mighty river which became the historic three-year Azusa Street movement in Los Angeles. Pentecostalism, which today represents the largest segment of Christianity apart from Catholicism, was born.[15]

Wales (1904)

Church membership was in decline. Keswick Conferences continued to be held. Seth Joshua asked God to raise up someone from the mines. God's answer was Evan Roberts. His meetings attracted large crowds, and more than 100,000 were added to the church in six months. Police reported a sixty percent decrease in drunkenness and forty percent fewer people in jail. Life in the mines was impacted. Cursing and profanity diminished. Pit ponies could no longer understand their drivers.[16]

Summary

What a legacy! God launched the 20th century with two major revivals. These and many of those that followed had their flaws, defects and aberrant behaviors. But in His sovereignty God used them even as they dealt with the heretical fringes and consolidated their Christology.

The following commentaries of earlier spiritual giants are encouraging as we await God's visitation early in the 21st century.

- "A religious movement almost always exceeds a just moderation. In order that human nature may make one step in advance, its pioneers must take many." (D'Aubigne)
- "Oh, Lord, send us the old revival, without the defects; but if this cannot be, send it with *all* its defects. We must have the revival!" (John Wesley)
- "Nature, along with Satan, will always mingle themselves, as far as they can, in the genuine work of the Spirit in order to discredit and destroy it. In great revivals of religion, it is almost impossible to prevent wildfire from getting in among the true fire." (Adam Clark)[17]

Let me add my own commentary: "Until we are ready to handle wildfire we will never experience real fire."

Let's consolidate our thinking regarding revivals by asking the question, "What do all these revivals have in common?"

- They were preceded by prayer.
- There were elements of surprise.
- There were evidences of the supernatural.
- They were born in a context of discontent.
- They sometimes included controversial manifestations or practices.
- They impeded and/or reversed historical drift.

Do Revivals Really Make a Difference?

We're talking about revivals in the context of historical drift. Considerable time has been spent on ways and means of impeding the seemingly inevitable process of drift. Such labor should be the everyday stuff of responsible Christian leadership. But, in God's graciousness and love for His Church, He sometimes intervenes sovereignly with times of refreshing which I'm calling revival—special but temporary divine occurrences with varying levels and length of impact.

We realize that most of Christian ministry happens between such "footprints of God." Revivals aren't intended to last. They come and go. Their transitory nature is inherent in the term revival—to resuscitate, relive, renew, recommit, return again to God. Revival is God's tender provision for His people who are prone to wander.

What, then, is the impact of revival? Let's begin by noting the impact of restored leaders. David's psalm of repentance is a prime Old Testament illustration. Following a series of pleas for pardon and cleansing, he declares: "Then I will teach transgressors your ways, and sinners will turn back to you" (Psalm 51:13).

There is also a New Testament reminder of the impact of revived leaders. Jesus' promise to a waffling Peter is a powerful example: "I have prayed for you, Simon, that your faith may not fail. And when you have turned back, strengthen your brothers" (Luke 22:32). Despite Peter's protestation to the contrary, he proceeded to deny his Jesus three times during the Passion Week. But, in answer to Christ's promised prayer, Peter repents. He's present in the upper room, awaiting Pentecost. As part of the 120, united in prayer, Peter is filled with the Holy Spirit. Christ's prophetic word that Peter would "strengthen his brothers" is dramatically fulfilled when he stands and preaches with anointing at Pentecost, the greatest revival recorded in Scripture.

What has been the impact of renewal in Church history? Succinctly stated: If God's people, led by revived leaders, had not responded to the Spirit's call to repentance, we would not have a Church today. Consider the following footprints of God and their impact on subsequent generations.

18th-Century England

Religion had hit a new low. Absentee clergymen were paid by the state. Poverty, crime, drunkenness, injustice and corruption prevailed. Into this desperate situation God brought the revived Wesley brothers. They had traveled to the New World as missionaries, but their ministry there was a dismal failure. Returning on a ship to England, they experienced stormy seas.

The testimony of Moravian missionaries on the same ship profoundly impressed the Wesleys. These Moravians had a peace of heart and total trust in God unknown by John and Charles Wesley. Upon returning to England, they had an experience with God at Aldersgate that transformed their spiritual lives. Their ministry became directed to the poor and was done outside and independently of the Church of England. Historians attest that the Wesleyan movement literally saved

England from a revolution such as the French endured. The event became known as the First Great Awakening.[18]

19th-Century North America

The Second Great Awakening spilled over into the 19th century (1790-1840) and impacted Yale, which became a strong church college. The businessmen's revival, 1857-59, in New York, began with six men and grew to 10,000 in six months. Impact? Revival became the major contributor to the establishing of many great and ongoing organizations: Faith Missionary Societies, the Bible school movement (Moody in Chicago 1885; Nyack in New York, 1882), prophetic ministries and, at the close of the century, the Student Volunteer Movement.

20th-Century World

The 20th century was launched by a mighty moving of God—the Wales revival in 1904. The Azusa Street events in Los Angeles came two years later. The Pentecostal movement dates its birth to the spiritual phenomena of 1906. Although its origin was controversial, it has experienced incredible growth worldwide.

What triumphs in world evangelization do we celebrate as we reflect on the 20th century? The following, each related to revival and awakening, are but three of many.

The Evangelization of Latin America

At the Edinburgh International Missionary Conference in 1910, South America was not even mentioned. However, by the end of the 20th century, strong national churches were established in every country, with the status of Cuba being somewhat undefined. Although again controversial at times, the Pentecostals have been the major player in this tremendous impact of the evangelical church in Latin America.

People Movements

People Movements, a version of an awakening and a term coined by Donald McGavran, have characterized the rapid growth of Christianity in animistic cultures. The term describes the conversion of ethnically defined groups which come to Christ en masse. Whole tribes have been reached through such movements: e.g., the Lisu tribe in Burma, 1916, and the Dani tribe in Irian Jaya, 1960s. In 1929, a Congo revival along tribal lines ignited a whole generation of African pastors.

Korean Revival (1939)

The rapid growth of the church in South Korea has impacted the entire evangelical world in the latter part of the 20th century. It began with the revival of 1939. With their trademark being the early morning prayer meeting, the South Korean Church continues to model not only prayer and growth, but also missionary vision. The initial revival also became the catalyst for the renewal movement in parts of China prior to the coming of communism in 1949.

~

Discussion Questions

1. Do you think John MacArthur's criteria for a genuine revival are adequate?
2. The author states "Until we are prepared to handle wildfire we will never experience real fire." Do you think this fear of "wild fire" is a significant deterrent to revival for Christian leaders? Why?
3. Which of the examples of "revivals that made a difference" catches your attention?

Good News

On the Move through Prayer

King of Kings Community Church (Christian and Missionary Alliance) in Manahawkin, New Jersey is on the move through prayer. "Prayer is behind everything we have done here," says Pastor Pat Sharkey.

In 1994, when Sharkey was appointed pastor, the congregation was thirty people. In 1999, more than 400 attend, much of the growth through conversions (220 in 1998 alone), and they are "bursting at the seams."

There are so many prayer groups it is impossible to keep track. One meets at 6 a.m. Monday through Saturday. And Thursdays are special—almost eight solid hours of prayer by various groups throughout the day. Kids, too, are learning to pray for such things as the nation's leadership, the sick and each other.

The congregation is in the process of expanding their facility by five times to include a gymnasium with basketball courts under one roof. "When they come in to play, they'll also get the opportunity to hear God's Word," says the six-foot-five-inch Sharkey.

This congregation on the Atlantic Ocean also believes that the tide of prayer will wash over other communities within a ten-mile radius. Despite major commitments to their own facility, the church is expanding to nearby Tuckerton where they will plant Lighthouse Alliance Church in keeping with the city's building project of a replica colonial seaport. In the process, King of Kings will give up seventy members—some of their best people—including their present assistant pastor, Steve Hartman.

"We're hoping that Tuckerton will give birth to a church of its own someday so that King of Kings can become a grandparent!" says Sharkey.[19]

"I would rather fail in that which will ultimately succeed than to succeed in that which will ultimately fail."

—Dr. Ralph Winter, Founder of
the U.S. Center of World Mission

17

Why the Passion for Revival?

Developing a Dissatisfaction with Comfortable Christianity

REVIVAL IS GOD'S COMPASSIONATE CALL to His people to re-vive—to live again. Immediately following our first parents' grievous sin, God reached out with hope, addressing the serpent: "And I will put enmity between you and the woman, and between your off-spring and hers; he will crush your head, and you will strike his heel" (Genesis 3:15). To remind them of His coming sacrifice as God, He "made garments of skin . . . and clothed them" (3:21).

Revival—It's the Heart of God

Again, God's persistent call through the prophets was, "Return to me, for I have redeemed you" (Isaiah 44:22). " 'Return, faithless Israel,' declares the LORD, 'I will frown on you no longer, for I am merciful,' declares the LORD" (Jeremiah 3:12). " 'Return to me, and I will return to you,' says the LORD Almighty" (Malachi 3:7).

Jesus, during His three years of ministry, tirelessly extended the invitation: "Come to me, all you who are weary and burdened, and I will give you rest" (Matthew 11:28). Even from the cross He issued one last call: "Father, forgive them, for they do not know what they are doing" (Luke 23:34). Then in His final words, following the resurrection, He gave an invitation to a church which had drifted: "Here I am! I stand at the door and knock. If anyone hears my voice and opens the door, I will come in and eat with him, and he with me" (Revelation 3:20).

Yes, I am passionate about revival because it is the very heart of God for His people.

Revival—It Addresses Historical Drift

I am also passionate about revival because I bumped into historical drift early. My spiritual life during my teens matched the double-minded man James describes, "unstable in all he does" (James 1:8). Then I discovered God had a higher road. I met the Holy Spirit—the missing Person in my life. My drifting life in my teens was transformed into a dynamic life of growth in the twenties.

At that time, in God's providence, He led me into a newly revived church. That church marked me for life in four key areas: 1) I saw and experienced the power of corporate prayer; 2) I was caught up in a holy enthusiasm for evangelism which was happening spontaneously; 3) I met my first "live missionary," and I discovered that missions was not a project but a passion. It seemed easy and natural in that church to respond to God's call to missions. But, 4) it was the church's commitment to what they called "the deeper life" that gave me a message for life. I learned that salvation is only the beginning of the Christian walk.

God's Spirit worked mightily in revival, especially among the leaders of that church, addressing historical drift. The imprint of that revived church hardwired me for life with a holy dissatisfaction with the status quo of a cozy, comfortable, cultural Christianity.

Revival—It's the Promise of Pentecost

We all acknowledge that the Day of Pentecost was a one-of-a-kind historical event. Peter explained it as the fulfillment of Joel's prophecy (Acts 2:16-21). Most agree that it marked the birth of the Church. I believe it is also the major biblical basis for expecting continued times of revival, times when God pours out His Spirit in special visitations.

Peter witnessed one of these *kairos* moments in the house of Cornelius, the Gentile. His response was: "Can anyone keep these people from being baptized with water? They have received the Holy Spirit just as we have" (10:47). Later, in Jerusalem, he explained this experience to the other apostles: "As I began to speak, the Holy Spirit came on them as he had come on us at the beginning" (11:15).

Peter connected what God did for these Gentiles as an extension of the Day of Pentecost. And Joel's prophecy (Joel 2:28-32), which Peter quoted, is set in the context of the last days. "In the last days, God says, I will pour out my Spirit on all people" (Acts 2:17). This is a familiar term used by most of the writers of the New Testament Epistles, e.g., Second Timothy 3:1; Hebrews 1:2; James 5:3; First Peter 1:20; First John 2:18 and Jude 18. It is generally interpreted as referring to the period beginning at Pentecost and culminating in The Day of the Lord and the unfolding end-time events.

I believe that during these last days we can expect times of revival and awakenings, times when God pours out His Spirit on all people (Acts 2:17). Note two of the characteristics of these visitations. It will be for both "sons and daughters" and "men and women" (2:17-18). A Spirit-sent revival takes care of the contentious issues such as gender equality in leadership roles. It also resolves the sometime preoccupation of churches to be generation specific; e.g., "Young men will see visions, your old men will dream dreams" (2:17). I believe these are clear indications that God is about to break in upon us again.

Revival—It's Our Greatest Need

The evangelical church in the West is strong. Numerically it has become an influential voice in the Protestant world. It has moved from being a sideline church to replacing the dying mainline churches. Politically, in the United States, evangelicals played a critical role in presidential elections in the second half of the last century, and they continue to dominate the religious media. Economically, evangelicalism is a growing giant. Its subsidiary enterprises are enjoying phenomenal growth in the marketplace, e.g., Christian bookstores, publishing houses, seminaries, colleges, retreat and counseling centers, parachurch movements, etc.

These observations defend success in our culture and increasingly in the evangelical church. However, from God's perspective, nothing has changed since the days of David's anointing. "The LORD does not look at the things man looks at. Man looks at the outward appearance, but the LORD looks at the heart" (1 Samuel 16:7). What does God see when He looks at the heart of evangelicalism?

From my vantage point as a Christian leader with broad exposure to a cross section of evangelicals, revival is desperately needed. The desperation becomes a stark reality, and our greatest embarrassment, when faced with interpersonal conflict situations and the inability to apply biblical principles to resolve conflicts in our churches and other Christian agencies.

We are the people who should best understand forgiveness. We have experienced it through Christ. We are the only ones to whom Christ gave the ministry of reconciliation. We have the message that everyone needs—reconciliation. And only we have it. But talk to bishops, superintendents, pastoral care personnel and Christian counselors who invest weeks and months mediating conflicts. The steps of Matthew 18:15-20 are rarely followed. The admonition of Paul in First Corinthians 6:1-8 against taking other Christians to court is summarily ignored in most cases.

Instead, we resort to secular answers: generous severance packages which become hush money; politically orchestrated transfers to another geographic jurisdiction; the intervention of Christian mediation groups; the use of legal counsel, to name a few. This has become our Achilles' heel, our most vulnerable area, our most public confession of our greatest impotence. It becomes the stuff the media plays up.

What is God's answer? "The sacrifices of God are a broken spirit; a broken and contrite heart, O God, you will not despise" (Psalm 51:17). Where are the Nathans who will say, "You are the man!" (2 Samuel 12:7)? And where are the Davids who will respond, "I have sinned against the LORD" (2 Samuel 12:13)? In most conflicts, if only one of the protagonists would make such a confession, the disputes would dissolve overnight. The appalling absence of brokenness over sin is the greatest indicator of our desperate need for revival.

Revival—I've Tasted It

Finally, I'm passionate about revival because I've tasted revival, and I refuse to be satisfied with anything less.

The setting was very much like the days prior to Pentecost. One hundred and twenty believers without a pastor began meeting together for prayer. The country was being governed by a leftist military junta. Their upper room in Jerusalem was in a large old colonial house on a busy avenue in the bustling city of Lima, Peru. Time? The early 1970s.

God answered their first prayer. He sent them a pastor from Argentina, then He responded above and beyond their expectations by recruiting two more outsiders, a Canadian missionary and an American businessman, who shared a vision. Their dream was to establish large urban churches throughout Latin America, located on highly visible streets and each seating 1,000 persons or more. Where would the first one be? Lima.

Funds became supernaturally available. Within months, the 120 people from the house church were meeting in a four-story Christian education building with a packed auditorium seating 450. From there they moved into the new sanctuary next door with a capacity for 1,000. "And the Lord added to their number daily those who were being saved" (Acts 2:47).

My family and I joined this moving of God in 1976. By that time, a second large church was being established across town. What we were about to experience would revolutionize the rest of our lives. I had been in ministry twenty-five years, but I had never experienced, nor would ever experience, what happened in Lima during the next three years. Here are but a few of the highlights:

- A Bumper Harvest: They had established a monthly rhythm—two weeks of an evangelistic crusade in the church followed by two weeks of Bible academy for teaching new believers. We would expect 100 professions of faith during each crusade. Often between 200 to 300 responded. This continued month after month during my three years.

- Simultaneous Baptisms: Less than half of those who responded followed through to baptism. Nevertheless, there were frequent and large baptismal services. The high numbers of candidates required lengthy services. The second large church, built for 2,000, found a creative solution. They built two baptismal tanks. Two pastors officiated. As one would question his candidate and then immerse the person, the other pastor would raise his hand to identify and baptize his candidate.

- Decision to Suspend the Harvest: I had never been in such a meeting before. The leaders, pastors and missionaries convened a meeting to deal with an urgent problem. The harvest was exceeding our ability to adequately disciple the large number of converts. The question became: "Should we suspend the harvest to do catch-up?" Around and around went the discussion looking for a consensus. (They had never heard of *Roberts' Rules of Order*.) Finally, a pastor said, "Brothers, if we stop evangelizing we will die." Everyone agreed. Meeting dismissed. *¡Adelante con la cosecha!* (*"Let's move ahead with the harvest!"*)

- Hunger for the Word: I have taught many students, but never had I faced a class where all were new Christians. In the monthly crusades, I watched them take copious notes of the messages of the visiting evangelists. The people came straight from their jobs, without eating, to attend the evening Bible school. One night, after I taught the importance of prayer in a class, I found a group praying on the stairs during the break. When crusades were on in the church next door, classes were dismissed early so the students could serve as counselors at the altar to lead people to Christ. Teaching new believers spoils you forever for teaching Ephesians for the fourteenth time to treadmill saints!

What Is Revival?

I was anxious for my students to hear about what God had been doing in the Western Canadian revival in 1971. My colleague, Pastor Walter Boldt, came and shared how revival had impacted him and his church. I waited almost breathlessly for the students' response. There wasn't any! Their body language seemed to say, "Well, what's so special about that?" Then it hit me. These young people had never lost their first love. Revival did not make sense to them.

Revival Impacts the Church

The revival, however, began to have its effect. Two pastors in the same church got crossways in their relationship. Their church was growing rapidly through the monthly crusades. The conflict was serious, so serious that it would have split ninety percent of the churches I know. They could have canceled all special meetings. But not these men. They believed that evangelism must continue. And it did. The conflict was resolved as a "tempest in a teapot" on the side, and God honored a church that honored His agenda of reaching lost people.

Revival Impacts Society

How do you reach a city of 4 million with the gospel? Attractive buildings? Good exposure? Radio and television ministries? Billboards? The Lima churches used all of these. But God's original plan still works—He uses salt and light to penetrate society. It became known that "the evangelicals were honest, hardworking people." Companies wanted to hire them. The international airport was plagued with corruption in their customs department. They heard about the evangelicals, hired people from our churches and bussed them to and from the airport.

Summary

What do you call the Lima story? In Spanish it was, *Lima al Encuentro con Dios*—Lima's Encounter with God. Was it just successful evangelism in a responsive culture? Was it revival? Was it an awakening impacting society? Answer: It was a wonderful inscrutable divine complexity of all the above.

All I can say is, "Oh God, do it again and again and again."

Discussion Questions

1. The author outlines four reasons for his passion for revival. Which of these resonate most with your heart?
2. What will it take to disturb our comfort zone with our cozy, cultural, version of Christianity?
3. Do businesses in your city or town want to hire evangelical Christians? Why or why not?

Good News

Sequel: Lima in the 1990s

I believe that the best church in the New Testament was Antioch, Syria. I am sure it would score high on Christian Schwarz' scale for "Natural Church Growth" and Dann Spader's "Perspective on Healthy Churches." More importantly, God gave the Antioch church high marks. The Holy Spirit selected Antioch over Jerusalem as the mother church for world evangelization. The missionary enterprise was born in that pagan city.

It's also significant that the disciples "were first called Christians in Antioch" (Acts 11:26, NKJV). The window on the church in Antioch, Acts 11:19-30, profiles a healthy body of believers effectively evangelizing and discipling "a great number of people" (11:21, 24). Then, in Acts 13:1-3, the Holy Spirit breaks into a time of prayer and fasting with a request: He asks them to include world missions in their vision.

I have introduced you to a Lima, Peru church powerful in evangelism. But, at the time of this writing, God is doing a new thing in Lima. The good news is that they are following the model of Antioch. To their aggressive evangelism, they have now added missions.

Early in the 1990s, the senior pastor of the mother church read a book that transformed his ministry. *A Passion for Souls* is one of the many books written by Oswald J. Smith of People's Church fame in Toronto, Canada. What Pastor Pepe Chavez heard God saying in that book was this: "Churches need to do what Antioch did—give their best to missions." He began encouraging several of the best pastors on his staff to move into church planting in the provinces, then he launched their first missionary convention.

I was asked to be one of their speakers at the second convention. I experienced one more of those never-before events. I couldn't understand why there would be lineups outside the church Sunday evening.

The answer: "It was the last free service before the missionary conference would begin on Monday." A registration fee equivalent to six dollars U.S. was being charged for the missionary conference that would
begin Monday and run through Sunday! And registrations were cut off
at 1,300! (The church officially seats 1,000.)

The schedule each evening started at 5:30 with a seminar. The evening featured special reports from their own missionaries whom they
had brought home, their church planters in the provinces and video
clips from overseas fields. The plenary speaker followed a brief food
break at 7:30.

On Friday I asked the senior pastor, "When does your staff rest?"

"Not for a while," he responded, "because next week we move into a
week of evangelistic services." (The provincial church planters, who
were part of the missions conference, would be the evangelists for the
following week.)

Lima's Encounter with God concept has spread to most of the countries of Latin America and into other parts of the world.

I visited Lima in February of 2000. When I left in 1978, there were
four Alliance churches in that city. I discovered that there are now
forty-two.

"I am willing to fail. Risks are not to be evaluated in terms of the possibilities of success but in terms of the value of the goal."

—Ralph Winter, *Christianity Today*, September 7, 1985, p. 18.

Part VI

HISTORICAL DRIFT REVIEWED

I've got good news for leaders. But before we explore that, let me crystallize my theses:

- Historical drift erodes all social structures including Christian organizations.
- Although it's inevitable, this subtle process can be impeded and even reversed.
- The biblical record demonstrates its effects and provides God's answers.
- The social sciences recognize, analyze and market techniques of response.
- Organizations don't drift—only the people who lead them.
- Culture and even the Church tend to address historical drift through structural renewal.

- God, in His response, focuses on the spiritual renewal of
  leaders.

My challenge to leaders is similar to what Francis Schaeffer, the
popular Christian apologist, bequeathed to the evangelical world
thirty years before this new millennium. He gave his life to coura-
geously confronting Western culture on the abortion question and related sanctity of life issues. His parting question to Christian leaders
was: "How shall we then live?"

I've attempted to grapple with the broader and more subtle issue—historical drift. My challenge to you in this closing chapter is:
"How must we then lead?"

"If we are not living our lives on the wave length of the Great Commission, our lives are irrelevant to the destiny of history."

—Robert Coleman, Professor at Trinity Evangelical Seminary

18

How Must We Then Lead?

Understanding the Times, Seizing the Moment

I'VE DESCRIBED SPECIAL VISITATIONS OF GOD as His footprints in history. We would all agree that much of Christian ministry happens between those footprints. The operative question becomes: "How do I lead my people in the in-between times?"

Western culture, especially in the latter half of the 20th century, prided itself in the departmentalization of life. One businessman confessed he operated with three consciences: one that works at home, a second in his office and the third in church on Sunday. This is heresy for Christianity. Jesus called those who operated with such duplicity "whitewashed tombs" (Matthew 23:27). He rebuked the Sardis church for having "a reputation of being alive," yet being dead (Revelation 3:1). Wisdom from Proverbs states it succinctly: "For as he [man] thinks in his heart, so is he" (Proverbs 23:7, NKJV). Paul, admonishing Timothy, a young leader, clearly links private life and public ministry with these words: "Watch your life and doctrine closely" (1 Timothy 4:16).

There must be a seamless blend of life and leadership. The inner and the outer must be congruous. Out of such integrity, I challenge you to lead and to impede drift. I believe the Holy Spirit is searching for leaders who will live and lead as Jesus did for such a time as this.

Leading from Our Knees

The day was special. An inner-city church was being officially organized with thirty-four charter members. Many had labored for seven long years to see this day. After the service, I commended the senior pastor's wife on their accomplishment. She responded quietly, "My husband leads from his knees."

Prayer is the Christian's vital breath and native air. We all promote it verbally. Every new initiative is launched with the reminder: "We must bathe this ministry in prayer." But our talk too often fails to match our walk. J. Oswald Sanders calls this a "strange paradox": "We pay lip service to the delight and potency and value of prayer. We assert that it is an indispensable adjunct of mature spiritual life. We know that it is constantly enjoined and exemplified in the Scriptures. But, in spite of all, too often we fail to pray."[1]

Prayer is the very essence of Christianity. It was the only thing Christ's disciples ever asked Him to teach them (Luke 11:2-4). Prayer is to be the heart of the Church. Jesus declared: "My house will be called a house of prayer" (Matthew 21:13).

A new staff member of a large church was unhappy that she was expected to attend an 8:30 prayer time each weekday. However, her attitude quickly changed when she discovered that her senior pastor came to the church at 5:30 each morning for prayer. It's a probing question: Are we leading from our knees? The following tough test questions will reveal the honest answer to that question:

- Personal Life: How important would your children consider prayer to be based on what they see in your private and family prayer life?
- Marriage: Would your spouse describe your leadership as "leading from your knees"?
- Professional Life: Is your prayer life commensurate with your sphere of ministry responsibility?
- Leadership: How would your staff rate the importance of prayer in ministry based on what they see in your leadership?

Leaders Who Lead with the Book

Before Youth for Christ coined their motto, "Anchored to the Rock but Geared to the Times," the Sons of Issachar had their own version. They were described as those "who understood the times and knew what Israel should do" (1 Chronicles 12:32). We all want this balance—elevating God's Word yet relating its truths to our generation.

John Wesley, the itinerant preacher, carried in his buggy a wide selection of classical literature and medical journals. Even though he was widely read, he was known as "a man of one Book." Our authority comes from the One Book. Jesus stood out in His day "because he taught as one who had authority" (Matthew 7:29). In today's milieu of religious pluralism, the Christian leader will command attention—especially if he or she believes Scripture is absolute truth in all that it addresses.

Protestantism has not fared well in holding to the authority of the Scriptures. Malcolm Muggeridge, for one, couldn't trust Protestants to hold firm. He converted to Catholicism. Why? Here's his answer: "It was the Catholic Church's firm stand against contraception and abortion which finally made me decide to become a Catholic."[2]

A.W. Tozer reminds us that evangelicals have drifted far from the authority of Jesus:

> Jesus Christ has today almost no authority at all among the groups that call themselves by His name. By these I mean not the Roman Catholics, nor the Liberals, nor the various quasi-Christian cults. I do mean Protestant churches generally, and I include those that protest the loudest they are in a spiritual descent from our Lord and His apostles, namely evangelicals.[3]

God's Word has always been counterculture. Although that sounds negative, it's actually very positive. As people trapped in a decadent society come to Christ, the quality of their lives becomes meaningful and their relationships are transformed. Evangelism doesn't just confront—it care-fronts with Christ's love.

In the last century, two gifted young evangelists were struggling with their doubts about the Bible. One decided to affirm its authority and work on his doubts along the way. The other chose to reject the Bible and go with his doubts. He left the faith. The first became famous for repeating the phrase, "The Bible says!" His name is Billy Graham. The other developed a career in the media. His name is Charles Templeton.

More Tough Test Questions

- Personal Life: When was the last time the Word of God caused me to confront drift in my lifestyle choices?
- Professional Life: Do I give priority to Scripture in my public ministry?
- Do I go to Scripture for answers when dealing with subtle evidences of drift in board meetings?

- How do I communicate the absolute authority of the Bible in my public worship services?

Thinking Christianly

Thinking Christianly? My computer rejects "Christianly" as proper English. The phrase implies the existence of a Christian mind. Consider the biblical evidence: "Blessed is the man who does not walk in the counsel of the wicked or stand in the way of sinners or sit in the seat of mockers. But his delight is in the law of the LORD, and on his law he meditates day and night" (Psalm 1:1-2).

Yes, there's a Christian way to think about everything in life. Paul assures us that we can "have the mind of Christ" (1 Corinthians 2:16). He admonishes us to nurture it: "Let this mind be in you which was also in Christ Jesus" (Philippians 2:5, NKJV). Our infatuation with brilliant secular minds makes us easy candidates for historical drift. Here's a wake-up call from Paul's understanding of the non-Christian mind:

- It is darkened: "You must no longer live as the Gentiles do, in the futility of their thinking. They are darkened in their understanding and separated from the life of God . . ." (Ephesians 4:17-18).
- It is corrupted: "Both their minds and consciences are corrupted. They claim to know God, but by their actions they deny him" (Titus 1:15-16).
- It is destitute of truth: "Men of corrupt mind, who have been robbed of the truth and who think that godliness is a means to financial gain" (1 Timothy 6:5).
- It is dead: "The mind of sinful man is death. . . . It does not submit to God's law, nor can it do so" (Romans 8:6-7).

If we would be leaders who impede drift, we must have a healthy distrust in the unregenerate human mind. Ever since the serpent in the

Garden of Eden, the focus of the battle has been the mind. Historical drift begins in the mind. As Spirit-filled leaders with transformed minds, we can and must help our people to think Christianly in every area of life.

The challenges are becoming ever more complex. What about going on the ultimate shopping trip to choose the genetic makeup of your baby? What about the morning-after pill? Is it a self-induced abortion? The German holocaust awakened the world to the depravity of the human mind. Highly educated individuals—and nations—are capable of executing holocausts and ethnic cleansings.

How will we protect our minds? The battle for the mind is becoming ever more intense. The venues for pornography have extended their devious tentacles into the privacy of our bedrooms and offices via video and the Internet. I agree with Billy Graham. "I'm shocked that I am no longer shocked!" Drift has already eroded my defense system.

More Tough Test Questions

- Personal Life: How does my thought life, as a Christian leader, align with Paul's counsel to the Philippians? "Finally, brothers, whatever is true, whatever is noble, whatever is right, whatever is pure, whatever is lovely, whatever is admirable—if anything excellent or praiseworthy—think about such things" (Philippians 4:8-9). How much of my counsel comes from the ungodly, e.g., respectable secular professionals?
- Professional Life: "How much of my strategizing in ministry comes from the voice of the marketer compared with the voice of the Maker? How well does my mind balance relevance and revelation?

With a Towel—Serving Selflessly

Servant leadership is affirmed by all but delivered by few. Every leadership seminar leader doffs his hat to it. After all, Jesus, the leader par excellence, modeled it. But the motivational seminar leader usually hustles on to the real issues: efficiency, expediency and excellence.

Back to my premise: "Organizations don't drift—only the people who lead them." Service is the buzzword in the marketplace: "When you buy from us, you buy service." It has, unfortunately, also evolved into a denominational headquarter's strategy: e.g., We must be perceived as serving the churches and adding value to our pastors. Servant leadership can easily degenerate into one more self-serving gimmick thinly veiled as a biblical model.

Let's recall the original model of "towel" servanthood. The room was pregnant with tension, and Jesus captured a teachable moment. The disciples had just come from that nasty discussion on the road as to who would be the greatest. Their feet were dusty and tired, but no one reached for a towel and a basin. So Jesus seized the opportunity. He took the towel and assumed the role of a servant, fully aware of the presence of Judas who would betray Him and of another who would deny Him three times (John 13:3-5).

What was and is the lesson? Those in authority must lead through humility. "I have set you an example that you should do as I have done for you. I tell you the truth, no servant is greater than his master, nor is a messenger than the one who sent him" (13:15-16).

A bishop who was highly esteemed always referred to the janitor at the office as Mr. Brown. His secretary questioned him: "How come everyone around this office calls him Ted, yet you refer to the janitor as Mr. Brown?"

"That's the way it ought to be," replied the bishop. Historical drift takes a major hit when genuine servants lead with a towel.

We need leaders who exert healthy pressure on the establishment. Genuine Christian servant leadership makes a counterculture statement to the corporate CEO image that evangelical leaders sometimes mimic. Jesus made it clear that the world system of leadership—lording it over their followers—would not be tolerated in His kingdom (Matthew 20:24-28).

Do you, do I identify with the author of the following lines?

> I am like James and John. Lord, I size up other people in terms of what they can do for me; how they can further my program, feed my ego, satisfy my needs, give me strategic advantage. I exploit people, ostensibly for your sake, but really for my own sake. Lord, I turn to you to get the inside track and obtain special favors, your direction for my schemes, your power for my projects, your sanction for my ambitions, your blank check for whatever I want. I am like James and John. Change me, Lord. Make me a man who asks of you and of others, what can I do for you?[4]

How do we reverse these subtleties so deeply entrenched in our lives? Here's Chuck Swindoll's suggested starting point: "Servanthood starts in the mind, with a simple prayer of three words: 'Change me, Lord.' "[5]

Ministering the Spirit

It was my twenty-fifth district retreat in a seven-year period. Most leaders choose "safe" speakers over "anointed" speakers. I knew this speaker well. He was one of the pastors from a neighboring district. The first night, he shared a "word from the Lord" which he received several years earlier. As he was driving to speak at a deeper life conference, God said, "Don't minister *about* the Word—minister the Word. Don't minister *about* healing—minister healing, and don't minister *about* the Spirit—minister the Spirit."[6]

On the third evening, he ministered the Spirit. He asked other pastors who felt God wanted to use them in ministering the Spirit to join him on the platform. About twelve responded. He then invited all who needed to be filled with the Spirit to come forward. Many moved to the altar. Result? From my perspective, it was the most effective and powerful pastors' retreat of the twenty-five I had attended.

Second- and third-generation leaders tend to preach and teach about Christian doctrines. This feeds the head, but often starves the heart. This kind of ministry makes historical drift feel comfortable and look respectable. However, we must lead by ministering the Spirit so that Christians, drifting into nominalism, will experience spiritual life and be restored.

More Tough Test Questions

- Personal: Is the Holy Spirit an it or a Person in my life?
- Ministry: Do I minister the Spirit or minister about the Spirit? Do I expect people to respond and experience truth?

With a Prophetic Edge

"Those who have most powerfully and permanently influenced their generation have been the 'seers'—men who have seen more and farther than others."[7] This becomes the lonely side of spiritual leadership. Often it translates into going with the minority report, e.g., Joshua and Caleb versus the majority: "We should go up and take possession of the land, for we can certainly do it" (Numbers 13:30). It means praying alone like Elisha that others will also see the invisible—"the hills full of horses and chariots" (2 Kings 6:17).

This approach to leadership is the opposite of the popular leadership by consensus practiced by savvy politicians. No leadership style breeds historical drift better than consensus.

What do I mean by "prophetic edge"?

God continues to raise up prophets. Prophets make us nervous. They come in one of two varieties: false and true. Inherent also in the prophetic role is the future focus. Certainly this aspect was prominent in the major and minor prophets of the Old Testament. However, upon closer scrutiny, the bold declaring of God's delivered message dominates their prophetic messages, i.e., forth-telling God's revealed will versus foretelling the unknown. Under the new covenant, the latter aspect has become the norm.

The comment tossed out by thoughtless Christians, "Only God knows the future," is heresy. Everyday Christians, who read their Bibles, know more about the future than do all the politicians, professional futurists, contemporary theologians and the most trusted financial gurus. God has made it abundantly clear that He "[does] not want [us] to be ignorant about" the future (1 Thessalonians 4:13).

Tragically, the doctrine of last things—eschatology— has been relegated by many preachers to the last thing they preach on. Our obsession with the here-and-now has left little time for the hereafter. Christ's coming is a purifying hope. Its neglect fosters drift away from holiness "without which no one will see the Lord" (Hebrews 12:14, NKJV).

What must leaders with a prophetic edge address? Let's leave the controversial chronological questions for heaven and proclaim the great events clearly outlined in Scripture:

- The personal and literal return of Christ (Acts 1:11).
- The judgment seat of Christ: "For we must all appear before the judgment seat of Christ, that each one may receive what is due him for the things done while in the body, whether good or bad" (2 Corinthians 5:10).
- The Great White Throne Judgment: "I saw the dead, great and small, standing before the throne, and books were opened. Another book was opened, which is the book of life.

. . . If anyone's name was not found written in the book of life, he was thrown into the lake of fire" (Revelation 20:12, 15).

- Heaven: "I go and prepare a place for you, I will come back and take you to be with me that you also may be where I am" (John 14:3). Heaven is a place absent of death, mourning, crying and pain (Revelation 21:4). Being in the very presence of Christ and joining in eternal worship with the multitude of the redeemed from every tongue and people group of all generations will make heaven heaven.
- The Marriage of the Lamb. "For the wedding of the Lamb has come, and his bride has made herself ready" (19:7). We live in the period of the bride, the Church, "making herself ready" for the wedding. Paul describes how she will look on her wedding day: "Radiant . . . without stain or wrinkle or any other blemish, but holy and blameless" (Ephesians 5:27).

How does your church compare with this description? Someone has suggested that the church we see is analogous to the typical bride on rehearsal night. It is difficult to identify her from the other participants. But on the wedding day, she becomes the central figure, adorned in white.

How then must we lead and impede historical drift? A prophetic voice will sound the warning. It will preach a message of hope. It will be a prophetic voice for revival, reminding God's people that judgment must begin first with God's people, that God historically has brought either renewal or judgment.

More Tough Test Questions

- Personal: What is the impact of God's revealed future events on my life? Does my appointment with Christ at the judg-

ment seat motivate me toward holiness? How would my
present level of godliness fit into the Bride of Christ described by Paul in Ephesians 5:27: i.e., holy, radiant, spotless, without wrinkle, glorious, etc.?

- Professional: Does my preaching anticipate future history?
Do I preach the whole counsel of God, including the end
times? Would my colleagues describe me as a leader with a
prophetic edge?

Summary

To be a leader who leads and impedes historical drift is a daunting
task. We need plenty of encouragement. Biographies abound of leaders
who have left their imprint on the world for time and eternity. One
such leader who has inspired many is Jonathan Edwards. I too am encouraged by his life because it reminds me that one leader, with God,
can make a difference.

Consider these characteristics of his life. One was its brevity—he
died at age fifty-five. His volume of writing was incredible. His vision
for both missions and the impacting of society was unusual. He experienced the high cost of impeding drift. His refusal to compromise as a
pastor cost him his job. He handled that by becoming a missionary.
His prayers and those of his wife for their children and yet unborn
grandchildren and great grandchildren are powerful reminders of
God's commitment to generations.

But most striking to me is his writing of seventy resolutions of his
life. Most of these were written when he was twenty years of age. It's a
spiritual retreat just to read them. Number seventeen is brief but powerful: "Resolved, That I will live so as I shall wish I had lived when I
come to die." Jim Elliot, one of the martyrs to the Aucas expressed a
similar thought: "When it comes time to die, make sure all you have to
do is die."[8]

Jonathan Edwards lived almost three centuries ago, yet through his writings he continues to mentor thousands of Christian workers. Few leaders have more effectively impeded historical drift and moved the Church forward than did Jonathan Edwards.

"Oh God, raise up a new tribe of the Sons of Issachar, leaders who will understand their times and will know what Your people ought to do. Amen."

~

Discussion Questions

1. The author begins by summarizing his theses regarding *historical drift*. Review and interact with each.
2. He outlines six answers to his bottom line question: "How Then Must We Lead?" Discuss the relevance of each of these in your role.
3. How then will you lead in your home, church, organization and vocation in life?

Good News

What Would Jesus Do?

T he first Christian book I read as a young man was *In His Steps* by Charles Sheldon. It impacted me profoundly. Simply doing what Jesus would do made good sense. It gave me a practical handle on living the Christian life. Thankfully, this book has been rediscovered, especially by the youth. A major industry of WWJD (What Would Jesus Do?) holy hardware has emerged in the Christian marketplace.

As I tried to do what Jesus would do, I soon discovered the same problem these thousands of young people wearing WWJD bracelets must face—the lack of power to walk as Jesus walked. His example inspires all who know His story, but without His indwelling presence I was, as they are, doomed to frustration.

As evangelicals our creed declares: "Jesus Christ is the same yesterday and today and forever" (Hebrews 13:8). Immediately after His ascension, two heavenly messengers assured His disciples: "This same Jesus, who has been taken from you into heaven, will come back in the same way you have seen him go into heaven" (Acts 1:11).

The book you hold in your hands has grappled with leadership. How should Christian leaders lead? How do we cope with the crosswinds of a decadent culture that threatens to send us adrift on the sea of life? What about the question, "What would Jesus do?" I believe it's valid. And the answers are more than guesstimates. We have available in the Gospels the fourfold composite record of what Jesus did and how He walked. We have not been left in the dark.

Let's wrap this up this way: The salient aspects of leadership as explained in those Gospels are five: mission, vision, strategy, personnel and historical drift.

Mission: Who Are We?

As a leader, Jesus knew clearly who He was. "I am the way and the truth and the life. No one comes to the Father except through me" (John 14:6). His disciples were expected to follow Him, even as martyrs. He made no apology for the cross, suffering or hardship. He and they were on the greatest mission.

Vision: Where Are We Going?

Jesus, as leader, set His face toward Jerusalem and the cross. Early in His ministry He cast the vision of His death, persecution, resurrection, the building of His Church and His return. Beyond God's provision for them here on earth they would receive a hundred times more than they gave up—plus eternal life (Matthew 19:29).

Strategy: How Will the Vision Be Realized?

How would a Church, opposed by Satan and culture, be built throughout the world? Christ would send the Holy Spirit to empower ordinary believers, then they would be sent to evangelize people groups everywhere. These churches would be indestructible. Undergirded by prayer, and armed with spiritual weapons, they would demolish strongholds (2 Corinthians 10:3-5).

Personnel: Who Will Help Us?

Jesus chose ordinary people, even weak people by worldly standards. He trained them on the job. His basic philosophy of education was simple—be with them. They would learn by observing and obeying their leader. And when they still felt incompetent, He would replace

Himself with the Holy Spirit. Unfettered by the human body, global expansion would be accelerated.

Historical Drift:
How Will Compromise Be Handled?

Christ schooled His people to expect hostility from the culture. Under His sovereignty this would become an effective strategy in realizing the vision. His people, who were recruited, directed and empowered by the Spirit, would be renewed constantly by that same Spirit. They would be deployed in teams. Authority would be decentralized right down to the smallest church. Christ would check the effectiveness of these churches regularly. Faithfulness and hard work would be commended, but He would be equally discerning in identifying drift: loss of first love for God, compromising of doctrinal truth, hypocrisy and self-sufficiency. Those who failed to repent would be subject to redemptive disciplinary action.

Reality Check:
What Did Jesus Do? What Would Jesus Do?

The real question is: "What is Jesus doing?" Although physically absent, He is, present tense, aggressively building His Church. He did say, "All authority in heaven and on earth has been given to me" (Matthew 28:18). This makes the Holy Spirit the key person in Christian leadership today. But, in most churches, He has become either the most forgotten Person or the most misunderstood Person. However, in times of revival, His role of renewing God's people is restored.

What would Jesus do? We know the answer from Scripture. It is our responsibility to join Him in what He is doing—present tense. He alone is the Ultimate Impeder of Historical Drift.

Appendix I

The United Church of Canada: "The Uniting Church"

Under the rubric, Built-to-Last Organizations, we have observed the success that some have experienced during two decades or more in holding to the core values of their founders. In contrast, this case study profiles a denomination which has experienced radical change over a similar period.

The United Church of Canada (UCC) is the largest Protestant denomination in Canada. Their 4,000-plus churches stretch from ocean to ocean, making it truly a national church. This national aspect was a significant factor in the 1925 union of three denominations, which created the UCC.

Why a "State" Church?

The initial proposal for a union of Methodists, Congregationalists and Presbyterians was voiced in 1904. Several influences drove this agenda. First, an emphasis on Christian unity was in vogue. Great gatherings such as the Edinburgh International Missionary Conference, 1910, issued the rallying call for "the evangelization of the world in this generation." A union of denominations, they thought, would certainly facilitate this noble thrust.

The second factor was the influx of one million immigrants who settled the West. The efforts of churches to minister to them resulted in duplication and, for those already initiating amalgamations, competition. Subsequent to the formulation of the Basis of Union in 1908, some congregations chose not to wait for the official union. This only increased the urgency.

Third, Protestants were aware that the new immigration was tipping the balance toward the Catholic Church. Union would bolster a united Protestant front.

The Basis of Union

The first General Council of the United Church of Canada convened in Toronto, June 10, 1925. In defense of the name, chosen eleven years earlier, the committee stated: "It shall be the policy of The United Church of Canada to foster the spirit of unity in the hope that this sentiment of unity may, in due time, so far as Canada is concerned, take shape in a Church which may fittingly be described as national."[1] There were twenty Founding Articles. These Articles constituted what is commonly called "the statement of faith."

Although the UCC union predates official recognition of evangelicals, their extensive doctrinal statement covered all the tenets of the emerging evangelicals twenty years later: e.g., God, revelation, divine purpose, creation, sin, grace, person of Christ, Holy Spirit, regeneration, faith and repentance, justification, sanctification, prayer, law, church, sacraments, ministry, church order, resurrection and Christian service.[2]

The founders essentially agreed to maintain their allegiance to the evangelical doctrine of the Reformation. Since then, and particularly since the 1988 decision to ordain homosexual ministers, several renewal movements emerged. Some withdrew while others, such as the National Alliance of Covenanting Congregations, chose to work for renewal from within the UCC. Eleven of the 360 churches in Alberta withdrew, formed the Association Churches of the UCC and reaffirmed the twenty articles of faith from 1925.

What is the present status of the UCC? During the 1960s, there was considerable unrest in the church. The introducing of a highly controversial new Sunday school curriculum in 1964 resulted in the first significant exodus of members. The second major exodus was precipitated by a decision in 1988 to ordain practicing homosexuals. Statements made in 1997 by the moderator, the Rt. Rev. Bill Phipps, created a new controversy. He questioned the validity of church creeds from the 3rd and 4th centuries and expressed doubts regarding the deity of Christ and His resurrection.[3]

How could a major denomination, founded upon solid biblical doctrines, shift to such a radical position within two generations? The UCC is a case study in unusually rapid historical drift. Four major factors contributed to an overly zealous commitment to ecumenism.

First, the strong ecumenical flavor of the Edinburgh International Missionary Conference in 1910 influenced some of the leaders of the 1925 Union. That conference's focus on unity was directed toward world evangelization. The UCC ecumenical passion was channeled toward Canadian nationalism. Ralph Milton in his popular book, *This United Church of Ours,* states: "From day one, back in 1925, the United Church has said that anyone who considers themselves a Christian can be a member of the United Church and all United Church people are eligible to be considered for the ordained or commissioned ministry."[4]

This all-consuming motif of uniting has, in retrospect, become their *raison d'etre.* This is eloquently illustrated in a book entitled: *Daring to be United: Including Lesbians and Gays in the United Church of Canada.*[5] It is a series of testimonies from across Canada expressing appreciation for a church that dared to unite everyone.

The second factor which contributed to ecumenism was an attitude of benign neglect toward orthodoxy and Scripture. A member of the UCC threatened to sue the church for changing its doctrinal position. The churches stated that they had not altered any one of the twenty articles of doctrine. In actuality, they have simply given them benign neglect. Ralph Milton, a popular UCC spokesman, when asked about orthodoxy, replied: "Orthodoxy is a theoretical concept that exists only in the minds of a few theologians, and few lay people ever ask themselves such a question."[6]

This attitude of indifference toward theology and Scripture was reflected in the reaction to the new Sunday school curriculum. Members charged that the materials denied or questioned such fundamental truths as the virgin birth, the deity of Christ, the inspiration and reliability of Scripture and creation. The curriculum's editor-in-chief, Peter Gordon White, responded: "It's not our business to protect United Church people against struggles with questions of faith. None of us have [sic] to protect God. The more disturbing the questions asked, the more likely is faith to be deep-rooted."[7]

The third factor in the shift to a radical position was a passion for relevance.

The UCC ordained its first woman pastor in 1936. When asked how they came to that position, the response was: "The decision to ordain women and homosexual persons happened because enough people in the church had come to that point that when a few persons articulated that idea, there was enough support for it to happen."[8]

When asked about the new curriculum, the response was that its purpose was "to restate the whole concept of Christianity in modern terms using the best available educational techniques."[9]

Referring to the General Council's decision to allow practicing homosexuals to be ordained, Milton defended them: "General Council's decision was made out of a deep sense of caring, of wanting to do what was just and right and fair.... Who knows? It may have been the wrong decision. But I think it's probably better to make the wrong decisions for the right reasons than the other way around."[10]

Leadership by consensus became the fourth factor that allowed such a radical shift in position in such a short time. In the preamble to doctrine in the founding documents, provision was made for substantial local church freedom while at the same time securing the benefits of a strong connecting tie and cooperative efficiency.[11] A redeeming factor, given the present controversy in the UCC, is that local churches, with few exceptions, still call their own pastors. Not even the moderator necessarily speaks for the church.

Unity in diversity is a strong core value. Huntly underscores this position: "The United Church never has required, or maintained, unanimity amongst its members."[12] Speaking to the question of ordination and how decisions are made, Milton made this comment: "The changes that happened in the United Church happened because those changes were happening in society. . . . The decisions were not arrived at through theological soul searching, much as some folks in the church would like to believe that.[13]

As one UCC pastor put it, "I need to know where my people are going so that I can lead them."[14]

Summary

Although the UCC, at the time of this writing, is approaching only seventy-five years, there's another component that must be factored into their rapid drift. The three amalgamating denominations brought considerable tradition to the union. Charles Johnston comments: "All three were certainly more conservative than they are today. However they all had 'liberal' elements in them. The liberal group from the Presbyterian denomination left to join what became the UCC."[15]

Nevertheless, there has been an appalling departure from their theological base as found in the twenty articles. The four positions they chose to assume should serve as a warning to all evangelicals. An inordinate passion for any number of good causes can result in benign neglect of doctrinal fidelity: e.g., missions, evangelism, relevance, social concerns, etc.

Appendix II

A Lonely Struggle
for Equal Rights

- 1965: The Melody Room opens on Church St., Toronto, Canada, and same-sex dancing is encouraged with the help of a front-door security system that alerts patrons to the arrival of police.
- 1969: Homosexuality between consenting adults is decriminalized in the Criminal Code in Canada.
- 1971: Despite several court actions, the first gay newspaper is published in Toronto.
- 1972: The American Psychiatric Association declassifies homosexuality as a disease.
- 1976: The 519 Community Center opens and offers the first gay program; it's called Gay Youth Group Toronto.
- 1981: The first Lesbian and Gay Pride Day is held in June, followed by the formation of the Toronto Gay Community Council.
- 1982: A Windsor, Ontario man becomes the first confirmed AIDS death in Canada, and the community begins to galvanize around the disease.
- 1986: The Ontario government amends the Human Rights Code to include sexual orientation as prohibited grounds for discrimination.
- 1989: The Supreme Court of Canada imposes new obligations on all governments to protect the rights of disadvan-

taged groups in its ruling on equality provision of the Charter of Rights and Freedom.

- 1990: Then-police chief, William McCormack, finally acknowledges publicly that the gay community is "a legitimate part of our community" and sets up a gay/police dialogue committee.
- 1992: The province is ordered by the Ontario Human Rights Commission to provide spousal survivor benefits to same-sex employees.
- 1995: Canada's Attorney-General concedes that limiting the definition of "spouse" in the federal Income Tax Act to persons of the opposite sex violates the equality provision of the Charter.
- 1998: In February, city council extends same-sex health benefits to all City of Toronto employees. In May, the federal government provides $145,000 for the first national survey of the gay and lesbian communities.[1]
- 1999: The province of Ontario grants full benefits to same sex partners.

Endnotes

Introduction (pages 1-7)

1. Robert Bork, *Slouching Towards Gomorrah*. New York, NY: HarperCollins, 1996, p. 2.
2. Elmer Towns, *America's Fastest Growing Churches*. Nashville, TN: Impact Books, 1972, p. 153.
3. Ibid.
4. Ibid.
5. Dean Kelley, *Why Conservative Churches Grow*. New York, NY: Harper & Row, 1972, p. 55.
6. In order to distinguish Christ's universal Church from local churches, I will use upper case "C" for the former and lower case for the latter.

Part I and Chapter 1 (pages 9-23)

1. Richard Niebuhr, *The Social Sciences of Denominationalism*. New York, NY: New American Library, 1957, pp. 19-21.
2. Henry H. Halley, *Halley's Bible Handbook*. Grand Rapids, MI: Zondervan, 1965, p. 411.
3. James Orr, General Editor, *The International Standard Bible Encyclopedia* (ISBE). Grand Rapids, MI: Eerdmans, 1939, pp. 2361-2362.
4. E.F. Scott, as quoted in William Barclay, *The Letter to the Hebrews*. Philadelphia, PA: Westminster Press, 1977, p. 3.
5. Origen, as quoted in William Barclay, *The Letter to the Hebrews*. Philadelphia, PA: Westminster Press, 1977, p. 3.
6. William Barclay, *The Letter to the Hebrews*. Philadelphia, PA: Westminster Press, 1977, p. 7.
7. Raymond Kincheloe, unpublished class notes, in which he identifies five warnings in the book of Hebrews: 2:14; 3:7-11; 5:11-6:3; 10:26-31; 12:14-17.
8. William Barclay, *The Letter to the Hebrews*. Philadelphia, PA: Westminster Press, 1977, p. 21.
9. Ibid.
10. Leon Morris, *The Revelation of St. John*. Grand Rapids, MI: William B. Eerdmans, 1978, pp. 57-58.
11. Jim Cymbala, *Fresh Wind, Fresh Fire*. Grand Rapids, MI: Zondervan, 1997, p. 11.
12. Ibid., 25.
13. Ibid.
14. Ibid., 27.

Chapter 2 (pages 25-41)

1. George Barna, *The Frog in the Kettle*. Ventura, CA: Regal Books, 1990, p. 21.
2. Ibid., pp. 25-26.
3. Ibid., p. 27.
4. Ibid.
5. Hayford endorsement of Barna's book, *The Frog in the Kettle*.
6. Kelley, pp. vii-viii.
7. Ibid., p. viii.
8. Max Weber, *Sociology of Religion*. London: Methuen, 1963, p. 175.
9. Kelley, pp. 99-100.
10. Franklin H.L. Littell, *The Origins of Sectarian Protestantism*. New York, NY: MacMillan Co., 1964, and *From State to Pluralism*. New York, NY: Doubleday, 1962, p. 104.
11. Kelley, p. 105.
12. Ibid., p. 110.
13. Ibid., pp. 63-64.
14. Donald McGavran, *Understanding Church Growth*. Grand Rapids, MI: William B. Eerdmans, 1970, p. 6.
15. Ibid., p. 5.
16. Mike Regele, *Death of the Church*. Grand Rapids, MI: Zondervan, 1995, p. 20.
17. Ibid., p. 19.
18. Ibid.
19. Ibid., p. 29.
20. Ibid., p. 35.
21. Keith J. Hardman, *The Spiritual Awakeners*. Chicago, IL: Moody Press, 1983, p. 98.
22. Ibid.
23. Ibid., p. 96.
24. Ibid., p. 106.

Part II and Chapter 3 (pages 43-64)

1. Niebuhr, pp. 19-21.
2. David O. Moberg, *The Church or a Social Institution*. Englewood Cliffs, NJ: Prentice-Hall, 1962, p. 100.
3. Elmer L. Towns, *America's Fastest Growing Churches*. Nashville, TN: Impact Books, 1972, p. 156.
4. *Webster's New Collegiate Dictionary*. Springfield, MA: 1975, p. 1044.
5. Bob, Buford, NET/FAX, "Jumping the Sigmoid Curve." Tyler, TX: Leadership Network, #8, December 12, 1994.
6. Ibid.
7. Robert D. Dale, *To Dream Again*. Nashville, TN: Broadman Press, 1981, p. 5.
8. Ibid., p. 143.
9. Ibid, pp. 117-126.

10. George Woodrow Bullard, Jr., "Congregational Passages," an occasional publication of the National Consultant for Denominational Transformation, 1996, Vol. One, No. One, pp. 1-2.

11. Ibid.

12. Ibid.

13. Eugene Peterson, *The Contemplative Pastor*. Carol Stream, IL: Word Publishing, 1989, p. 126.

14. Peter Laurence, *The Peter Principle*. New York: Bantam Books, 1969, pp. 63, 68.

15. K. Neill Foster, *Classic-Christianity e-zine*, December 1999, p. 2.

16. B. Carlisle Driggers, *Empowering Kingdom Growth*. South Carolina Southern Baptist Convention, paper distributed at the Leadership Network Conference for Denominational Leaders, March 24-26, 1996, pp. 1-9.

17. Ibid.

18. Ibid.

Chapter 4 (pages 65-81)

1. James C. Collins and Jerry I. Porras, *Built to Last*. New York, NY: HarperCollins Publishers, 1994, pp. 22-23.

2. Willow Creek Association Leadership conference, 1997.

3. Op. cit., p. 44.

4. Ibid., p. 81.

5. Ibid., pp. 201-202.

6. Adizes, *Corporate Lifecycles*, pp. 56-59.

7. © 1988 Ichak Adizes, Ph.D. in *Corporate Lifecycles*. Paramus, NJ: Prentice Hall, 1988, p. 103.

8. Adizes, *Corporate Lifecycles*, pp. 61-63.

9. © 1988 Ichak Adizes, *Corporate Lifecycles*, p. 268.

10. Ibid., p. 202.

11. Ibid., pp. 56-59.

12. Ibid., p. 204.

13. Ibid., p. 63.

14. Collins and Porras, p. 202.

15. George Woodrow Bullard, Jr., seminar presentation for The Christian and Missionary Alliance, Toronto, Canada, September 29-30, 1999.

16. Ibid., p. 227.

17. David F. Wells, Ligonier Conference, Toronto: December 3, 1995.

18. Carl F.H. Henry, quoted by Les Thompson, *Christianity Today*, May 1993, p. 10.

Chapter 5 (pages 83-95)

1. Billy Graham, *Christianity Today*. No. 1, October 5, 1956.

2. Elisabeth Elliot, *Christianity Today*. No. 7, January 7, 1957.

3. Frank E. Gaebelein, *Christianity Today*. No. 9, February 4, 1957.

4. Nelson Bell, *Christianity Today*. No. 24, September 16, 1957.

5. L.L. King, "The Christian and Missionary Alliance, As I See It, Beyond 1987." An unpublished paper by Dr. King, president of the C&MA U.S., 1987, pp. 2-3.

6. ISBE. Grand Rapids, MI: Eerdmans, 1939, Vol. 2, p. 1199.

7. Bork, p. 2.

8. *The Toronto Star,* June 6, 1998, p. 7. (See Appendix II.)

9. C. Peter Wagner, *The New Apostolic Churches.* Ventura, CA: Regal Books, 1998, pp. 16-18.

10. Ruth A. Tucker, "Worldwide Church of God Sees the Plain Truth." *Christianity Today,* July 15, 1996, pp. 26-32.

11. Joseph Tkach, Jr., "Forgive Us Our Trespasses." *Plain Truth,* March/April, 1996, as quoted by Ruth A. Tucker in *Christianity Today,* July 15, 1996, p. 30.

Part III and Chapter 6 (pages 97-112)

1. *The Globe and Mail,* March 30, 1998, p. C 3.

2. Bruce Wilkinson and Chip MacGregor, *First Hand Faith: Recapture a Passionate Love for the Savior.* Gresham, OR: Vision House Publisher Inc., 1996, pp. 13-20.

3. Eddy Gibbs, *In Name Only: Tackling the Problem of Nominal Christianity.* Tunbridge Wells, Kent, England: Monarch Publications Ltd., 1994, pp. 1-21.

4. Ibid., p. 21.

5. Ibid., p. 23.

6. Harold Voelkel, revised by Will Bruce, *Oh God, Revive Us Again.* Mississauga, ON: OMF International, 1996, pp. 2-3.

Chapter 7 (pages 113-132)

1. Os Guinness, "Recycling the Compromise of Liberalism," *Tabletalk.* May 1992, p. 51.

2. Ibid.

3. Marvin Mayers, *Christianity Confronts Culture.* Grand Rapids, MI: Zondervan, 1987, p. 156.

4. Edward R. Dayton, *What Ever Happened to Commitment?.* Grand Rapids: Zondervan Publishing House, 1984, p. 129.

5. John Piper, Message Preached, U.S. C&MA Council, June 1997.

6. Lillian Cox, *Men of the Morning.* London: Epworth Press, 1938, pp. 37-38.

7. Kenneth Scott Latourette, *Christianity Through the Ages.* New York: Harper and Rowe, 1965, pp. 296-97.

8. Harold Lindsell was a former professor. His book, *The Battle for the Bible,* 1976, chronicles the controversy during the 1960's.

9. David Hubbard was president when the decision to alter their position on the Bible was made.

10. Paul K. Jewett, *Man as Male and Female.* Grand Rapids: Eerdmans, 1976, p. 112.

11. John Stott and David L. Edwards, *Evangelical Essentials*, Downers Grove, IL: InterVarsity Press, 1989, pp. 312-321. *Evangelical Essentials* is a liberal-evangelical dialog between David L. Edwards and John Stott. In Stott's response to questions on hell and judgment, he explains how he has come to his position of accepting some form of annihilation (pp. 319-320).

12. Robert Shindler, "The Down-Grade," *The Sword and the Trowel*. March, 1887, p. 122.

13. Ibid., p. 170.

14. Charles Spurgeon, "Another Word Concerning the Down-Grade," *The Sword and the Trowel*. August, 1888, p. 399.

15. Ibid., p. 465.

16. John F. MacArthur, Jr., *Ashamed of the Gospel: When the Church Becomes Like the World*. Wheaton, IL: Crossways Books, 1993, p. 225.

Chapter 8 (pages 133-148)

1. Joseph M. Stowell, *Shepherding the Church into the 21st Century*. Wheaton, IL: Victor Books, 1994, p. 15.

2. Rick Warren, *The Purpose Driven Church*. Grand Rapids: Zondervan, 1995, pp. 103-106.

3. Christian A. Schwarz, *Natural Church Development*. International Centre for Leadership Development and Evangelism Conference, Toronto, ON, May 20-21, 1999, pp. 20-37.

4. Dann Spader, *Growing a Healthy Church*. Elburn, IL: SonLife, 1998, p. 4.

5. Robertson McQuilkin, "What Is Your GCQ?" *Trinity World Forum*. Trinity Evangelical Divinity School, Winter 1997, pp. 1-2.

6. Ibid., p. 2.

7. Ibid.

8. Ibid., p. 4.

9. Ibid.

10. Ibid.

Part IV and Chapter 9 (pages 149-164)

1. Charles Swindoll, "The Temptations of Ministry: Improving Your Reserve." *Leadership*, Fall 1982, pp. 16-27.

2. J. Oswald Sanders, *Spiritual Leadership*. Chicago: Moody Press, 1967, p. 146.

3. Laurence J. Peter, *The Peter Principle*. New York: Bantam Books, 1975.

4. Wagner, pp. 45-58.

5. Merriam-Webster, p. 232.

6. Bruce L. Shelley, *Church History in Plain Language*. Waco, TX: Word Book Publisher, 1982, p. 260.

7. Kent and Barbara Hughes, *Liberating Ministry from the Success Syndrome*. Wheaton IL: Tyndale House, 1988, front cover flap.

Chapter 10 (pages 165-176)

1. *Webster's Ninth New Collegiate Dictionary*. Springfield, MA: Merriam-Webster, 1983, 1991, p. 49.
2. Francis A. Schaeffer, *The Great Evangelical Disaster*. Westchester, IL: Crossway Books, 1984, p. 37.
3. Ibid.
4. William A. Heth and Gordon J. Wenham, *Jesus and Divorce: The Problem with the Evangelical Consensus*. New York: Thomas Nelson Publishers, 1984, pp. 13-16.
5. John Piper, "On Divorce & Remarriage in the Event of Adultery," http://desiringgod.org/resources/divorce/Div&rem-adultery.htm, March 9, 1999.
6. Ibid.
7. Excerpted from *The Pentecostal Testimony*, Jan.-Feb., 2000, back cover.

Chapter 11 (pages 177-194)

1. James C. Collins and Jerry I. Porras, *Built to Last: Successful Habits of Visionary Companies*. New York: HarperBusiness, 1994, p. 217.
2. George Sweeting, "Talking It Over." *Moody Monthly*, Oct. 1986, p. 4.
3. _____, "Celebrating 75 Years of God's Faithfulness," March 1998.
4. Joy Ridderhof, quoted in "Celebrating 75 Years of God's Faithfulness." Columbia International University, March 1998, p. 36.
5. _____, "The Past with Gratitude." Peoples Church, 60th Anniversary, 1988.
6. Lois Neely, "Dr. Oswald J. Smith: Beloved of Canada, Owned by the World," *Faith Today*. Toronto: March/April 1986, p. 12.
7. Ibid.
8. John Hull, "Preparing the Peoples Church, Toronto for a Third Generation of Ministry." An unpublished doctoral thesis, Toronto: 1996, pp. 3-7.
9. Ibid., p. 61.
10. Ibid., pp. 35-39.
11. Edward E. Plowman, "Pressler Pressure," *WORLD*. July 3, 1999, p. 38.

Chapter 12 (pages 195-208)

1. Gilbert Bilezikian, *Beyond Sex Roles*. Grand Rapids: Baker Book House, 1985, pp. 9-13.
2. _____, "The Cambridge Declaration." Abridged quote from *Modern Reformation*, July/August 1996, pp. 34-36.
3. Millard Erickson, *The Evangelical Left: Encountering Post-conservative Evangelical Theology*. Grand Rapids: Baker Books, 1997, p. 26.
4. James Davison Hunter, *Evangelicalism: The Coming Generation*. Chicago: University Press, 1987, p. 32.

5. Roger E. Olson, "Post-conservative Evangelicals Greet the Postmodern Age," *Christian Century.* May 3, 1995, p. 482.
6. James Montgomery Boice, "Recovering Our Lost Confessions," *Modern Reformation,* January/February 1999, p. 40.
7. Ibid.

Chapter 13 (pages 209-230)

1. Latourette, Kenneth Scott, *A History of Christianity, Volume 2.* San Francisco: Harper and Row, 1975, p. 756.
2. K. Neill Foster, *Binding and Loosing.* Camp Hill, PA: Christian Publications, 1998, p. 173.
3. Ibid.
4. Ibid.
5. K. Neill Foster, "A Theology of Historical Drift Impedance," an unpublished paper, May 1991, p. 4.
6. See Good News Vignette, at end of chapter.
7. Proceedings, "Brief Statement," adopted as part of the doctrinal statement by the Lutheran Church—Missouri Synod, 1932, p. 1543.
8. Philip Teng, *Crises in the Apostolic Church.* Bombay: Gospel Literature Service, 1980), pp. 5-64.
9. Diana S. Frazier, "Musings on Commerce: a Review of the Christian Booksellers' Association Convention." *Modern Reformation,* January/February, 1999, pp. 36-37.
10. Robert Shaker, memo from owner of Reformation Book Services, 2045 ½ , Avenue Road, Toronto.
11. David F. Wells, *No Place for Truth or Whatever Happened to Evangelical Theology?* Grand Rapids: Eerdmans, 1993, pp. 207-211.
12. Brochure of Christian Publications, Inc. (CPI), Harrisburg, PA., n.d.
13. *Christianity Today,* December 12, 1998, p. 18.
14. Jim Collins, "One-on-One with Jim Collins and Bill Hybels." WCCC Leadership Conference, Chicago, 1997.
15. Norman Geisler excerpts from plenary lecture given at Evangelical Theological Society, ETS, Orlando, Florida, November 19-21, 1998.
16. Ibid.
17. "ACTS Seminaries and Some Trends in Contemporary Evangelicalism," Langley B.C., February 2, 1999, p. 1.
18. Jerry Rankin and Avery Willis, "The Southern Baptists Restructure to Reach the Unreached Peoples," *Mission Frontiers,* July-October, 1997, pp. 15-18.
19. Russell G. Shubin, "Fueling the Passion in the Pew," *Mission Frontiers,* September-December, 1998, p. 9.
20. Ibid., p. 11.
21. Ibid., p. 12.

Part V and Chapter 14 (pages 231-246)

1. Erroll Hulse, *Spirit of Revival.* Buchanan, MI: Life Action Ministries, Vol. 29, Number 1, February, 1999, pp. 24-26.
2. William Strauss and Neil Howe, *Generations: The History of America's Future, 1584 to 2069.* New York: William Morrow, 1991, pp. 28-31. These authors identify six awakenings during the period of 1584 to 1990.
3. J.R. Green, *A Short History of the English People.* New York: Harper and Brothers, 1898, p. 736.
4. A.W. Tozer, *Tozer on the Holy Spirit.* Camp Hill, PA: Christian Publications, Inc., 2000, October 5.
5. David Needham, *Birthright.* Portland: Multnomah Press, 1979, p. 82.
6. John Piper, "Training the Next Generation of Evangelical Pastors and Missionaries." The Evangelical Theological Society, Orlando, FL: November 20, 1998.
7. Nancy Leigh DeMoss, *Brokenness: The Heart That God Revives.* Video available from Life Action Ministries, P.O. Box 31, Buchanan, MI. Message given at a staff conference of Campus Crusade for Christ at their U.S. headquarters, July 7, 1995.
8. Ibid.

Chapter 15 (pages 247-258)

1. Richard A. Swenson, *Margin: Restoring Emotional, Physical, Financial, and Time Reserves to Overloaded Lives.* Colorado Springs: Navpress, 1992, pp. 91-182.
2. Richard A. Swenson, *Hurtling Toward Oblivion: A Logical Argument for the End of the Age.* Colorado Springs: Navpress, 1999.
3. Kevin Jenkins, speaker at Ontario Prayer Breakfast, Toronto, April, 1993.
4. Les Thompson, "Put Faith Back into Management," *Christianity Today,* January 1989, p. 10.
5. A.W. Tozer, *The Size of the Soul.* Camp Hill, PA: Christian Publications, 1992, p. 15.
6. John Piper, "Lecture on Preaching and Worship," Trinity Theological Seminary, Deerfield, IL., 1997.
7. A.B. Simpson, *Missionary Messages.* Camp Hill, PA: Christian Publications, n.d., 115-149.
8. Ron and Patricia Owens, *Return to Me: A Fresh Encounter with God through Song.* Nashville, TN: Lifeway Press, 1993, pp. 11-12. Used by permission.
9. Al Henson, Flames of Freedom Conference, Rives Junction, MI, September 1997.

Chapter 16 (pages 259-270)

1. John MacArthur, Jr., *Reckless Faith: When the Church Loses its Will to Discern.* Wheaton, IL: Crossway Books, 1994, pp. 225-231.
2. Russell G. Shubin, "Winds of Renewal," *Mission Frontiers,* January/February, 1999, p. 7.
3. Ibid.

4. Ibid., p. 8.
5. Russell G. Shubin, quoted in Zondervan News Service, January 19, 1999.
6. Ibid.
7. Shubin, p. 6.
8. Lyle Eggleston, *Can Revivals be Prayed Down?* Regina, SK: Canadian Revival Fellowship, 1991, pp. 17-19.
9. Ibid.
10. Robert Coleman, *One Divine Moment.* New Jersey, Fleming H. Revell, 1970, pp. 14-18.
11. Eggleston, pp. 13-15.
12. J. Edwin Orr, *Evangelical Awakenings: Eastern Asia.* Minneapolis, MN: Bethany Fellowship, 1975, p. 56.
13. Eggleston, pp. 8-9.
14. Ibid., pp. 7-8.
15. Frank Bartleman, *Another Wave of Revival.* Springdale, PA: Whitaker House, 1982, p. 7.
16. J. Edwin Orr, *The Flaming Tongue: The Impact of the Twentieth Century Revival.* Chicago, IL: Moody Press, 1973, pp. 1-28.
17. Ibid., pp. 43-44.
18. The Moravians were a strong missionary movement originating in the early 18th century under Count Ludwig von Zinzendorf.
19. Based on an article from *Pray!* Magazine, Issue 14, September-October 1999, Colorado Springs, CO: pp. 26-30.

Chapter 17 (pages 271-281)

There are no endnotes in this chapter.

Part VI and Chapter 18 (pages 283-300)

1. J. Oswald Sanders, *Spiritual Leadership.* Chicago: Moody Press, 1967, p. 6.
2. Malcolm Muggeridge, *The Most of Malcolm Muggeridge.* New York, NY: Simon and Schuster, 1988, p. 140.
3. A.W. Tozer, *The Waning Authority of Christ in the Church.* Harrisburg, PA: Christian Publications, 1963, p. 6.
4. Charles Swindoll, *Improving Your Serve: The Art of Unselfish Living.* Waco, TX: Word Books, 1981, pp. 94-95.
5. Ibid.
6. Wayne Boldt, District Retreat, Pentictan, B.C., November 1999.
7. Sanders, p. 48.
8. *Life* magazine, January 30, 1956, Volume 40, Number 5, p. 11.

Appendix I (pages 301-305)

1. "The United Church of Canada: Record of Proceedings of the First General Council," 1924, Toronto, pp. 239-242.
2. Ibid.
3. Leslie Scrivener, *Toronto Star*, October 29, 1997, p. C3.
4. Ralph Milton, *This United Church of Ours*. Kelowna, BC: Wood Lake Books Incorporated, 1991, p. 112.
5. Alyson Huntly, *Daring to Be United: Including Lesbians and Gays in the United Church of Canada*. Toronto, ON: United Church of Canada Publishing House, 1998.
6. Ralph Milton, in correspondence with Menno Fieguth, October 9, 1998.
7. Peter Gordon White, editor-in-chief of United Church Sunday school publication, *United Church Observer*, May 15, 1964, as quoted in "Faith Today," July/August, 1987, p. 26.
8. Milton, written response to Menno Fieguth, researcher.
9. White, p. 26.
10. Milton, p. 112.
11. "UCC: Record of Proceeding of the First General Council, 1924."
12. Huntly, p. 160.
13. Milton, correspondence with Fieguth.
14. Ibid.
15. Charles Johnston, Librarian at St. Andrews College, Saskatoon, SK: interview with Menno Fieguth, March 1999.

Appendix II (pages 307-308)

1. "A Lonely Struggle for Equal Rights," *Toronto Star*, June 6, 1998, p. F7.

Bibliography

Adizes, Ichak. *Corporate Lifecycles*. Englewood Cliffs, NJ: Prentice Hall, 1988.

Barclay, William. *The Letter to the Hebrews*. Philadelphia, PA: Westminster Press, 1977.

Barna, George. *The Frog in the Kettle*. Ventura, CA: Regal Books, 1990.

Bartleman, Frank. *Another Wave of Revival*. Springdale, PA: Whitaker House, 1982.

Bell, Nelson. *Christianity Today*. No. 24 (September 16, 1957).

Bilezikian, Gilbert. *Beyond Sex Roles*. Grand Rapids, MI: Baker Book House, 1985.

Boice, James Montgomery. "Recovering Our Lost Confessions," *Modern Reformation*. (January/February, 1999).

Bork, Robert H. *Slouching Towards Gomorrah*. New York, NY: HarperCollins, 1996.

Buford, Bob. NET/FAX, "Jumping the Sigmoid Curve," Tyler TX: Leadership Network, #8 (December 12, 1994).

Bullard, George Woodrow, Jr. "Congregation Passages," an occasional publication of the National Consultant for Denominational Transformation, Vol. One, No. One, (August 1996).

Consulting session with The Christian and Missionary Alliance, Toronto, Canada, (September 29-30, 1999).

Coleman, Robert. *One Divine Moment*. Old Tappan, NY: Fleming H. Revell, 1970.

Collins, James C., and Porras, Jerry I. *Built to Last: Successful Habits of Visionary Companies*. New York, NY: HarperCollins, 1994.

Collins, James. "One-on-One with Jim Collins and Bill Hybels." WCCC Leadership Conference, Chicago, 1997.

Cox, Lillian. *Men of the Morning*. London, England: Epworth Press, 1938.

Cymbala, Jim. *Fresh Wind, Fresh Fire*. Grand Rapids, MI: Zondervan, 1997.

Dale, Robert D. *To Dream Again*. Nashville, TN: Broadman Press, 1981.

Dayton, Edward R. *What Ever Happened to Commitment?* Grand Rapids, MI: Zondervan, 1884.

Driggers, B. Carlisle. "Empowering Kingdom Growth." South Carolina Southern Baptist Convention, paper distributed at the leadership Network Conference for Denominational Leaders, March 24-26, 1996.

Eggleston, Lyle. *Can Revivals be Prayed Down?* Regina, SK: Canadian Revival Fellowship, 1991.

Elliot, Elisabeth. *Christianity Today*. No. 7 (January 7, 1957).

Erickson, Millard. *The Evangelical Left: Encountering Post-conservative Evangelical Theology*. Grand Rapids, MI: Baker Book House, 1997.

Foster, K. Neill with Paul L. King. *Binding and Loosing: Exercising Authority over the Dark Powers*. Camp Hill, PA: Christian Publications, 1998.

_____. *Classic-Christianity e-zine* (December 1999).

_____. "A Theology of Historical Drift Impedance," an unpublished paper (May 1991).

Frazier, Diana. "Musings on Commerce: a review of the Christian Booksellers' Association Convention," *Modern Reformation* (January/February, 1999).

Gaebelein, Frank E. *Christianity Today*. No. 9 (February 4, 1957).

Geisler, Norman. Excerpts from plenary lecture given at Evangelical Theological Society, ETS, Orlando, FL (November 19-21, 1998).

Gibbs, Eddy. *In Name Only: Tackling the Problem of Nominal Christianity*. Tunbridge Wells, Kent, England: Monarch Publications Ltd., 1994.

Graham, Billy. *Christianity Today*. No. 1 (October 5, 1956).

Green, J.R. *A Short History of the English People*. New York, NY: Harper and Brothers, 1898.

Guinness, Os. "Recycling the Compromise of Liberalism." *Tabletalk* (May 1992).

Halley, Henry H. *Halley Bible Handbook*. Grand Rapids, MI: Zondervan, 1965.

Hardman, Keith, J. *The Spiritual Awakeners*. Chicago, IL: Moody Press, 1983.

Hayford, Jack. Senior Pastor of The Church on the Way. Endorsement of *The Frog in the Kettle* by George Barna, 1990.

Henry, F.H. Quoted by Les Thompson, *Christianity Today*, May 1993.

Henson, Al. "Flames of Freedom Conference," Rives Junction, MI, 1997.

Heth, William A. and Wenham, Gordon J. *Jesus and Divorce: The Problem with the Evangelical Consensus*. New York, NY: Thomas Nelson Publishers, 1984.

Hughes, Kent and Barbara. *Liberation Ministry from the Success Syndrome*. Wheaton, IL: Tyndale House, 1988.

Hull, John. "Preparing the Peoples Church, Toronto, for a Third Generation of Ministry." An unpublished doctoral thesis, Toronto, 1996.

Hulse, Erroll. *Spirit of Revival*. Buchanan, MI: Life Action Ministries, Vol. 29, Number 1, February 1999.

Hunter, James Davison. *Evangelicalism: The Coming Generation*. Chicago, IL: University Press, 1987.

Huntly, Alyson. *Daring to Be United: Including Lesbians and Gays in the United Church of Canada*. Toronto, ON: United Church of Canada Publishing House, 1998.

Ironside, H.A. *Expository Notes on the Gospel of Matthew*. Neptune, NJ: Loizeaux Brothers, 1948. (Quoted in Foster *Binding and Loosing*, p. 173.)

Jenkins, Kevin. Speaker at Ontario Prayer Breakfast, Toronto (April 1993).

Jewett, Paul K. *Man: Male as Female*. Grand Rapids, MI: Eerdmans, 1975.

Johnston, Charles. Professor at St. Andrews College, Saskatoon, SK, interview, March 1999.

Kelley, Dean M. *Why Conservative Churches Are Growing*. New York, NY: Harper and Rowe, 1972.

Kincheloe, Raymond. Unpublished class notes, in which he identifies five warnings in the book of Hebrews: 2:14; 3:7-11; 5:11-6:3; 10:26-36; 12:14-17, 1956.

King, L.L. "The Christian and Missionary Alliance, As I See It Beyond 1987." An unpublished paper by Dr. L.L. King, president of the C&MA U.S., December 1987.

Latourette, Kenneth Scott. *Christianity Through the Ages*. New York, NY: Harper and Rowe, 1965.

Laurence, Peter. *The Peter Principle*. New York, NY: Bantam Books, 1969.

Lindsell, Harold. *The Battle for the Bible*. Grand Rapids, MI: Zondervan, 1976.

Littell, Franklin H.L. *The Origins of Sectarian Protestantism*. New York, NY: MacMillan Co., 1964.

MacArthur, John, Jr. *Reckless Faith: When the Church Loses Its Will to Discern*. Wheaton, IL: Crossway Books, 1994.

McGavran. *Understanding Church Growth*. Grand Rapids, MI: Zondervan, 1970.

McQuilkin, Robertson. "What Is Your GCQ?" *Trinity World Forum*. Trinity Evangelical Divinity School, Winter 1997.

Mayers, Marvin. *Christianity Confronts Culture*. Grand Rapids, MI: Academie Books, imprint of Zondervan, revised, 1987.

Merriam-Webster, A. *Webster's New Collegiate Dictionary*. Springfield, MS: G. & C. Merriam Company, 1975.

Milton, Ralph. *This United Church of Ours*. Kelowna, BC: Wood Lake Books Incorporated, 1991.

Moberg, David O. *The Church or a Social Institution*. Englewood Cliffs, NJ: PrenticeHall, 1962.

Mohler, R. Albert, Jr. Quoted in James Montgomery Boice in "Recovering Our Lost Confessions," *Modern Reformation* (January/February, 1999).

Morris, Leon. *The Revelation of St. John*. Grand Rapids, MI: Eerdmans, 1978.

Muggeridge, Malcolm. *The Most of Malcolm Muggeridge*. New York, NY: Simon and Schuster, 1988.

Needham, David. *Birthright*. Portland, OR: Multnomah Press, 1979.

Neely Lois. "Dr. Oswald J. Smith: Beloved of Canada, Owned by the World," *Faith Today*, Toronto (March/April 1986).

Niebuhr, Richard. *The Social Sources of Denominationalism*. Hamden, CT: Shoe String Press, 1954.

Olson, Roger E. "Post-conservative Evangelicals Greet the Postmodern Age," *Christian Century* (May 3, 1995).

Origen. Quoted by William Barclay, *The Letter to the Hebrews*. Philadelphia, PA: Westminster Press, 1977.

Orr, James. General Editor. *The International Standard Bible Encyclopaedia*. (ISBE). Grand Rapids, MI: Eerdmans, 1939.

Orr, J. Edwin. *Evangelical Awakenings: Eastern Asia*. Minneapolis, MN: Bethany Fellowship, 1975.

_____. *The Flaming Tongue: The Impact of the Twentieth Century Revival*. Chicago, IL: Moody Press, 1973.

Owens, Ron and Patricia. *Return to Me: A Fresh Encounter with God through Song*. Nashville, TN: Lifeway Press, 1993.

Peterson, Eugene. *The Contemplative Pastor*. Carol Stream, IL: Word Publishing, 1989.

Piper, John. Message preached at U.S. C&MA Council (June 1997).

_____. "On Divorce and Remarriage in the Event of Adultery." [http://desiringgod.org/resources/divorce/Div&rem-adultery.htm] (March 9, 1999).

_____. "Lecture on Preaching and Worship," Trinity Theological Seminary, Deerfield, IL (1997).

_____. "Training the Next Generation of Evangelical Pastors and Missionaries." Given at the Evangelical Theological Society, Orlando, FL (November 20, 1998).

Plowman, Edward E. "Pressler Pressure," *WORLD* (July 3, 1999).

Rankin, Jerry and Willis, Avery. "The Southern Baptists Restructure to Reach the Unreached Peoples." *Mission Frontiers* (July-October, 1997).

Regele, Mike. *Death of the Church*. Grand Rapids, MI: Zondervan, 1995.

Sanders, J. Oswald. *Spiritual Leadership*. Chicago, IL: Moody Press, 1967.

Schaeffer, Francis. *The Great Evangelical Disaster*. Westchester, IL: Crossway Books, 1984.

Scott, E.F. As quoted by William Barclay in *The Letter to the Hebrews*. Philadelphia, PA: Westminster Press, 1977.

Scrivener, Leslie. *Toronto Star* (October 29, 1997).

Shelley, Bruce. *Church History in Plain Language*. Waco, TX: Word Books Publisher, 1982.

Shindler, Robert. "The Down-Grade," *The Sword and the Trowel* (August 1888).

Shubin, Russell G. "Winds of Renewal." *Mission Frontiers* (January/February, 1999).

Simpson, A.B. *Missionary Messages*. Camp Hill, PA: Christian Publications, n.d.

Spader, Dann. *Growing a Healthy Church*. Elburn, IL: SonLife, 1998.

Spurgeon, Charles. "Another Word Concerning the Down-Grade," *The Sword and the Trowel* (August 1888).

Stephens, W.P.S. *The Theology of Huldrych Zwingli*. Oxford, England: Clarendon Press, 1986. (Quoted by Foster in *Binding and Loosing*, p. 173).

Stott, John, and David L. Edwards. *Evangelical Essentials*. Downers Grove, IL: InterVarsity Press, 1989.

Stowell, Joseph M. *Shepherding the Church into the 21st Century*. Wheaton, IL: Victor Books, 1994.

Strauss, William and Howe, Neil. *Generations: The History of America's Future, 1584 to 2069*. New York, NY: William Morrow, 1991.

Sweeting, George. "Talking It Over." *Moody Monthly* (October 1986).

Swenson, Richard A. *Margin: Restoring Emotional, Physical, Financial, and Time Reserves to Overloaded Lives*. Colorado Springs, CO: Navpress, 1992.

_____. *Hurtling Toward Oblivion: A Logical Argument for the End of the Age*. Colorado Springs, CO: Navpress, 1999.

Swindoll, Charles, "The Temptations of Ministry: Improving Your Serve." *Leadership* (Fall 1982).

_____. *Improving Your Serve: The Art of Unselfish Living*. Waco, TX: Word Books, 1981.

Teng, Philip. *Crises in the Apostolic Church*. Bombay, India: Gospel Literature Service, 1980.

Thomson, Les. "Put Faith Back into Management," *Christianity Today* (January 1989).

Tkach, Joseph, Jr. "Forgive Us Our Trespasses." *Plain Truth* (March/April 1996).

Towns, Elmer. *America's Fastest Growing Churches*. Nashville, TN: Impact Books, 1972.

Tozer, A.W. *Tozer on the Holy Spirit*. Compiled by Marilynne E. Foster. Camp Hill, PA: Christian Publications, 2000.

_____. *The Size of the Soul*. Camp Hill, PA: Christian Publications, 1992.

_____. *The Waning Authority of Christ in the Church*. Harrisburg, PA: Christian Publications, 1963.

Tucker, Ruth. "Worldwide Church of God Sees the Plain Truth." *Christianity Today* (July 15, 1996).

Voelkel, Harold. *O God, Revive Us Again*. Mississauga, ON: OMF International, 1996.

Wagner, C. Peter. *New Apostolic Churches*. Ventura, CA: Regal Books, revised by Will Bruce, 1998.

Weber, Max. *Sociology of Religion*. London, England: Methuen, 1963.

Wells, David F. R.C. Sproul conference, Toronto, December 3, 1995.

_____. *No Place for Truth or Whatever Happened to Evangelical Theology?* Grand Rapids, MI: Eerdmans, 1993.

White, Peter Gordon. *United Church Observer* (May 15, 1964).

Wilkinson, Bruce and MacGregor, Chip. *First Hand Faith: Recapture a Passionate Love for the Savior.* Gresham, OR: Vision House Publisher, 1996.

Winter, Ralph. *Mission Frontiers Bulletin,* Vol. 21, Num. 1-2 (January-February, 1999).

Recommended Reading

Collins, James C., and Porras, Jerry I. *Built to Last: Successful Habits of Visionary Companies.* New York, NY: HarperCollins Publishers, 1994.

Cymbala, Jim, *Fresh Wind, Fresh Fire.* Grand Rapids, MI: Zondervan, 1997.

Foster, K. Neill with Paul L. King. *Binding and Loosing: Exercising Authority over the Dark Powers.* Camp Hill, PA: Christian Publications, 1998.

Gibbs, Eddy. *In Name Only: Tackling the Problem of Nominal Christianity.* Tunbridge Wells, Kent, England: Monarch Publications Ltd., 1994.

Hardman, Keith, J. *The Spiritual Awakeners.* Chicago, IL: Moody Press, 1983.

Heth, William A. and Gordon J. Wenham. *Jesus and Divorce: The Problem with the Evangelical Consensus.* New York, NY: Thomas Nelson Publishers, 1984.

Hughes, Kent and Barbara. *Liberating Ministry from the Success Syndrome.* Wheaton, IL: Tyndale House, 1988.

Kelley, Dean M. *Why Conservative Churches Are Growing.* New York, NY: Harper and Rowe, 1972.

Lindsell, Harold. *The Battle for the Bible.* Grand Rapids, MI: Zondervan, 1976.

MacArthur, John, Jr. *Reckless Faith: When the Church Loses Its Will to Discern.* Wheaton, IL: Crossway Books, 1994.

Owens, Ron and Patricia. *Return to Me: A Fresh Encounter with God through Song.* Nashville, TN: Lifeway Press, 1993.

Piper, John. "On Divorce and Remarriage in the Event of Adultery." [http://desiringgod.org/resources/divorce/Div&rem-adultery.htm] (March 9, 1999).

Sanders, J. Oswald. *Spiritual Leadership*. Chicago, IL: Moody Press, 1967.

Schaeffer, Francis. *The Great Evangelical Disaster*. Westchester, IL: Crossway Books, 1984.

Swenson, Richard A. *Hurtling Toward Oblivion: A Logical Argument for the End of the Age*. Colorado Springs, CO: Navpress, 1999.

Tozer, A.W. *Tozer on the Holy Spirit*. Compiled by Marilynne E. Foster. Camp Hill, PA: Christian Publications Inc., 2000.

Voelkel, Harold. *O God, Revive Us Again*. Mississauga, ON: OMF International, 1996.

Wagner, C. Peter. *New Apostolic Churches*. Ventura, CA: Regal Books, 1998.

Wilkinson, Bruce and MacGregor, Chip. *First Hand Faith: Recapture a Passionate Love for the Savior*. Gresham, OR: Vision House Publisher, 1996.

Scripture Index

Author and Subject Index

A

B

S